What other reviewers have to say about
Seraffyn's European Adventure

"Full of people and places that delight readers who are armchair sailors. Serious sailors will be pleased with the last 67 pages of specific boat information with illustrations."

Margaret Wiggs, *Fort Wayne News-Sentinel*

"If you've ever dreamed of making an extended cruise in a sailboat, this bright chronicle will confirm your expectations—it can be a glorious way to go. This book is a rich compendium of nautical lore."

Warren Wightman, *Rochester Democrat and Chronicle*

"Captures the characters of the people and places visited...Good sound advice is given throughout the book."

John Kenny, *Library Journal*

"There is a lot of vicarious enjoyment packed in this volume...a worthwhile book for those who do, or would like to, live the cruising life."

Dix Brow, *Rudder Magazine*

"Although this book is not specifically a how-to-cruise book, I would highly recommend it to anyone with the itch to go...There is surely more to be learned here about the joy of cruising than in dozens of heavy-weather how-tos. It is an enticing nudge away from the television fantasy world many of us associate with adventure and includes a healthy dose of an exciting world much closer to us than we generally realize."

Geoff Heath, *The Small Boat Journal*

"This book reads equally well as a study of the attributes of a successful liveaboard cruiser, as a travelogue, or as a study of human relationships. As a pleasing combination of all three, it is particularly worthwhile reading."

Ann M. Hays, *The Chesapeake Boatman*

"The Pardeys are an articulate, self-reliant couple who view small-boat cruising as a way of life, their personal freedom. With only the forces of nature for power, they explore, sail, and work their way, putting winds and tides to work for them. And that's what sailing is all about. The Pardeys tell a charming tale, laced with humor without overlooking the difficulties of small-boat sailing."

Bud Wacker, *Buffalo New York News*

"It is these people [the people the Pardeys met] whose brief appearances...raise this book above the ordinary seafaring tales. Lin Pardey, who does most of the writing, lets us see, hear, and smell every aspect of a voyage that was every bit as rewarding as it was tedious."

Jeffrey Schneider, *The Monthly Book Review*

Seraffyn's
European
Adventure

Richard Blagborne

Seraffyn's
European Adventure

by

Lin and Larry Pardey

Pardey Books

Printing history
Originally published by W.W. Norton, New York, NY, 1979
ISBN 3-393-03231-0
W.W. Norton Paperback, second edition, 1984
Pardey Books, third edition, 1998

Library of Congress Cataloguing in Publication Data
Pardey, Lin.
Seraffyn's European adventure
1. Seraffyn (cutter) 2. Sailing—Europe
I. Pardey, Larry, joint author.   II. Title
GV822.S39P38   1979   797.1'24   78-32032
ISBN 09-646036-4-0

This book is set in Janson and Perpetua
Manufactured by Thomson-Shore Inc.
Designed by Jacques Chazaud
Third-edition production by Allison Peter
Cover design by Rob Johnson
Printed in the United States of America
Published by Pardey Books and distributed by Paradise Cay Publishing,
Box 29, Arcata, CA 95518-0029, tel. 800-736-4509, fax 707-822-9063

2 3 4 5 6 7 8 9 0

To Leslie Dyball

the kind of shipmate we'd enjoy cruising or racing with,
anytime, anyplace.

Contents

Preface

~~~~~~

Cruising, like the rest of life, has its different paces, its different moods, its highs and lows. During the first three years of our cruising life we sailed almost fifteen thousand miles. We spent our time learning to live free of schedules, learning to know our boat, ourselves, and the seas around us. During the next two and a half years, the ones covered by this book, we voyaged less than six thousand miles. We saw a completely different world and we came to marvel at the variety of opportunities our life on *Seraffyn* opened to us.

Acknowledgements

Besides the people who went to a lot of trouble to provide the information that appears in Appendix B, we would like to thank Mike Hope, Chris Field, and Phil Lum who took some of the photographs used in this book.

Our appreciation goes to people like Tom Nibbea, Jonathon Blair, Bruce McElfresh, and Tom Smith at National Geographic, who helped us learn to use a camera with more success. And to Julia Stansby and Irene Khor, who helped with the typing of the manuscript. Thanks also to Humphrey and Mary Barton, who edited the first half of Seraffyn's *European Adventure* in Malta, making helpful suggestions. It was at their insistence that Larry and I stopped dropping our anchor and started letting it go. John Dodd, Jim and Ann MacBeth, Peer Tangvald, and Brian Merrill each read parts of this manuscript in rough typewritten form and made very useful suggestions that we know improved it. Eric Swenson, Eleanor Crapallo, Richard Whittington, Dick Rath, John Delves, Shelley Heller, Linda Moran, and the crew of *Boating* magazine gave us their kind assistance in New York, and Shiela Waygood handled our mail and photographic problems in England. Patience Wales and the staff of *Sail* magazine helped us locate information when we needed it. Without these helping hands it would have been a lot harder to coordinate this book, especially since we have been cruising on as we wrote it.

Some people we'd especially like to remember here are the members and staff of the Parkstone Yacht Club in England and the Alborg Yacht Club in Denmark, plus all of those other people we met and shared wonderful moments with but just couldn't mention because of the limited spaces on these pages.

Finally, we'd like to thank the thoughtful people we have never met who took the time and effort to write us letters saying, "We enjoyed your first book, when do we get to read the sequel?" People like Dennis Walsh, Tor Christiansen, Bob and Sandy Levesque, and many others. We hope they are not disappointed.

Seraffyn's
European
Adventure

CHAPTER 1

$\sim\sim\sim$

Dragons and the Sea

St. George had his dragon, I had the Atlantic. We had built *Seraffyn* strong enough to sail almost anywhere. We'd cruised from California along Mexico's west coast to Costa Rica and Panama, north through the Caribbean and past the Florida Keys to the Chesapeake, wandering along like gypsies for three years, singing, swimming, playing, and occasionally working. Always there'd been land within three or four hundred miles of our tiny floating home. So as the time came closer for our plunge across the forty-two hundred miles of North Atlantic that blocked our path to England, I kept telling myself, "It's nothing different, Lin, just a few more days at sea than usual."

Larry had none of these concerns. He'd been sailing since he was a kid. He'd made two passages across the Pacific on an eighty-five-foot schooner. He'd been skipper on a fifty-three-foot charter boat in Newport Beach, California, for two years, and had raced competitively in his home port of Vancouver, British Columbia, for five. He was a sailor who loved every mood of the sea. Seasickness? Larry didn't know what the word meant. The only thing in the sailing world that bothered him was being becalmed in our engineless boat near heavy shipping. The Atlantic would be a relief after the crowds of shipping we'd met in the Straits of Florida. So Larry looked forward to the crossing, dreaming of the other side long before we cast off our mooring lines.

Forty-two hundred miles! The North Atlantic! Storms! No land for twenty or thirty days! Each thought filled me with apprehension. I'd had almost no sailing experience before I met Larry. My father had owned a fourteen-foot lapstrake sloop until I was five years old, but then we'd had to sell it because the family was leaving Michigan to move to California. Each summer after we arrived in Los Angeles, we would make a one-day pilgrimage to Newport Beach, ninety miles from our home. We'd play on the yellow sands, intimidated by the roaring Pacific. We'd eat our picnic lunch of fried chicken and potato salad. Then would come the event my dad had waited for. He'd walk across the narrow peninsula, my brother Allen by his side, pay for one hour's rent of a sixteen-foot sloop, prepare it for us, and we'd step aboard and skim down Newport Bay, dad's face turned upward toward the dirty, battered sails, excitedly telling Allen, "Trim the jib, duck, watch the boom." Mom and my baby sister Bonnie would try to sunbath on the tiny foredeck. I'd look at dad with admiration. He was happy, king of his world, thoughts of house payments, a car that needed new tires, a job filled with petty conflicts far behind him. Then twenty minutes later he'd glance at his watch and the dream would vanish. He'd say, "Got to head back, take us much longer to beat up the bay."

So we'd set to work short-tacking past the glowing white yachts tied in front of luxury homes, through moorings filled with gray and blue swordfish boats, their fantastic bow platforms stretching twenty feet ahead of them. Dad would time his hour to the second, handing the painter on the rental boat to the dock man with reluctance, and all three of us kids would rush past him as he gazed at the seemingly unobtainable world that that battered rental boat represented. Now came *our* favorite event of the day. Mom would buy each of us kids the treat only Newport Beach offered, a frozen chocolate-covered banana on a stick. Then sticky, wind blown, sandy, and tired, we'd hunt up the car, scramble inside, and head for home. As mom, Bonnie, Allen, and I slowly nodded off to sleep, dad would wistfully say, "Nice sail, wasn't it?"

By the time I was fourteen I'd become like most teenage girls. A day on the beach with the folks? Wouldn't be caught dead, not when I could be chasing around with some girlfriends chattering about boys. So sailing for me was a memory of the one day a year when my dad was king.

I met Larry accidently when I was twenty. He invited me for an afternoon's sail. I couldn't resist and two hours later I was in a world neither my dad nor I had ever dreamed of. We powered over a glassy sea in the fifty-three-foot ketch, the throb of a diesel engine beneath our feet, huge white glowing sails over our heads. I fell in love that day: with the laughing blue-eyed Larry; with the sheen of white sails, varnished wood, and creaking blocks; and with the same dream I'd noticed once a year in my father's eyes, the dream of far-off lands, of freedom and tranquility.

Two weeks later I was working with Larry, learning to help him build the twenty-four-foot cutter he planned to cruise in. My every thought turned to boats: lumber, nails, varnish, sails, sailing. When I drove to visit my folks once or twice a year I'd spent half the day talking boats with dad who was saving up to buy his own day sailer. I don't think my folks really believed Larry and I would sell out, move all our remaining worldly possessions onto our beamy little turtle shell of a boat, and sail off "forever." In fact, I didn't believe it myself until the day we launched *Seraffyn*, three and a half years from when she entered my life.

With six years of Larry's patient training behind me, fifteen thousand miles of sailing and countless hours spent reading every cruising book I could find, I was still apprehensive about the Atlantic. Gordon Yates, a friend we'd made while cruising in Mexico, used to say, "If you're not afraid, you just don't know the facts." I knew I'd occasionally be seasick. That was no problem, just a nuisance. But would I have enough food on board? Had I found enough books to read? Would I hate being at sea for weeks on end?

By the time we cast off our mooring lines, I'd used up every worry I could think of and, as usually happens, the Atlantic crossing turned into a daily affair, each morning different from the one before, each day filled with easy companionship. Some good weather, some bad. Some fabulous sailing, some frustrating as hell. We'd had to beat most of the last twelve-hundred-mile leg from the Azores to Falmouth, England. But as Larry said, "If it's this much work, it must be worthwhile." We'd sailed into Falmouth the night before and let go our anchor. I cried in Larry's arms, thrilled with the dragon I'd slain. I'd done it. There was still twenty gallons of fresh water in our tanks, lots of good food left hidden away in various lockers. Both of us were healthy and unbelievably happy. I knew then that I'd stood my test of fire.

Love the sea? Not really. I didn't trust it enough. Love sailing? With Larry, yes! Love cruising? Yes, completely!

As we climbed into bed together for the first time in three weeks, Larry kissed me and teased away my tears. "Just think, Lin, tomorrow we get four months' worth of mail from home. Then there's the whole of Europe to explore."

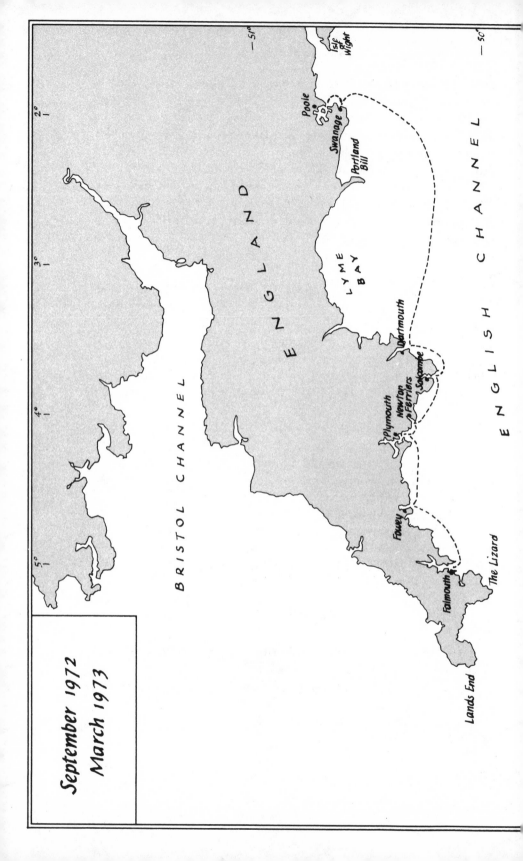

September 1972
March 1973

BRISTOL CHANNEL

ENGLAND

ENGLISH CHANNEL

ENGLISH CHANNEL

Isle of Wight

Poole

Swanage

Portland Bill

LYME BAY

Dartmouth

Salcombe

Newton Ferriers

Plymouth

Fowey

The Lizard

Falmouth

Lands End

CHAPTER 2

~~~~~

Falmouth for Fun

An early-morning sun glowed through our portholes. *Seraffyn* dipped to a passing wake. Larry roused me by crawling out of our double sleeping bag. It took me some time to remember where we were —Falmouth! No more ocean passages for a while; just lovely day hops ahead, no matter which way we chanced to go!

Larry called to me as he slid the companionway hatch open. "Hurry, Lin, come see them. They're everywhere!" Larry sounded like a kid let loose at the zoo.

I crawled out of the warm down bag and immediately knew we were in England. It was cold! I pulled on woolly socks, jeans, and a sweatshirt at the same time as I tried to climb through the small companionway into the main cabin, and whacked the back of my head soundly. But I barely felt it in the excitement of my first daylight glimpse of the Old World.

The first sight of any port in daylight after a nightime entry is a bit magical. But Falmouth is in a class by itself. They were all around us—boats like *Seraffyn*, boats we'd read about in books by Uffa Fox and Peter Pye. Not fifty yards away was the transom of *Victory*, a seventy-year-old Falmouth oyster dredger, her hull looking just like ours, but without a cabin. Her bowsprit was fourteen feet long at least, seven feet longer than ours. Instead of the tall Bermuda-rigged mast we had, hers was short and stout with all the gear of a big gaff sail. Not far from *Victory* lay two other oyster dredgers, one red, the other turquoise and black.

Larry's coffee started to perk, filling the boat with a homey aroma. But we ignored it as a fleet of swans came alongside. I'd never seen a

The swans of Falmouth kept us fascinated.

wild swan, and to have one followed by six speckled cygnets not two feet from our floating home was irresistible. We pulled the drop boards out, I grabbed some stale bread, and we scrambled on deck. The swans knew a pair of suckers when they saw one, and started preening their feathers for us when our last piece of bread was gone. I was rummaging for something else to feed them when the forty-foot Customs boat came alongside.

Clearance was more a matter of being welcomed by the smiling officials than paperwork. Even our still-plentiful stock of duty-free liquor caused no problem since the English rule, which we'd read in Reed's *Almanac,* is that any yacht owned by a member of a recognized foreign yacht club may carry as much spirits and liquor as would "be reasonably consumed on board during the intended length of stay."

"The holding ground is poor here. Besides, the yacht club always has a mooring free for transatlantic sailors," the Immigration officer called as he left after finishing a cup of coffee.

So as soon as we'd cleaned up, we set sail toward the Royal Cornwall Yacht Club. A handsome twelve- or fourteen-foot varnished launch set off from the shore as we tacked through the club moorings.

"You the *Seraffyn*?" the young curly-haired launchman called as he approached. "Follow me. Thank God you're here; your post has filled our safe."

Over the chonk, chonk, chonk of his little Stuart Turner engine Leslie introduced himself to us. He handed up a mooring pennant and said, "Grab your shower kit. Hot water's on and the secretary is waiting."

We climbed into his launch, laden with fresh clothes and the unavoidable sailbag full of dirty laundry that every cruiser seems to have after a passage. Leslie gave us a running commentary in heavily accented West-country English. Then Larry started to say, "You Englishmen . . ." He got no further. Leslie drew himself up to full height and, fuming with regional pride, announced, "I'm not *English*, I'm *Cornish*!"

The door of the hundred-fifty-year-old gray stone home, now used by the yacht club, was flung open as we climbed the steps from the landing. A formidable-looking gray-haired woman approached us and announced, "Welcome to England! Now, do you wish to shower first or read your post?" Before either of us could say a word, she answered, "No, if you start on that pile of letters you'll never have time for a shower. You, up the stairs; men through the bar." She grabbed our sack of laundry, shoved it in a corner of the foyer, and steamed majestically off into the nether regions of the clubhouse.

"God, that shower felt good," Larry sighed when we met at the foot of the stairs forty-five minutes later. "That's one of the treats of cruising. If you could have a hot shower anytime you wanted, you'd never appreciate them at all."

Mrs. Muirhead, the club secretary, must have been listening for us. She hustled into the foyer, finally introduced herself, and said, "When you wrote four months ago, you said some of your post might contain important documents, so I put it all in the safe. Had to take the cash box out three weeks ago to make room for your things." I laughed inwardly when I remembered our letter politely asking the secretary to put our mail in a safe place. The important documents I had been referring were only travelers check receipts.

Mrs. Muirhead led us to a small round table piled six inches deep with letters. Then she went on, "Arnold Gee over there has bought you lunch and promised not to disturb you until you've read your post."

So Larry and I sat down and began opening almost a hundred letters as we devoured a chicken and ham salad without even noticing it. We read how my father's knee had healed perfectly, long before we read the letter telling how he had broken it in a boating accident. We had unexpected checks from articles we'd written during our previous winter in the Chesapeake Bay, greetings and news from friends, "When are you coming home?" from parents. Not one bill. That's why mail calls are such a treat for us.

It was at least three hours before we were sure we'd read everything. I stood up and stretched and the man who'd bought us lunch came over. Arnold Gee was a sixty-five-year-old sailor we came to know well. He had twinkling gray eyes, set in a completely bald round head, and a charming English manner that fitted perfectly with the Old World atmosphere of the gray-carpeted, bay-windowed clubhouse.

"Now come into the bar and meet some sailors," he insisted.

The first sailor was Mayne, the Irish bartender who worked as a fisherman during the winter. Mayne poured Larry his first draft Guinness. Then he asked the question that we were to answer a hundred times during our cruise in England: "Why did a North American build an English boat?" We looked at *Seraffyn*, sitting proudly on her mooring in front of the club's lawn, and Larry answered, "*Seraffyn*'s designer, Lyle Hess, tried to combine the best of both worlds, the seakeeping ability of the long-keeled English cutters with the room and stability of the beamy American bottom."

I broke in, "I think he succeeded. We averaged a hundred miles a day for the whole forty-two-hundred-mile voyage and made several runs of a hundred forty miles a day between Bermuda and the Azores in a twenty-four-foot boat." And so the afternoon evaporated as Arnold and Mayne introduced us to a dozen more sailors.

As it grew dark, Larry asked Mayne for the location of a self-service laundry and the name of the best restaurant in town. Mayne called a cab after explaining we could drop our laundry at a little shop just up the lane where they would wash and dry it for us at no extra charge. "That's great," Larry replied. "Now for a good dinner ashore. Lin deserves one after cooking aboard for the past twenty days."

As soon as we entered the carpeted foyer of the Green Lawns Hotel a hostess came to escort us to the sitting room. She took our order for drinks and handed us a menu. A waiter arrived soon with my sherry and Larry's Irish whiskey. He took our pâté order for starters, then chateaubriand for two, grilled tomatoes, and chef's oven-sauteed potatoes, to be followed with English raspberry trifle and a cheese board. We lounged in the overstuffed chairs sipping our drinks and had just finished when our waiter reappeared, "Your table is ready." He escorted us to a spot overlooking the lights of Carrick Roads and we found a salad-like display with fresh pâté and toast waiting for us surrounded by polished silver and crystal. Almost an hour later, after one last nibble at a delicious round stilton cheese, our waiter escorted us to another lounge full of comfortable couches where coffee and tea were served. Although that dinner cost us nearly twenty dollars, we didn't mind at all. We'd spent nothing during three weeks at sea, and the food, wine, and service were excellent.

As we walked through the yacht club that evening, Mayne stopped us and introduced two more local sailors. Frank and Irene Jarrett invited us to come to their home for dinner the next evening. Then Frank said, "Last club race of the season is Sunday. Care to go?"

"Sure," Larry answered. "Will you two crew for us? Can we get a rating in time for the race?"

Frank looked a bit surprised and said, "I was thinking of finding a crew spot for you. Sure you want to take your boat out racing so soon?"

"Why not?" Larry replied. "We've got a great spinnaker."

So after a meeting time was set, Frank borrowed a club member's dinghy and rowed us home since the club launch had stopped running hours before.

We climbed between our last set of clean sleeping-bag sheets, tired and happy but reluctant to go to sleep. "All the talk about English reticence must be a myth," I told Larry as we reviewed our list of invitations from only one day ashore.

By Saturday noon, two days later, we were tired of answering letters. So when we noticed some men hauling up a fifteen-foot-long jackspar to set a topsail on the oyster boat nearest us, Larry yelled, "Where are you headed?" The oysterman and his crew yelled, "Regatta day—starting line is off the yacht club. Come on, set your sails and join us." The oystermen looked disappointed as we hoisted our triangular sail. Although *Seraffyn*'s sister ship had been designed with a gaff rig, we had decided against one for cruising because Larry was concerned that I wouldn't be able to handle the running backstays and gaff. We were under way in minutes and reached alongside the smallest of the oyster dredgers, the twenty-two-foot *Magdelena*. Her owner yelled over, "Tea and sticky buns after the regatta at the Flushing Yacht Club on the quay over there." He pointed toward the opposite shore and then tacked to run down to the starting line. Over twenty engineless dredgers beat across the line, high peaked gaffs sheeted in amazingly flat. Each carried a flying jib, and under that, a long, overlapping staysail. How they flew under their massive spread of canvas! We watched them overtake IOR boats to windward in the Force 3 winds. I turned to Larry and said, "So much for modern yacht design." But Larry answered, "The oyster boats must be sixty percent ballast, no interior, no engines. Besides, with those large open cockpits, they couldn't even be out in winds over Force 7."

When we joined the finishing get-together for the strong milky tea the club was serving with sugar-coated sweet rolls, Arfie Trenier,

The only modern thing on these workingboats are their well-cut synthetic sails.

Magdelena's owner, told us how one of the oyster dredgers had sunk during the previous season's last race. "Was blowing Force 7. She was on a broad reach inside the bay, bit of a gust hit her off the shore and that was all. Sank like a stone. Lucky a local yachtsman was watching only a few feet away in his power launch. Grabbed the six crewmen as they popped to the surface. One fellow came to the surface sole first, his hip waders full of air. Probably saved him, 'cause he couldn't swim. Couple of local divers had the boat off the bottom a week later. No damage. Nothing the water could hurt in an oyster boat. No engine, no electrics. Lost a few pair of shoes, though." At 1730, Mayne appeared from the Royal Cornwall Yacht Club to join in the more serious drinking that was going on now that the club could officially open its bar. He told us how thirty-four of the thirty-nine oyster boats still afloat in the Falmouth estuary actually were used to dredge oysters in the winter. "Good catch can make a man a hundred pounds a week.

Evelyn is flying a borrowed starcut spinnaker with two knots tied into its head.

George Glasson is dried out on the shore of Flushing Creek opposite the town of Falmouth.

Not bad when you consider how little maintenance these boats need compared to a normal powered fishing boat. Then you consider the dragging hours are limited by local law to 9 A.M. to 3 P.M. Man goes sailing to work, sails while he's working, sails home from work, and is sitting feet up in front of his fireplace by dark. Then when the oyster season has closed, he has a good boat to race, and the races have a cash prize. Yup, fifteen pounds to the first boat today. *George Glasson*, the turquoise and black dredger over there, has been in the same family for three generations."

The next morning we had *Seraffyn* in "race trim" when Irene and Frank arrived one hour before the 1300 starting time. All "race trim" meant was "dinghy off, spare water jug in the dink." I set out lunch as Larry showed our crew what strings went where. We were soon off the mooring and on our way toward the harbor entrance. The starting line was between the two guardian castles built during the 1400s at each side of the entrance to the Falmouth estuary. It was to be a pursuit race, each boat starting separately according to its rating, smallest boats first. That way the winner was the first boat to cross the finishing line. Larry suggested we try out our spinnaker before hand since it was to be a downwind start. Frank let out a happy shout as he watched our thirty-two-foot-wide, thirty-four-foot-high, bell-shaped spinnaker fill. "Never seen a spinnaker that big on anything but a forty-footer," he commented as a light gust hit us on the beam and sent Irene and me scrambling after sandwiches and coffee mugs.

Because *Seraffyn* is a cutter with a bowsprit, her spinnaker can have a very wide foot and still carry no penalty on most race rating systems. Although we were mainly a cruising boat, we'd decided to buy a spinnaker when we first set off, and we were glad we had. We rarely used it at sea, but when we were day-hopping along coasts with diurnal wind patterns, that 1,050-square-foot spinnaker sometimes made the difference between spending a night at sea or getting our anchor down before dark. When we were sailing alone, we made it a rule to get the spinnaker down before the winds reached fifteen knots. But when there was a chance to join some club's local racing we carried extra crew, so we flew that spinnaker as long as it was possible.

We roared across the starting line with that blue and white balloon dead before us, one minute behind a Folkboat. We soon overtook the four smaller boats in the ten-knot breeze. Before we reached the first mark our crew was handling the boat like champs. Irene constantly trimmed the mainsheet as if she'd been racing on *Seraffyn* for seasons. Frank helped Larry get in the spinnaker and set the genoa. I tightened the staysail using our windward sheet winch. I kept glancing over my shoulder as the larger boats slowly gained on us. I was a bundle of excitement as we reached around the mark, Mr. and Mrs. Muirhead only feet to windward in their thirty-foot Sparkman and Stephens sloop *Jemalda*. A gust hit us and I slid down the cockpit and landed across the tiller. *Seraffyn* headed straight at *Jemalda*. Larry yelled, "Get off the tiller!" straining against my weight. I struggled to extricate myself—and we cleared *Jemalda* with only inches to spare. What a disaster it would have been if we'd hit the commodore's boat! Larry and I were still a bit shaken as we roared toward the Helford River with the front of the fleet. Our crew worked silently and competently, easing and tightening sheets as we worked the puffs that came off the shore. The close-quarter sailing was an exciting change from our usual life of cruising alone, and sometime during that long reach we were near enough to two other racers to hear someone say, "If that funny little cruising boat wins, I'm going to protest its rating."

Our competitor needn't have worried. As we worked back toward the entrance of the river for the beat home, we saw some of the local boats shortening sail. But we didn't take notice and put our side decks under water as we cleared the point. By the time we'd dug out our lapper (a 110 percent genoa) dropped our big genoa and staysail, and gotten under way again in the short choppy tidal sea, we were almost the last boat in the fleet. When we finally beat across the finishing line in twenty-five knots of wind an hour later, Mrs. Muirhead called, "Come aboard for tea."

The first thing she said as we climbed out of the club launch onto *Jemalda* was, "Real light-wind flyer you've got there. Wouldn't have minded you beating us to the mark if we hadn't seen the crop of goose barnacles hanging under your stern."

On September 30, 1972, the English cruising season was officially over, but the days, although getting shorter, were often sunny. We were preparing to sail eastward after three wonderful weeks in Falmouth when a Swedish couple arrived in an International Folkboat and picked up the mooring next to us. We met them in the clubhouse an hour later and soon the four of us were in the local fish-and-chips

Sunday sailors on Falmouth estuary.

shop trading sailing stories. Ingrid and Khristan Lagerkrantz had left Sweden that spring after graduating from the university, and were headed for Yugoslavia via Spain and Portugal. Ingrid had her degree as a police psychologist and Khris was an anthropologist. He hoped to write his master's thesis on the people of the Dalmatian Islands. The conversation turned to a discussion of their twenty-five-foot boat.

"Sure she's a bit limited in space," Khris told us. "But I could never afford to go to Yugoslavia to live and roam and study in the islands for a year any other way."

Ingrid added, "We've got a good big bed. Khris has promised to fix up the galley for me. When we get where it's warmer, we'll be able to live on deck much of the time so our space will be doubled."

We've met several other people cruising on Folkboats, both wooden ones and the slightly more roomy fiberglass version. Some of them add a masthead lightweather genoa to the standard three-quarter rig, then use an outboard motor or long sculling oar during calms (see Appendix B). The boats are minimal for a couple, but as the Lager-krantzes agreed, "Our Folkboat is good and seaworthy. And we'd rather be a bit cramped some days than working at a desk in Sweden full time."

We woke up the next morning to our tiny traveling alarm's amaz-ingly loud buzz. It was 0625, time for the maritime weather forecast. We argued about who was going to climb out of the warm bunk and turn on the radio. England has one of the best maritime weather forecast systems we've come across. Updated reports, consisting of a general weather synopsis, a forecast for each of twelve areas of the British Isles, and finally actual reports from twelve shore stations, are broadcast four times daily on the longwave band. Wind direction, visibility, and sea state are given. We found these reports amazingly accurate, although sometimes we heard forecasts like "Force 2 to 3 southeast with possible increase to 5 or 6; chance of gales later" and we figured the weather man was covering himself against future com-plaints.

The morning forecast was for light offshore winds. So I dug out the tidal charts that are like a Bible for sailors in English waters. Wouldn't pay to leave before the tide turned fair at noon. We poked our heads out to say good-bye to Khris and Ingrid who were setting sail for sunny Spain, four hundred miles south, then clambered back into the still-warm bunk.

~~~~~

CHAPTER 3

A Cruise in Company

An English single-handed sailor we'd met in the Azores, Brian Crai-gie-Lucas, said, "I've cruised on three continents now and the south coast of England still beats them all, especially if you cruise it out of season." He'd given us his rubberband-bound *Shell Guide to the South Coast of England* and we thumbed through it as we cleared the entrance to the River Fal with our lapper and mainsail set to catch the northerly breeze. The guide showed a tiny fishing port called Mevagissey, just up the coast from Falmouth, but like half the man-made ports of England, it dried out at low tide. To visit it we would have had to lie up against a seawall since we weren't equipped with legs or bilge keels like so many English boats. Instead, we set our course for Fowey (pronounced Foy), twenty miles east.

Fowey's narrow entrance would have required some tricky sailing as we tacked in, but the two-knot incoming tide flushed us quickly through. A tiny city, built all of gray stone and topped by black slate roofs, nestled along the river, backed by steep green hills. If the cars were removed from the waterfront, Fowey would have looked the same as it had three hundred years ago. We were anxious to go ashore to explore but couldn't find a clear spot to anchor. Our harbor chart and the *Shell Guide* showed a ferry crossing, but we watched for five or ten minutes as we reached up and down the four-hundred-yard-wide river and saw nothing that looked remotely like a ferry. So we let go our anchor, furled our mainsail, bagged our jib, and launched the dinghy. A husky fisherman rowed alongside in a fourteen-foot skiff. "Ya can't anchor here! You're in my way! I'm the ferry," he proclaimed.

I looked at the hundred feet of clear water all around us. "Surely you can row past us," I replied.

"Nope," the ferryman growled, "Law says this is the ferry lane and you got to get out of it."

Larry noticed me getting ready to explode and whispered, "Lin, we're guests here; let's not argue." So, while the ferryman stood watching from his oar-powered fourteen-foot ferryboat, we unfurled the mainsail, weighed our anchor, and set off. We found another clear spot a quarter mile upriver and set our hook, furled the sail, and started to climb into our dinghy. A powered launch came chugging alongside before we'd cast off. "See that mooring over there?" the young boatman said, pointing to a green can about a hundred fifty feet away. "That's the tugboats' mooring. You won't want to anchor here."

By this time I was getting uptight, but again Larry signaled to me and said, "Surely a hundred fifty feet is enough clearance for any tug that would work on a river this small."

The boatman shrugged his shoulders and pointed upriver to where a green tug was just coming into view, a three-hundred-foot ship on a tow line. We couldn't believe our eyes—that tug must have been one hundred fifty feet long! We didn't need any more urging. "Come on, let's sail somewhere else," I said impatinetly. Larry was just about ready to agree when a rubber dinghy buzzed up, driven by the inevitable Seagull outboard motor. "Follow me!" the yachtsman in it yelled, "I've been watching your problem and I know where there's a good clear spot for you." David Burnett introduced himself, then waited while we again weighed anchor, set our mainsail, and got under way. We followed him through the moorings, crowded with local fishing boats, tour boats, and decommissioned yachts, past a glorious hundred-twenty-foot ketch and, sure enough, right in the middle of the crowded moorings was a clear spot just large enough to allow us to anchor with a scope of three to one. We let go our anchor right where David suggested. Then we invited him on board. David went off to get his wife Chris, and returned for drinks. He was a ship's master on holiday in his thirty-foot twin-bilge-keeled yacht. He must have noticed us glancing uneasily around, for he kept reassuring us, "Don't worry, you really can stay here. I know this harbor well." Dark fell while we all chatted and, besides, we thought it wise to be around in case any of the returning fishermen claimed our spot. We never did get ashore that day.

There was an hour and a half of flood tide when we finally roused ourselves the next morning. The wind was light. "Come on," Larry urged, "let's use the tide to go upriver and see where that big ship came from."

We drifted slowly upriver, using our sail power to stay in the center of the four-fathom-deep channel as the incoming tide did most of the work. Around the first bend, out of sight of the peaceful little city, lay a noisy commercial dock covered with china clay heaps. Two large ships were loading there and two more ships lay tied bow and stern to big mooring buoys. They took up over a third of the river's width. It started to rain just as we reached the point on the river where the shoals and oyster beds began. We donned wet-weather gear as *Seraffyn* was caught by the turning tide and began her trickle downstream. I watched the rain running off our decks and got a bright idea. Now would be a good time to give our decks the scrubbing they needed. I rushed below and squirted dish soap into a bucket, then took my dish scrubber, a Golden Fleece pad, and set to work. I rubbed the teak in a circular motion and the rain did the rinsing. Soap suds ran down our topsides as I scrubbed and we drifted within yards of a fisherman cleaning his nets at his mooring. The fisherman glanced our way, then gave a questioning look at me. Larry shrugged his shoulders and said, "Nesting urge, happens every year about this time."

I had the decks glowing by the time the tide carried us back past the sheep-spotted hills and commercial docks to the anchorage. Every stain from buttered popcorn feeds, fried chicken, and spilled wine lifted right off the teak decks and cockpit sole with the help of lots of dish soap and some light scrubbing.

The rain slowed to a drizzle as we moored up, then had lunch. So Larry rowed me into Fowey to shop for some dinner treat, then set off to look at an old shipyard across the way. I left my yellow oilskins in the Fowey Yacht Club locker room and wandered over the slippery cobbled roads, past vine-covered fishermen's cottages to the center of town. Tiny tea shops and tourist stores were almost deserted now. Only the local bakery was alive, its Georgian window filled with cakes and raisin buns. I was drooling over them and trying to decide which ones Larry would like best when a very tall fellow came purposefully toward me, towing a brown-haired girl behind him. "Hello there," he said in the wonderful accent Americans associate with England. "Lovely yacht you have. Where have you sailed from?" I was puzzled.

I hadn't noticed him on the dock when we came ashore. In fact, there had been absolutely no one around. But I answered, "Falmouth, yesterday."

"No," he interrupted, "I mean, where did you come from originally? Where did you buy her?"

So I told him we'd built *Seraffyn* ourselves in California.

He asked me, "Will you join us for a cup of tea and hot scones? I'm Ted Welstead; this is my crew, Jonquil." I finally had to ask, "How did you know I was from *Seraffyn*?"

Ted laughed as he said, "Easy, you're wearing well-worn seaboots." Ted and Jonquil were on the homeward leg of a month's cruise in Ted's thirty-seven-foot Buchanan-designed sloop *Quinag*. "We've moored up just astern of you," Jonquil explained. "Join us for dinner."

I showed them the package containing a nice Scottish beefsteak I'd bought for dinner and Jonquil, in the practical manner we came to know well, said, "Good idea. I'll buy a steak for Ted and myself and we'll grill them together on *Quinag.*"

We separated and I hunted up Larry, which wasn't very hard as he was being treated to a drink at the yacht club bar by another of *Seraffyn*'s new admirers.

Over a very companionable dinner that evening the four of us agreed to a casual cruising race eastward. Ted's home port and our immediate goal were the same, Poole Harbor. We had mail and money waiting for us there. Brian Cooke, another sailor we'd met in the Azores, was a bank manager near Poole and had suggested that he and his wife handle our post for us.

So we got under way early the next morning after consulting the tide tables and watched as Ted and Jonquil lifted their anchor. They soon gave up trying to tack out in the three-knot breeze and powered past us, yelling, "Got to make a phone call by 1400. Meet you at the yacht club in Plymouth." Twenty minutes later they were hull down as we worked to pick up each puff of wind. Although it was the middle of October, the day seemed warm until a cold breeze filled in from astern. I piled into two more sweaters while we started gaining on *Quinag* as if she were standing still. We flew into Plymouth just minutes behind her, and stood clear as Ted picked up a visitor's mooring smartly under sail. Then we sailed in and anchored.

Ted yelled over, "Lost our gearbox. Guess we'll have to look for help. Seems serious." Ted spent most of the afternoon looking for a mechanic. "It's all right for you to say, 'Forget the motor, sail without it.' You two have been doing it for years," he told us that evening.

By morning a strong southerly wind was making the anchorage in front of the yacht club unsafe. The forecast was for gale-strength winds. Larry yelled across to Ted, "I'm sailing up the river to find a quiet anchorage. I'll come back and help you if you need it."

Ted shook his head, "Be a challenge to get out of here."

Running along the coast of England with our working jib on the spinnaker pole.

The wind was now Force 6, directly onto the forty-foot-high rocky cliffs under the clubhouse. Our two moorings were only a hundred yards from the cliffs. We watched *Quinag* maneuver out perfectly, Jonquil at the helm, Ted handling the sails. Then we set out. In tandem we ran upriver, fighting a two-knot ebb. An hour later we anchored near the famous River Tamar Railway Bridge, designed by Brunell.

Ted and Jonquil rowed over to have lunch with us and Larry said, "If you can sail out of a tight spot like that, you can sail anywhere. Why put up with a halfway repair job here. Take *Quinag* to Poole and give that gearbox a proper overhaul this winter."

Ted now readily agreed, "I'm not going to let an engine ruin the last of a good holiday. I'll do it without power."

And so we wandered onward in company, joining each other after the day's sail or whiling away the stormy days, visiting pubs or chattering in one boat or the other. Ted regaled us with stories of the Royal Air Force. He'd signed out after nine years as a pilot and was looking for work with a commercial airline so he could have more free time for *Quinag*. He had a hundred questions for us—he too hoped to cruise off someday. We matched him question for question about England.

We loved the southwest coast of England and sailed up each river that had enough water for the two boats. We hid from storms two or three days at a time in the Tamar River, then the river at Salcombe. One rainy, windy day Larry and I donned our wet-weather gear for a walk ashore. We were anchored a mile upriver from the village, so we landed on a tiny shingle patch next to some heavy woods and pulled the dinghy clear of the high-water mark. Then we scrambled through the woods until we came to a bramble hedge, the last of its berries long since turned to seed. Larry searched along the hedge to find a hole. He helped me through, holding the bigger branches out of my way, and then I helped him. Then hand in hand, chatting about nothing in particular, we strolled up the grass-covered hill toward a distant gate. Something made me turn my head. Standing not a hundred yards from us, slowly pawing the ground and snorting, was the biggest, blackest bull I've ever seen close up. I jerked Larry's hand and pointed. He didn't pause. He dragged me along, running as best he could in bulky wet-weather gear. We headed for the nearest hedge and literally dove through the first hole we saw. We came out the other side slightly scratched and breathing like runners from the four-minute mile. Then Larry found a place to look over the six-foot-high hedge and let out a wonderful peal of laughter. "Bull never moved an inch. Couldn't, Lin. He's chained to a big stake." Then Larry set to work pulling brambles from my hair.

Two weeks later, we approached the entrance to the River Dart. Ted and Jonquil waved good-bye. They had a fair wind and tide for home, and commitments. We had no schedule and we didn't want to miss the home of England's famous naval college. Besides, friends we'd met along the way had told us that the seawall in front of Dartmouth town was a perfect place to dry out. After almost four years of constant sailing we were beginning to be tormented by a loud clicking sound when we lay at anchor. We'd traced the sound to our gudgeons and pintals. They had worn and become sloppy. So Larry wanted to remove the rudder, bore out the gudgeons, and insert nylon bushings to stop the gradual wearing of bronze against bronze.

The tide was against us, flowing out of the narrow entrance of the River Dart at four knots. So we found a shallow spot, near a tiny old stone water mill perched on the steep shore, and let go our anchor. That evening's weather forecast was for the usual easterly winds, the same winds we'd been beating against for most of the past two weeks, so we lay comfortably in the lee of the land all night.

I was first on deck in the morning. A small fishing boat was headed into the river and I waved. The fisherman yelled, "Want a crab?" I called back, "How much do they cost?" He came carefully alongside and insisted, "Go get your biggest cooking pot." I looked at the beautiful live crabs crawling out of boxes and around the fisherman's heavily booted feet and Larry was almost instantly on deck with our eight-quart stewing pot. The fisherman picked up one crab after another, then finally settled on one that could just be squeezed into the pot if he held the claws under the crab. "That's enough for the two of you; give me five shillings." The fisherman didn't wait for our thanks but putted off with our sixty cents while we let our delicious-looking four-pound friend loose in our big plastic washbasin. Then we prepared to sail in with the tide.

CHAPTER 4

Of Rudders and Surveys and Ladies

As we short-tacked past the old verandaed buildings of the Royal Dart Yacht Club, Larry asked me to set our Canadian ensign. I climbed aft of the boom gallows and reached up to hook the flag onto its grommet on the backstay. Larry called a regulation "Ready about," then brought *Seraffyn* up into the wind. I snapped the lower hook of the flag in place and moved clear of the boom as *Seraffyn* paid off on the other tack. Then I let out a shriek, "Come about quick!" A big hunk of my long unruly hair had gone into the double mainsheet block. Some very quick work on Larry's part saved me from being scalped, and we continued up the otherwise beautifully placid river, stray black hairs hanging from the block.

There's nothing quite like meeting an old cruising friend in a new port. As soon as we spotted *Mouette* I rushed below to start a pot of fresh coffee and Larry yelled, "Hey, Brian, come on over for breakfast. How long'd your trip from the Azores take?"

Brian Craigie-Lucas was alongside as soon as we'd set our anchor. Over sausages and eggs we thanked him for the *Shell Guide*. Then Brian reached into his pocket and presented us with two unpolished whale's teeth. "Your friend, Anton, in Horta, came running down to the harbor to give these to you the day you were leaving. You didn't hear him calling, so he gave them to me in case I saw you somewhere in England," Brian told us as he dug into his breakfast. Brian is over six feet tall and on the thin side. I always worried that he wasn't getting enough to eat. Yet when we'd been invited for dinner on board *Mouette* in the Azores, Brian had served us a plentiful, tasty meal. Brian had made a single-handed voyage to the Cape Verde Islands in thirty-five-year-old *Mouette*. Her engine had had a broken crankshaft when he bought her, so Brian sold the engine and did without. Now he was waiting for fair winds for the voyage up channel to his home on the Hamble river. "Most frightening part of any voyage," Brian told us, "so much shipping, bad visibility, tides. Have to stay awake for at least twenty hours to keep a lookout past Portland Bill and St. Albans. Be glad when it's over." (See Appendix B for details on *Mouette*.)

When Larry mentioned wanting to dry out, Brian grabbed our tide tables from the shelf. "Get her next to the wall by noon, then you'll have most of the afternoon to work," he said.

I was really concerned about this idea of laying our five-and-a-quarter-ton pride and joy against a stone wall, then letting her dry out. It was okay for Brian tell us not to worry. He'd been sailing around these waters for thirty years and as he said, "I've never once paid to haul *Mouette*. Why should I spend money when I can dry her out for free?"

Larry wasn't concerned either because he'd used a tidal grid at his yacht club in West Vancouver. But when we sailed across the river an hour later and tied to the iron guardrail posts lining the edge of the main street in Dartmouth, I rushed around like a nervous clucking hen. I watched as the tide rushed quickly out and *Seraffyn*'s keel nestled into the hard sand bottom. Larry tied her so she leaned against three fenders, a line from her mast secured to the iron posts, a long bow and stern line and two springs holding her in position. Slowly *Seraffyn*'s bowsprit lowered as the water ebbed away. I tried to find work to keep me busy, but each time *Seraffyn* wiggled or squirmed during the two hours it took for the tide to flow out from under us, I'd yell out, "Sure she won't fall?"

"Come on, be logical," Larry kept saying. "There's the whole town of Dartmouth holding her up on one side, and a twelve-inch-wide, three-thousand-pound lead keel trying to stay in one place. How can she go anywhere?" When I climbed on deck, looked overboard, and saw less than a foot of water around us, I realized Larry was right. But I still walked around on deck light-footed.

We had a cup of tea in the cockpit as the last of the water rushed away. Larry glanced up at the iron post right above our heads and joked, "Sure would be funny if some dog decided to use that particular post." He wasn't laughing when, not more than five minutes later, a spotted mongrel did just that. Larry was prancing around like a whirl-

Seraffyn's full-length keel and outboard rudder make her easy to haul, and now we found her easy to lay against a seawall for a quick scrub and rudder repairs. Our CQR anchor has lived in this position for forty thousand miles and never caused a problem.

ing dervish, screaming at the top of his lungs, trying to avoid that dog's yellow stream. His shouts cut short the dog's activities and a few buckets of sea water washed away the evidence.

Outboard rudders make sense for a cruising boat. Ours was off in less than ten minutes. The harbormaster came by as Larry was inspecting the wear on our manganese bronze gudgeons. He charged us twenty-five pence a day for using the town hard. So the complete slippage bill for the job came to seventy-five pence, or $1.80 for three days. If we'd had an inboard rudder we'd have had to be lifted by a travel lift or gone on a ways car with enough room below it to drop the rudder and shaft. Our outboard rudder had two other major advantages. We'd been able to fit the least expensive, simplest homemade type of self-steering gear. And if our rudder was ever damaged at sea we could get at it to work on it.

We scrubbed the slime off *Seraffyn*'s bottom, and Larry searched around town until he found a machine shop that could make the nylon shoulder bearings he wanted. We turned in after an early dinner, weary from the day's work. Normally we sleep with our heads toward *Seraffyn*'s bow, feet under the bookshelf that is attached to the bulkhead between the forepeak and main cabin. But *Seraffyn* was lying bow down at an angle of six or eight degrees because of the shape of her forefoot and keel. So I changed the bedclothes around and our feet pointed toward the bitts and chain locker. It was quite comfortable, and since I had finally gotten over worrying about leaning against the quay with no water around us, we both fell asleep quickly. At about two in the morning the tide started slowly to lift *Seraffyn*'s bow. A fishing boat plowed up the river and its wake caused *Seraffyn* to thump loudly twice. Larry was up like a shot. He threw the bedclothes off, and by force of habit rushed toward the foot of the bunk to climb out and see what was happening. He collided soundly with the bits and got caught in the chain locker, his heart pounding so loudly I could hear it. Finally he realized we'd been sleeping wrong way round, unscrambled himself from the chain locker, and found the companionway. *Seraffyn* lay perfectly calm. But it took a shot of brandy before Larry was calm enough to sleep again.

Many interesting people stopped to chat with us as we worked just below the sidewalk on Dartmouth's riverfront. One couple came by and said, "Hello. Know you're busy, but how about joining us in the park to share our picnic lunch?" Instead, we invited them on board and

I added tea and fruit to their spread of sandwiches and cheese. Nigel and Jan Hudson had saved all they could by working at several jobs in Australia. They'd sold everything they owned and, at about twenty-five years of age, set off with ten thousand Australian dollars (about thirteen thousand U.S. dollars) to look for a yacht to live on. They'd had an adventurous journey starting first in Singapore then leading across Asia, through the Himalayas, across Turkey, around the Mediterranean, and finally to England. They'd traveled by hitchhiking, bus, train, airplane, and foot. Now they owned a tiny old Austin estate wagon which they used as a caravan. After much consideration, they'd decided that a Vertue-class twenty-six-foot sloop would be a practical cruising boat. Nigel and Jan had come to Dartmouth to look at a nine-year-old Vertue that was advertised for four thousand pounds (about nine thousand U.S. dollars). Two days after our picnic lunch, they asked us to take a look at the boat they liked. We looked it over and agreed that it would be a fair buy if it passed survey.

"Survey?" Nigel replied. "Why should I pay seventy dollars for someone to look at a boat for me? I know enough about boats to look her over myself. Don't worry, I'll be careful before I spend my money."

Larry shook his head and explained, "I built my own boat and spent ten years repairing other people's boats, and I'd still employ a surveyor. That way a disinterested person would be double-checking it for me. He wouldn't be prejudiced by having fallen in love with some beautiful but possibly rotten old classic. He might catch all sorts of things I'd miss. Besides, I've rarely heard of a good surveyor who couldn't save you at least the cost of his fee when it came to negotiating the final price."

Jan and Nigel went away that evening discussing Larry's words. They came back the next day and told us they'd made an offer for the Vertue, subject to survey. They'd refused to use the local surveyor suggested by the owner's agent and instead hired one from out of town. We watched the surveyor at work the next day and he was good. His hammer and awl searched everyplace you might expect to find trouble. He pulled every sail from its bag. He climbed the mast, carefully removed several fastenings from the hull and pieces of ceiling from the boat's interior. Then he gave Nigel and Jan a typed list of all the defects he'd found and suggested a reduced offer. After the surveyor left, Nigel told us, "Best seventy dollars I ever spent. I learned seventy bucks' worth just watching him survey the boat. There's about three thousand dollars' worth of repairs needed to get the boat seaworthy. Won't buy it unless the owner either lowers the price or pays for the repairs."

Negotiations fell through on the Vertue, but we kept in touch with Nigel and Jan as they wandered around England for four months more looking for the perfect small cruising boat. Then they headed back to Australia and a year later wrote us, "We've started building our own twenty-eight-footer. Seems there are no cheap good small boats to be had anywhere in the world."

After three days we sailed *Seraffyn* away from Dartmouth's town quay, anchored, and rowed ashore with a bag of dirty laundry. We put our clothes in the coin-operated machines and Larry suggested a cup of tea. The closest tea shop had a window full of delicious-looking fat pills and we were soon digging into a plate of tea cakes and raisin buns. A diminutive gray-haired, sixty-five-year-old lady trundled in, flower-print dress covered by a tidy handknit sweater, white gloves immaculate. She set her large shopping bag down next to the window table and ordered tea from the smiling waitress, who addressed her as "Mrs. Smith." I whispered to Larry "Perfect English lady," as Mrs. Smith carefully removed her gloves and skillfully poured tea.

We went back for our laundry and the next time we saw Mrs. Smith was an hour later at the town quay. She was dressed from head to toe in baggy black oilskins with knee-high seaboots. She dragged an Avon dinghy through the thirty-feet of mud between quay and water, and rowed out to an antique-looking sloop. Larry and I were stopped in our tracks by this transformation, and rowed by her boat on the way home.

"Hello there," Esther Smith yelled. "You must be off that little Canadian yacht. Come on board." We gladly accepted and explored *Essex Breeze*, a 1930 Alfred Milne–designed thirty-two-foot sloop. Although someone had shortened the original ten-foot bowsprit on *Essex Breeze*, they'd never touched the magnificent thirty-foot-long boom. Esther had a fire roaring in her tiny coal-burning stove when we came below.

"I'm the worst sailor in Dartmouth," she proudly announced. Then she told us her story. "I always wanted to learn to sail, ever since I was a tiny girl, but my father wouldn't hear of it. And then when I got married my husband told me, 'Sailing isn't for ladies.' Well, my husband died when I was fifty-five so I hired a man to look after our farm for a few months, then I bought this sailboat. I figured I didn't have much time at my age to learn to sail properly. I just had to go out and *sail. Essex Breeze* has taken good care of me. But I always warn everyone to stay out of my way."

We both were enchanted by Esther, and before we left that evening we'd planned an exploratory sail upriver in company. Larry rowed me over to *Essex Breeze* the next morning, and rowed home to get *Seraffyn* under way. Esther and I had a great time running before the strong, fluky winds with the tide under us. Then without warning that six-inch-diameter, solid-pitchpine, thirty-foot-long boom came whistling by, clearing the top of my head by inches. I'd heard it coming. Most booms are quiet until they reach the end of the jibe. Esther's enormous boom gained so much velocity as it flew across a seventy- or eighty-foot arc that it actually started whistling, just like a dive bomber. I must have looked startled when I turned to where Esther was complacently steering upriver, tiller under her seaboot. "Oh yes," she chirped. "Should have said 'Jibe ho,' shouldn't I."

We anchored four miles farther upriver, near the shipyards at Galmpton, and Larry moored *Seraffyn* alongside. Clad in oilskins, the three of us climbed into our six-foot eight-inch pram *Rinky Dink* for a row ashore and a tromp through the drizzle and woods. I suggested dinner on board *Seraffyn* when we came back, and Esther excused herself for a few moments. When I set the hot beef stew on the table, Mrs. Smith from the tea room sat next to Larry, gloves on the settee, a garnet brooch on her shoulder.

Once again a pile of mail lay ahead of us. We were also almost out of money. Brian Cooke had both waiting for us in Poole. We'd sent some checks ahead to him and asked him to open a checking account for us (current account in English). But now we had less than twenty-five dollars on board, and although Poole was only about eighty miles east of us, easterly gales were blowing through the whole of the English Channel. In desparation I walked into a branch of Brian's bank in Dartmouth and asked for the manager. He laughed at my concern and explained the exceptional services offered by the National Westminster Bank of England. An account in any branch of that bank is good in any other branch with only ten minutes' delay. Although it's handier to have a checkbook from your own branch, it's not necessary.

He also told us about the most convenient way to handle money we'd ever run into—Eurochecks. Once our account was established, our bank manager would issue each of us with a Eurocard. This card would have our name, account number, and special check-cashing number. By presenting this card to any participating bank in any European country, plus twenty-four other countries, like Malta, Lebanon, Turkey, or Egypt, we could cash a check for thirty pounds each day. The National Westminster Bank would guarantee these checks as long as our special number was on the back. During the next four years of cruising in fourteen countries, we've had no need for travelers checks. All of our banking was done through our British External Account. (Any European bank can arrange Eurochecks for you.) Meanwhile, the Dartmouth bank manager gave us thirty pounds in cash and we rushed off, rich again, to buy a steak for dinner.

Easterly winds were followed by dense fog, then more easterly gales. We were tired of sitting in the River Dart. We'd rigged up a workable heater by lashing a big pot lid as a reflector in the back of

Brian and Sheena Cooke were a constant source of help during our stay in England. We'd first met Brian in Horta as he sailed the fifty-six-foot *British Steel* home from the 1972 Observer Single-handed Transatlantic Race. This photo was taken on board *British Steel* just before the race. *Mike Hope*

our Primus one-burner stove, but rain and wind kept us confined inside the boat too much. So we asked Brian Craigie-Lucas to watch *Seraffyn* for a day, and after filling and lighting our kerosene anchor light, we hitchhiked to Poole and spent the night with Brian Cooke and his wife Sheena. Brian took the morning off and showed us a safe and inexpensive marina in Poole where we could spend the winter tied to a dock with electricity and water available. Then we hitchhiked back to Dartmouth. It was dark when we arrived at the river. But we could easily spot *Seraffyn* because that little anchor light with its half a cup of oil was still burning, thirty-six hours after we'd lit it.

For three weeks the gales blew. We'd spend our mornings on board writing, then we'd wander around visiting new friends. Some afternoons we'd read books to while away the time. We had all sorts of plans for the winter months when we would hopefully be tied alongside a quay; meanwhile, we sat and waited for the weather to clear, getting up to catch each weather forecast. One day the rains let up, but the wind was still reported as gale force easterly for the Channel. When the sun came out Larry said, "Come on, let's you and me sail around the river again. At least we won't be sitting around moping all day." I pulled on my warm jacket and joined him on deck, still in short temper after three weeks of wishing for fair winds.

"Come on, Lin, get that mainsheet cleated and haul in the jib," Larry yelled from forward, as he secured the anchor. He came aft and took the tiller from me. "Ease the main," he called. I turned to ease the mainsail. "The outhaul needs tightening" was his next command. "Free the telltale," he called.

I blew up. "Stop bossing me around," I yelled. "I can sail this boat as well as you can!"

Larry merely let go of the tiller and walked away. "Do it then!" *Seraffyn* beat down on the boats moored ahead. I took hold of the tiller, brought her about, got the jib in on the other tack, and sat smugly steering close-hauled toward the boats on the other side of the channel.

"Not bad," Larry commented as he came on deck with a hot mug of coffee, "but you're pinching."

I pulled the tiller toward me.

"I'd come about now if I were you, Lin. . . . Too quick. . . . You're too far off the wind. . . . Why don't you watch your telltale?" Larry's criticisms fell on me like stinging shots of hail as my silent temper grew blacker and blacker.

When I finally tried, I found I
could even handle *Seraffyn's*
sixteen-foot-long spinnaker
pole. But it was more difficult
than we liked so Larry has
since designed a much easier
arrangement.

I tacked to clear the stern of a sloop moored near the shore. I was so angry by this time I couldn't see straight. Then the jib sheet got in an override on the winch. I bashed the back of my hand as I cleared the snarl up, balancing on one leg, the other stretched behind me, foot on the tiller. Still, Larry sat on the cabin top issuing commands—"Shouldn't have come through the wind so quickly. Jib sheet wasn't cleared before you tacked."

I finally let go. "I'm never going to sail with you again if you don't shut up right now!" I yelled so loud a cormarant flew squawking from the boat near us. In seven years together, I'd only once before screamed at Larry. He almost fell over and his shocked look set me laughing. "Now get to the end of the bowsprit where I can't hear your silly comments," I told him. He went meekly and sat at the forward end of the bowsprit while I short-tacked through the mooring-filled river, past the narrows in front of Agatha Christie's summer home, past the bend at Galmpton, tack on tack. Without Larry's nagging, I soon set my own pattern for each tack. I never missed a move, as I planned how to get the jib in before I needed to use the winch. An hour later I turned and ran downriver right to our mooring spot, let go the anchor, furled the sails, then glared at Larry.

He came back from his perch of exile and wrapped his arms around me. "That's the first time you've really taken charge and sailed this boat yourself, Lin. You did a hell of a job. Anytime you want to be in charge from now on, tell me and I'll play flunky."

~~~~~~

CHAPTER 5

To Find
a Winter Haven

Another 0630 weather forecast of heavy fog sent me back into the warm sleeping bag. "Come on, Larry, dream up something to do today." He yawned, wrapped his arms more tightly around me, and sighed, "Just have to spend the day in bed, I guess."

The three-knot ebb of the tide past our anchor chain and stem gurgled and boiled. *Seraffyn* sounded as though she were under way. I listened to the water rushing past and thought of the three weeks we'd been anchored in Dartmouth waiting for fair weather. Portland Bill, with its tidal race and one of the heaviest concentrations of shipping anywhere in the world, lay between us and Poole. Each time there had not been reports of easterly gales there had been reports of fog. Not only did we feel it was wise to wait for a fair wind, we also wanted a twenty-four-hour period with good visibility. We'd feel like sitting ducks if we became becalmed in the English Channel. Twice we'd doubted the weather forecasts we heard on the radio, and twice we'd set sail, only to run into a sheet of fog rolling and boiling at the river's mouth. Each time we'd turned back to anchor and wait some more. I was bored. November. Days getting shorter and shorter. Cold. I wanted to settle someplace for the winter where we could get ashore without rowing, and Dartmouth didn't have room at its marina. Besides, we needed a new mainsail and Larry had a good idea. "I'll ask around till I find a sailmaker who's overworked, then ask if I can work for him in exchange for the materials for our new sail. That way I'll learn something about sailmaking and I can finish our mainsail to my own specs." Dartmouth had no sailmaker.

We read until lunchtime, propped against the hull in our forward

Seraffyn's Sony casette stereo
works off a six-volt dry-cell battery,
the same type we use for our
quarter-mile flashlight. The battery
gives us power for 100 to 150
hours of music.

Filling the tea kettle is easy with
Seraffyn's gravity-fed day tank
water system. No pumps to rebuild,
no parts to replace. Headroom
under the skylight is 5' 6" and
under the two hatches its 5' 9",
enough for Larry.

The table slides out easily from
under the cockpit and seats four.

bunk, then got up and dressed to share a big lunch. Fog rolled past our port lights. We couldn't see the boat on the next mooring although it was less than a hundred feet away.

Larry got out our cribbage board and beat me at another series, best of three games. We heard the buzz of an outboard. Someone yelled, "Pardeys, you there?" Larry knocked the cards off the table in his rush to open the companionway hatch. He yelled "Over here" into the thick whiteness.

Henry North appeared through the fog. "Thought you might like a ride around the moors. Grab your boots and come with me." We'd met Henry with his long gray beard, flying brown hair, and perpetual Harris-tweed, elbow-patched jacket when we'd dried *Seraffyn* out. But we'd only chatted casually with him as he worked on one or the other of the three small charter boats he owned.

"Best put on an anchor light," Henry suggested. "I've told my wife to expect you for dinner." We putted across the river then scrambled into Henry's old car, shoving boat gear out of the way. Henry inched slowly through fog-shrouded Dartmouth, then up the long steep hill past the naval college. When we reached the moors, visibility improved until we could see a mile ahead over the moss- and fern-covered rolling hills. A few shaggy dripping ponies huddled in a tiny valley by the road side, a small remnant of the herd of wild Dartmoor horses.

We rode across mile after mile of gray and brown soggy desolation until suddenly the hulking gray walls of Dartmoor prison rose through the gloom. Henry's great-great-grandfather had captured many of Napoleon's soldiers who'd later perished in this infamous fortress. So Henry was able to give us a running commentary of heroic escape attempts and prison stories. We turned into the courtyard of a slate-roofed pub and parked. Henry led us through the leaded-glass door and we were greeted by the roar of an open fire that sent flickers of light across black leather seats and red carpets. We snacked on tiny hot pies filled with beef and onions while Henry chatted on. "This is where the prison warders have hung out for the past three hundred years." After exhausting his collection of prison stories, Henry pointed at some hunting prints on the wall. "Always preferred punting myself. My dad built a special boat. When you got in it, the gunwale was almost level with the river. Had a real cannon of a shotgun bolted on the deck. I'd lay in it among the reeds of the river till a flight of ducks landed. Then I'd let fly. That gun could take thirty sitting ducks at a shot."

We reluctantly left the warmth of the pub to drive on to a wood. We followed Henry through the damp grass and birch trees until we were at the top of a small rise. "You're standing on a fortress from the Bronze Age," he announced. Henry and his father had dug at this site and uncovered Bronze Age tools and household utensils. "Come on, let's get back to the house," Henry called as he turned to go back to the car, "I've got lots there to show you."

When we arrived at Henry's hundred-fifty-year-old rambling house, perched on a ridge a thousand feet above the River Dart, there wasn't the slightest chance of getting the car into the garage—it was filled to overflowing with boat gear. Three sailing dinghies littered the tiny lawn. We'd just reached the door when it was flung open by a big, buxom, raven-haired woman. "Come in, come in." She led us into the cluttered entry hall, peeled our coats from us, flung them onto an already-overheaped chair. "I'm a lousy housekeeper, but then I've got an excuse. My family always had servants before," she said with a wink. "Now I'm decadent aristocracy!"

We almost tripped over two children lying next to the fire, eyes glued to the television. "Off with the moron-a-scope!" Henry roared, "we've got company." He cleared a pile of books from two chairs. The children joined in as Henry pulled one nautical antique after another from the crowded shelves. Josephine rolled a tray of drinks into the room muttering, "Neither of our families ever threw anything away. Come on, Lin, I've got something more interesting than these silly old pieces of brass to show you." We crossed the entrance hall into a large dining room filled by a magnificent mahogany table for ten. One complete side of the room was covered by a doll's house. "Forty rooms, every bit of furniture built by my father," Josephine explained as she showed me perfectly scaled, two-inch-high, plush-covered sofas, quarter-inch-high chamber pots, and miniature silver tea services. "But that's not what I want to show you." I turned reluctantly away from the thirteen-foot-long, five-foot-high doll's house.

Josephine opened the lid on a cedar-lined chest that was as long as the doll's house and almost four-feet deep. Piles of handmade lace petticoats burst from it as she burrowed deep into its interior. "All the clothes my mother, grandmother, and great-grandmother owned. Here it is! I'm sure my grandmother was exactly your size when she was young." Before I could protest, Josephine pulled my sweater over my head and began lacing me into a whalebone, blue-ribboned corset, then a wicker bustle. Over this she dropped two lace-covered petticoats. "My ancestors were Scottish lairds, had the same family of seamstresses living in the castle since 1800. Two women worked full-time making grandmama's clothes." I looked over the fine handstitiching of the petticoats while Josephine dug deeper into the chest. She pulled out a white silk blouse with a high lace ruff, then a blue-and-white-striped silk skirt and waistcoat with the same tiny stitching. Soon I stood tightly laced while Josephine combed my hair smooth. I glided slowly into the drawing room, silk rustling about me, stopped just inside the door, and dropped a curtsy as best I could from memories of Scarlett O'Hara and *Gone with the Wind.* My entry was a complete success. Larry and Henry stopped talking and stared. I turned to show off my bustle and my skirt lifted a bit. Henry toasted me with his glass of whiskey, then cocked his head to one side and stated, "Magnificent, magnificent! Fits you perfectly, but those seaboots aren't quite right, are they?"

I sat on a stool at dinner, bustle behind me, skirts in a sweep around my feet. I sympathized with the ladies of 1850 as my intake of the bountious roast-lamb dinner was limited by the tightly laced corset. I climbed reluctantly back into my slacks and bulky sweater after dinner. Without the corset I was really able to dig into the lucious strawberry trifle that was served with coffee in front of the drawing room fire.

Henry took us home through the fog and we arrived just in time for the 0030 forecast. Northerly winds, Force 4 to 5, visibility improving. A wonderful day with the incredible Norths, a good forecast for the next day. We consulted our tide tables, planned for a late-afternoon departure, then got a good night's sleep.

We sailed out of the River Dart on a westerly wind less than twenty minutes after the 1800 forecast. It was dark and we could see Start Point light twenty miles southwest of us. The lights of shipping showed around the horizon. I chose the first watch, so Larry helped me set the lapper on the spinnaker pole, then went below. Wing and wing, we flew through the night. Larry had a shot of brandy, then started to pull his shoes off as I watched him through the half-open companionway. We cleared the point of Lyme Bay and the wind shifted ninety degrees without warning. Helmer, our steering vane, changed course to compensate. "How about a hand to take the pole down?" I called to Larry. He pulled on his shoes and came up. "It'll be wet when you put her on a beam reach," Larry told me as he surveyed the situation. "I'll get the pole down; you get your wet gear on."

After pulling on another sweater, then my anorak, boots, and wet-weather gear, I struggled through the companionway feeling like a kid ready for the snow. I took over from Larry, sheeted in the jib, and reset Helmer.

Seraffyn's bowsprit pointed east again. Her bow shoved aside rolls

Waterproof gloves and good foul-weather gear are a must to enjoy English winter sailing.

of water and showers of spray burst over her windward side. I was glad of my waterproof gear as I huddled against the back of the cabin trying to shield myself from the spray and cold. *Seraffyn* reached over the tide-tossed seas of Lyme Bay at over five knots. The northerly wind had thirty miles of fetch and kicked up a nasty sea. Normally I'd have left Helmer to steer and gone below to make a hot drink of tea, but now we were surrounded by heavy shipping. When I climbed on top of the dinghy I counted the lights of twenty-six ships. They stayed well clear of us and I spent most of my time trying to keep warm. Our ship's clock rang each half hour and I woke Larry eagerly when three hours had passed.

His Canadian blood must be thicker than mine because what to me had seemed like a hell of cold and wet drew comments of delight from Larry. We steered a course to clear Portland's race by seven or eight miles. Although this put us right in the shipping lanes, it kept us clear of the tidal overfalls.

As the sun rose, we saw Portland Bill looking like an island and slowly the wind died. The tide carried us east. The sun dried our decks. By noon we had our jackets and sweaters off. Larry was shirtless. The white chalk cliffs of Lulworth Cove slid slowly past us. Then, just at four o'clock, tea time, our northerly breeze came back. God, it was cold! Larry took charge and sailed us past St. Albans Head. He piled on all the clothes he could, including his wet-weather gear although there was no spray at all. I stayed warm in the cabin, passing up mugs of hot chocolate and navigating as we beat in, looking for Poole Harbor light. "What kind of sequence is that light supposed to have?" Larry asked again.

"One flash every five seconds."

"Only light anywhere near my course is a quick flasher," Larry announced.

He came below and together we studied the chart. There was a nasty-looking mile-and-a-half-long submerged breakwater shown at the entrance to Poole Harbor. Miserable thing to bump into at night. We were trying to find the buoy that marked its end. Larry went on deck and looked again, then called, "Anywhere else we can go and anchor for the night? The lights are different from the light list. Not worth taking a chance."

I studied the chart. "Do you see a red flashing light about two miles away, right on our beam?" I asked.

"There's a red flasher on what looks like a pier," Larry called down. "Great! Head for that and drop the anchor anywhere you want. But don't go inshore of the pier. Lots of protection from this wind."

As we reached slowly in toward the Swanage pier on the dying northerly breeze I chatted with Larry through the three-quarters-closed companionway feeling only slightly guilty about being so warm as he steered with the tiller between his legs, hands in his pockets. We talked about other times we'd made a landfall after dark only to find the lights or landmarks didn't line up with the chart. Each time, we'd chosen an alternate anchorage or hove to until morning. Each time, when daylight came we'd found we'd made the right decision. (We later learned that the light on the Poole Harbor entrance buoy had been changed to a quick flasher only two weeks before.)

We spent a peaceful night anchored in Swanage, disturbed only slightly by a southeasterly swell. By morning a southerly gale was blowing and only the reef off the southern tip of Swanage protected us. We ran into Poole Harbor under the gray, lowering sky, picking our way through the shoals, and tied up at Poole Town Quay as the first squalls of rain came down.

Brian Cooke arrived minutes after our call to take us home for showers and Sheena's wonderful steak-and-kidney pie. The storm was over when Brian drove us home late that evening. We noticed ice forming on the puddles along the quay. Our breath froze in the air of *Seraffyn's* cabin as we got ready for bed. By morning there was snow on our decks.

Larry looked out at the glistening white covering our cockpit, shook his head, and said, "Looks like time to winter."

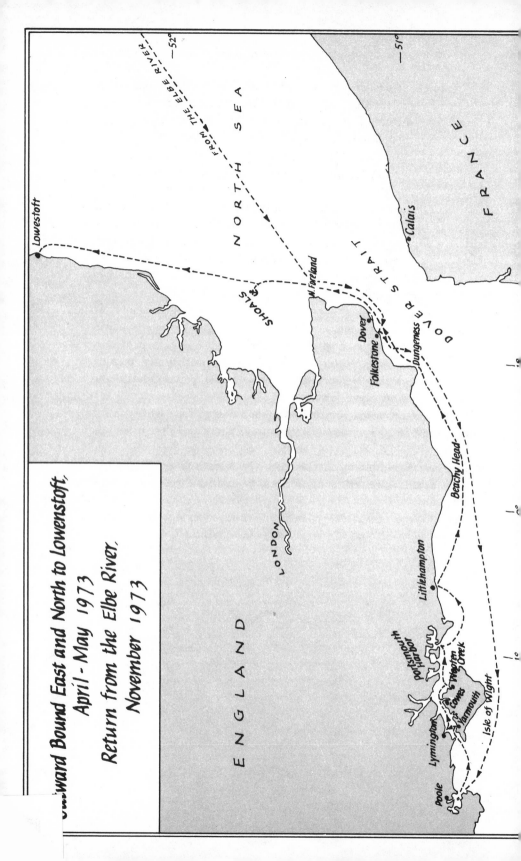

Outward Bound East and North to Lowestoft,
April - May 1973
Return from the Elbe River,
November 1973

FROM THE ELBE RIVER

52°

51°

Lowestoft

NORTH SEA

SHOALS

N. Foreland

Dover

Folkestone

Dungeness

DOVER STRAIT

Calais

FRANCE

Beachy Head

Littlehampton

LONDON

ENGLAND

Portsmouth Harbor

Lymington

Cowes

Wootton Creek

Yarmouth

Isle of Wight

Poole

1°

2°

1°

CHAPTER 6

Winter

Poole Town Quay—it sounds so safe and comfortable. But the name doesn't tell about a rushing five-knot current. Nor does it indicate the ten-foot rise and fall of the tide. What appeared to be husky pilings at high tide became worm-eaten scraggle-toothed monsters as the water ebbed away. We found a ten-foot-long two- by eight-inch plank and made it into a fender board. But when the wind blew strong from the east, a nasty swell ran through the channel. Then fenders popped from behind the board and lines chaffed around rusty metal securing rings so that gear had to be tended constantly. A slimy twenty-foot steel ladder was my low tide doorway to the upper world. Not twenty feet from *Seraffyn,* double-decked red buses rushed by shaking the street. Two tugs tied just ahead and often woke us with the roar of their engines and wash of their propellors.

After the quiet of river anchorages, this hustle would have been a trial but for the people we began to meet the moment we sailed in. Basil Bennet took our lines and promptly invited us to lunch at the Parkstone Yacht Club the next day. Basil could only be described as loquacious, and after overwhelming us completely with a flurry of new people, presented us to the club secretary who gave us a handwritten card that said "L & L Pardey are honorary members when ever they arrive at the Parkstone Yacht Club on board *Seraffyn.*" When we told Basil of our desire to find an overworked sailmaker, he assured us, "Should be no problem at all. Every sailmaker for miles around is overworked."

The next morning Larry left the boat early. He was back within an hour. "Found our sailmaker. His loft is only two blocks from here.

He'll come by with his girlfriend at 7 P.M. for a drink. I start work tomorrow for three weeks; then he'll help me build our new mainsail."

So our days fell into a pattern. I'd work on writing each morning while Larry went off to learn sailmaking. I'd often bring Larry a packed lunch and join in as Paul Lees told us about sails. Paul was only twenty-one but had worked two and a half years with Hood's of Lymington. He was an avid dinghy sailor and had won the National Yachting Monthly Day-Boat Championships two or three years running. As he learned sailmaking, Paul began doing repairs at home for his dinghy-sailing friends. This grew until he had to ask his mother to help with the machine work. He'd finally opened his own loft just four months previously, and he and his mother really appreciated Larry's help, especially because they didn't have to pay in cash, a commodity that is scarce in most new businesses. Paul's loft rang constantly with taped pop music. The tea kettle had a place of honor on the cluttered workbench.

"You're right about building a mainsail without battens," Paul told us as he sipped his tea. "Look at that pile of repairs. Every mainsail has ripped or chafed batten pockets." One corner of the loft was filled with a ceiling-high pile of bagged sails waiting for repairs. Larry spent most of his working day on these. He showed me headboards that were ripped loose, seams that needed restitching, weak reefing clew patches. So when it came time to build our own mainsail, Paul selected unfilled 6.5-ounce U.S.-weight Terelyne (the English brand name for Dacron) and laid it out so it would need no battens or headboard. Each seam was triple-stitched, and three rows of reefpoints were sewn in place, with the clew and tack patches strongly reinforced. Then Larry set to work using his new skills to handsew the boltrope. He handstitched every ring into the sail. The results were great. In four years not one ring or seam has needed repairs. We've also been able to hoist, lower, or reef the sail on any point of the wind, no battens or headboard to catch under the spreaders, shrouds, or lazy jacks.

"What do you think of making a genoa with a row of reef points in it?" Larry asked when Paul took the two of us to lunch at his favorite pub. "Great idea," Paul answered as he dug into his venison sausages. "That way you'll have one jib taken the place of two. Put a rope luff in—it's easier to sew a reef cringle to a rope than a wire. You'll have draft control that way, too. Want to work off that genoa now?" Larry declined the offer since our headsails still had some life left in them.

But Paul's enthusiasm set us thinking about how much space we'd save below decks by having reefpoints instead of extra sails.

As soon as Larry was finished with our sails, we decided to leave noisy Poole Town Quay and sail under the lifting bridge separating us from a huge tidal bay that contained Cobbs Quay marina. The bridge opened only four times a day, so sailing would be difficult once we were through. But Cobbs Quay had floating docks next to each boat and we could secure *Seraffyn* and not worry about tides or tugs. We used a fair tide and a light easterly breeze to sail through the bridge. Then we threaded our way up the narrow, twisting channel, nudging the muddy sides twice when we took too long to tack. I looked around at the miles of dull-brown, reed-covered tidal swamp. Cobbs Quay came into view, not a tree in sight. Two hundred deserted-looking boats were tied forlornly in the water; three hundred more were ashore for the winter, covered with tarpaulins. The low gray clouds added to the neglected, end-of-the-season mood I felt as we warped into our mooring and Larry made fast six lines to hold us in position. I went below out of the drizzle. The tide fell slowly and mud banks became my only view as I looked out the galley port light. Our little butane heater glowed bravely, but its heat didn't dispel my gloom. Larry came in as *Seraffyn*'s keel nuzzled into the soft mud below us. It was only 1600 and already dark enough to need our oil lamps.

It was extreme low tide when we got up the next morning. I couldn't believe my eyes. Mud, nothing but mud. Larry and I pulled on jeans, seaboots, two sweaters, and jackets, then climbed on deck. *Seraffyn* had made herself a nest in the mud. The floating pier next to us sat on the mud. The nearest water was twenty-five feet away where the once-wide channel was now merely a trickle. My depression became overwhelming. "We may be safe," I moaned, "but what fun is that? We're miles from everything, no people around, can't go sailing, it's cold, it's months till spring, the weather is miserable." Larry didn't look convincing when he entreated, "Come on, Lin, look at the bright side. *Seraffyn* is absolutely safe here no matter what blows up."

I was close to tears when two swans spotted us standing on the foredeck. They swam to the edge of the tiny dredged channel, then plodded toward us, sinking up to their bellies in mud. By the time they reached *Seraffyn*'s side the two normally snowy-white birds were speckled with mud, from orange beak to wingtips. Larry was quaking with laughter. I ran below to get some slices of bread as the swans begged with hissing noises. A man popped his head out from under the brown canvas cover on a deserted-looking varnished sloop moored two boats away. "It's those damn swans again," he muttered. "Don't encourage them." We turned to him in bewilderment, wondering who could dislike such glorious birds. Then the two swans spotted him and struggled through the gooey mud toward his boat. "Go away, scram!" the head growled as they approached. The two swans ignored him, waddled right up to his boat, hissing, then began to peck at his varnished rub rail. "Look at this," he called. "Not one bit of varnish left since I stopped feeding the beggars."

We walked over and watched as chip after chip of varnish came loose. Mike, who lived on the varnished sloop, introduced himself. "Come over for breakfast in ten minutes," Larry suggested.

Larry buttered toast while I scrambled eggs. "Bus is only three-quarters of a mile away, place isn't deserted, we've got neighbors. Spring's less than three months from now. London Boat Show starts this week and we've got an invite to stay with Alf Taylor in London. Gordon and Annabelle Yates will be here for a visit in four weeks. Winter is going to fly," I told Larry as we waited for Mike. "That's right," he answered. "We'll buy that little Ford Anglia and then do some exploring."

The London Boat show turned out to be a week filled with new ideas, new people. Thousands thronged the huge exposition hall, yet at each corner we'd bump into sailing friends from all parts of the world as we looked at gear from all over Europe.

We tore ourselves away from the boat show to look into visas for our summer's cruise. Sweden, Finland, Denmark, each embassy loaded us with travel brochures and said "No visas needed." The Polish Embassy was a different story: "Fill out these three forms in triplicate, bring four photos each, and pay us four pounds. Then leave your passports with us for ten days so we can decide if we can issue you a visa." We took our forms, kept our passports, and headed toward the Russian Embassy.

Few spy thrillers could have caught the oppressive atmosphere we met there—armed guards, one-way glass doors, heavy drapes, and silent watchers. "Why don't you fly to Russia," the consular officer asked us when we reached his office after a forty-five-minute wait. "I don't know of any yacht that has ever entered socialist Leningrad or Tallinn and I have no idea if it can be arranged. First, you must have a place to keep the boat. Then you'll need a pilot for your voyage up the Neva. Not an easy thing to arrange. Try our shipping company. If you can provide for the boat, I'll provide for the people."

The man at Aeroflot shipping (we've eliminated names for the protection of people who were most kind to us) was delighted by the idea of an engineless twenty-four-foot yacht trying to arrange berthage. "Our country needs visitors like you. I'll set to work immediately on this. No charge, it will be my pleasure. Call me in one week." He took *Seraffyn*'s tonnage, draft, total berthage length (which came to thirty-four feet including bowsprit and boomkin), and cargo—two curious people. "In any country but ours this would be an easy matter," the official told us, "but the Soviet Union? We're very friendly people but our officials are afraid to make unusual decisions." We left his office determined to visit Russia.

We rejoined Brian Cooke at the National Westminster Bank stand he was working on at the boat show and over lunch told him about our adventures. "I have a Polish sailing friend. Maybe you should write her. Theresa Remiszewski represented Poland in the last single-handed transatlantic race." We took her address, then set off on our two-hour drive back toward Poole.

Both of us used sheet after sheet of tissue as we sniffled from winter colds. We stopped at Brian's house to relay a message to Sheena. She took one look at Larry and all her nursing training came into play. "You're not going back to that cold, damp boat. You're climbing right into our guest bed and staying until you're well." We had no choice. We both felt like pampered children as Sheena made us a hot dinner, then tucked us in. "Come now," she admonished, "admit it, you're crazy to live on such a small boat for the winter. You could have rented a flat for eight pounds [twenty dollars] a week."

As our health improved we came to agree with her. A twenty-four-foot boat is wonderful in the tropics, or even for three or four weeks on a winter cruise. But it *is* too small to winter in. We talked of having a boat big enough to heat with a coal-burning stove. Later, when we were given clean bills of health we went to visit Fiona and Hank who were wintering in Lymington on their fifty-seven-foot cutter. *Senta* was a magnificent yacht built in San Francisco by Lester Stone—teak and mahogany, a huge main saloon, central heating. We found that Fiona and Hank had the same complaints we did. "Never going to spend another winter on a yacht in England. It's just too damp. Everytime you go out you have to walk miles to get anywhere. Get wet and come below and then the cabin sole gets wet. Have to keep everything closed up all the time. Never enough space to spread out. Be cheaper and more comfortable to put the boat on a mooring, rent a flat, and live ashore. Boats are for sailing, not sitting in port." Hank and Fiona had the right to say this. They'd sailed from California and raced and cruised through most of Europe. We left *Senta* with our plans for a bigger boat, complete with coal-burning heater, shelved for a while.

Theresa Remiszewski replied within a week. "Come to Gydnia, be a guest of our sailing club." We called our friend at Aeroflot shipping. "I have it," he said happily. "There's a Telex from Tallinn giving you berthage for the yacht *Seraffyn* and a pilot." So we took a flying trip to London. Theresa's letter got immediate results. Our passports were stamped by the Polish Embassy and returned in ten minutes. The Russian visas were still a problem. "It will take at least three weeks," the Russian consul-general told us, but he then assured us our telegram from Tallinn would solve all problems. So we left our passports and returned to *Seraffyn*.

Winter was flying. Days were growing perceptibly longer. The sun poked its head out at least four days a week. To spice up February, Annabelle and Gordon Yates arrived. We'd first met the Yateses in Baja California two months after our cruising life started. They'd sailed from San Diego on their thirty-two-foot trimaran. We spent wonderful days with them, meeting in scattered rendezvouses from La Paz to Acapulco. We'd get together to share fish recipes and rum punches while we discussed and solved all the world's problems. Then the Yateses turned north to sell *Amøbel* while we headed south toward Panama. We met again in Florida where they were living on an English twenty-two-foot Westerly Cirrus. After three years of cruising the Bahamas and Florida Keys, they'd decided they needed a slightly bigger boat so their grandchildren could come and visit for a few weeks. Now they were bound for Denmark to take possession of a brand-new Great Dane 28 (see Appendix B). For three days Gordon and Annabelle stayed in a rooming house a street away from us and we used our rickety old car to explore all the boatyards and marinas within thirty miles. We talked late into the night and their visit was like a tonic.

As spring grew closer, we set to work on *Seraffyn*'s refit. Larry was busy doing some alterations to the cockpit, so I sanded the starboard bulwark and waterway, dusted it, got out the paint, and started to put it on. I'd removed the ventilator that leads into our chain locker so I could paint around it more easily. With atrocious luck and no small amount of clumsiness, I knocked over the half liter of white paint. Then I let out a shriek as half of it poured down the ventilator hole and the other half ran in a stream down the bare teak decks. "Larry! Get me some kerosene, quick! Rags! Paper towels! Rush!" He came forward to see what was causing the ruckus, looked down at the mess quite calmly, and said "Excuse me." Then he walked off the boat. I ran for kerosene, took one look into the varnished chain locker with its liberal dose of white paint, scrambled back on deck, poured kerosene on the teak, and started rubbing. Just then Paul Lees and his girlfriend Vicky arrived. "Where is Larry?" Paul asked. I looked up from my frantic work and pointed toward the end of the pier two hundred yards away where Larry was yelling at a flock of seagulls. "What is he doing?" Vicki asked. I guiltily answered, "Shouting at the gulls instead of me."

The white paint wiped easily off the varnish of the chain locker. But in spite of scrubbing with a gallon of kerosene, spots of it still decorate the teak deck four years later.

CHAPTER 7

I'd Rather Go
to Sea

I stood at the helm, foghorn in hand. Larry rowed *Seraffyn,* making about one knot. The tide was just beginning to ebb as we approached the closed Poole Town bridge. I blasted the required signal with the horn when we were within a quarter mile of the bridge, then went forward as Larry suggested, to make sure our anchor was ready to let go if a sudden change of current threatened to drag us into danger.

There was a clanging of bells from the bridge control tower. Red lights flashed to stop the Sunday traffic. Guard gates fell into position and slowly the bridge formed a vee, then split in two. Larry kept up a strong, steady rhythm with our fourteen-foot oar and *Seraffyn* moved majestically forward. A back eddy around the bridge structure slowed our progress. The line of waiting cars quickly grew longer. People climbed out of their cars to stand in the sunshine and see what was causing the holdup. The bridgekeeper climbed down from his tower to see where we were. *Seraffyn* stood almost stationary under the bridge, Larry sweated against the oar, yet we made only inches against the back eddy. The bridgekeeper climbed back into his tower. "Get that bloody mast out from under my bridge," he called through a loudspeaker, "you're holding up half of Dorset County." That seemed to do the trick. The ebbing tide caught us at last and we burst free. I hoisted our mainsail to catch the tiny breeze that whispered along the quay. *Seraffyn* heeled lightly, then we skimmed away from the bonds of winter.

We sailed through the deepwater channel of Poole Harbor with Leslie Dyball, the sixty-six-year-old treasurer of the Parkstone Yacht

Club, on board, enjoying the warmth of early spring. Leslie seemed to make up his mind as we short-tacked back toward the club later that afternoon, "If you come back to England next summer, will you crew for me on *Chough* in the two-man Round-Britain Race?" he asked Larry.

"If things work out, I'd love to," Larry answered, and his attitude made me sure things *would* work out.

We hauled and painted *Seraffyn* at the ever-helpful Parkstone Yacht Club, disposed of our rattletrap car, had farewell dinners with wonderful winter friends. Then, laden with stores, we set off for the Baltic on the fourth year of our cruise. A dozen people had come to see us leave and yell good wishes. We set our lapper and mainsail, then reached out of the Poole Town Quay with a fair tide under us. I waved until we couldn't make out any faces while Larry steered through the intricate maze of buoys and stakes marking the shoal patches. "That's the one thing wrong with our way of life," I told Larry when I finally went below to start lunch. "You meet wonderful people who invite you into their lives. Then before you know it, it's time to leave."

"Maybe that's good," Larry answered. "We stay just long enough to learn the good things about people and we leave before they learn our faults or we learn theirs."

We came abeam of Brownsea Island castle just as my soup was ready to serve. "How about dropping the hook for lunch?" Larry suggested. I readily agreed and went forward to douse the lapper. And so ended the first leg of our Baltic cruise, although we hadn't cleared Poole Harbor and were less than three miles from where we'd started.

Brownsea Island is a one-mile-square bird sanctuary nestled just inside Poole Harbor's entrance. Once the home of royalty, it is now under the National Trust and a summer tourist spot. A small pond and swamp attracts migrating birds from all of Europe. We launched *Rinky* and rowed ashore after lunch. The caretaker met us at the ferry landing. "I'm sorry," he told us, "the island is closed to visitors until the first of May."

I was disappointed and my face obviously showed it since the caretaker asked, "Can't you come back in a month. It's only a short sail across the bay."

"We're leaving England, bound for Denmark," Larry replied. With that the caretaker seemed to notice *Seraffyn* with her Canadian flag lifting to the breeze. He asked, "Did you sail across the Atlantic?" We talked about sailing as the caretaker took us on a short tour of the main buildings. He was a keen dinghy sailor and the idea of crossing oceans under sail intrigued him. Then he remembered some work he had to do. "I must go back, but if you promise not to bother the peacocks, you can go for a walk on your own. Have a pleasant afternoon and good sailing when you leave."

Larry and I strolled hand in hand across the green meadows dotted with golden daffodils. We lay on the sun-warmed grass while a flock of glistening blue, green, gold, and brown peacocks strolled within four feet of us to investigate. We walked on, the calls of ten or twenty different species of birds echoing over the trees. When we reached the shore on the far side of the island, low tide had exposed miles of gray-brown mud dotted with tidal pools. Right on the edge of the bank we noticed an old man walking, head down, stooping to pick up something he tossed into the battered bucket he carried. I ran over to him to ask, "What are you catching?"

"Must be the people off the yacht anchored at the castle," he commented as he showed Larry and me a pile of oysters, cockles, and tiny twirled shellfish I didn't recognize. "These are winkles; ever had one?" He showed us how to remove the meat from the thumb-sized twirls. "Hang a bucket of these overboard for two days. That'll get the sand out. Then eat them as they come."

Larry was more interested in the oysters. "Aren't they polluted? Who owns them?" The fisherman had a twinkle in his eye when he answered, "The townfolk think they're polluted. But my family and I've been eating these oysters for years. No sewers around here, tide sweeps up the channel bringing fresh water twice a day to keep them clean. Wouldn't eat the oysters you'd find next to the town, though. No one owns these oysters, all strays from the commercial oyster beds upriver." We found a plastic bag in the tide line, then worked alongside the fisherman for a few minutes to see how he spotted the mud-colored oysters. Then we worked back toward the landing as the tide slowly began to cover the shoals. We had three dozen three-inch oysters, forty or fifty cockles (clams), at least a hundred winkles, muddy shoes, and soaked pantlegs by the time we reached our dinghy. The sky had clouded over and the wind was rising. We rowed out to *Seraffyn* and I climbed on board to start our cabin heater while Larry shucked the oysters in the dinghy. Then we turned on our stereo and feasted on a tossed salad with blue-cheese dressing, oysters on the half shell, then cheddar and stilton cheese on biscuits, all washed down with a bottle of white Spanish wine. Outside, the wind whistled through the rigging, wavelets slapped against our bow and *Rinky*'s clinker hull chattered to the tide.

Two lazy days later the sun came back and we set sail with the ebbing tide. The winds were light so we missed the fair tide into the Solent. It took us three hours to make two miles through Hurst Narrows against the three-and-a-half-knot ebb. When we reached the tiny port of Yarmouth, we tried to beat through the entrance but just couldn't beat the tide. We anchored outside the harbor and three hours later, when the tide was slack, we set our sails again, lifted anchor, and worked into the harbor, Larry steering, me on the foredeck warning him when I could see the rocks getting close to the surface. We secured between two pilings eight hours and seventeen miles from Brownsea. An engine would have made it easier, but nowhere near the fun. Besides, what did time matter to us? We had all the food we could use for two or three months, enough money for eight months, and our only scheduled date was on our Russian docking permit, on the first of August.

We spent a week in Yarmouth, riding bicycles through the hills of the flower-covered Isle of Wight. On Friday the thirteenth of April, I took the laundry ashore even though it would have been a lovely day for sailing. As I said to Larry, "You may not be superstitious, but I am. It's bad luck to start a voyage on a Friday." As I rowed back at noon with a load of groceries, Larry greeted me with "Come on, let's forget your superstitions and just take a day sail across to Lymington."

I agreed with him after I looked out onto the Solent. It was twinkling with sunshine, ruffled by a six-knot northerly. Lymington was in view about five miles to windward. I stowed my gear and we set off, lunching as we sailed. We easily found the entry marks and began to tack up the river to Lymington Town. Within minutes we ran aground on the east side of the river. "Friday the thirteenth," I called to Larry as he laid out our kedge anchor. "Just didn't tack soon enough," he called back. We beat upriver as soon as we were free, and four tacks later hit the mud and stuck again. "Don't say it," Larry mumbled as he climbed back into the dinghy to lay out the kedge. As soon as he dropped the anchor I bent to the winch handle and whispered "Friday the thirteenth" as I worked to winch us free again.

We tied up at the Royal Lymington Yacht club and the dockmaster took *Rinky* around behind the main pier to the dinghy dock. We called Alf Taylor and said, "Come join us for the weekend." We'd spent several days basking in Alf's warm hospitality during the previous winter, using his home as a base while we explored London. Now we were glad we could reciprocate in our own way.

Alf arrived from London early the next morning and we were soon skimming down the river. He relaxed against the lifelines and surveyed *Seraffyn* as we ran dead before the wind. "Boat looks great, but what have you done with your dinghy?" Alf asked.

Larry and I both looked behind us and said in unison, "*You* forgot *Rinky!*" Alf roared with laughter while we hardened in the sheets to beat back upchannel. "Friday the thirteenth," I muttered as we tacked well inside the marks. "Nope," Larry answered, "it's Saturday today. Blame that one on forgetfulness."

With *Rinky* once again trailing docily behind us, we spent the next two days wandering through the Solent. We visited Cowes, tacked up the Medina River almost to Newport, then ran down with the tide. With Alf on board telling us about the scenery we passed, it was special fun. Alf was amazed by *Seraffyn*'s light-air performance. He took the helm to work her upriver and couldn't believe it when she just about sailed herself, even without the self-steering vane connected. He thought the vane was magic and, like most newcomers to self-steering vanes, started to grab the tiller each time "Helmer" reacted to a windshift. Before the weekend was over he'd decided to sell his own twenty-six-foot sloop and ask Lyle Hess to design him a thirty-two-foot *Seraffyn* for his retirement home.

At the end of the weekend we sailed up Wooten Creek to take Alf to his ferry. The tide was falling but we had an introduction to Jack Whitehead, the figurehead carver who lived up the creek. Our Royal Cruising Club guide and our Admiralty chart both showed six feet of water in front of the Wootten Yacht Club at low tide. But they were wrong. Inside the mouth of the river, just past the ferry dock but a hundred fifty yeads short of the club moorings, we ran aground. Before we had a chance to consider kedging off, *Seraffyn* began to tilt. We knew the tide had about seven feet to fall and, while there was still a thin sheet of water over the tidal flats, Larry rowed Alf and his dufflebag ashore. When Larry came back, he said, "I met the club's dockmaster. He told me the British Railway Ferry has made this pool silt up over the last two years." The club was trying to get the railway to

Aground in Wootten Creek.

provide a dredger to clear the pool (we heard two years later that they had succeeded and the Wootten Creek Yacht Club had again become a favorite cruising man's weekend retreat, complete with water).

Meanwhile, the water ebbed away until there was mud in every direction for at least three hundred yards. Twenty mooring buoys sat on the mud in front of the club like colored balloons. On one of the moorings a twin-keeled "mud duck" showed her stuff, settling evenly into the mud. But *Seraffyn* lay on her bilge, tilting at a forty-five-degree angle. Larry assured me there was nothing to worry about. "*Seraffyn* is built stout enough, and the bilge stringer is taking any extra strains. It would be nice to have legs, though, like the Falmouth oyster boats do." So, after joking about our situation and remembering when a friend in Falmouth had said "Only man who never ran aground, never went anywhere," we both took books onto the "upper deck" and lay in the sun waiting for the water to return.

About three hours later a thin sheet of water came creeping toward us. *Seraffyn* began to lift so Larry said, "Come on, Lin, let's row up the river and meet Jack. There's four more hours of rising tide. We can sail off this evening." We piled fifty feet of chain and our CQR anchor into the dinghy, rowed it out, then dropped the anchor and set it by shoving its bill into the mud with the dinghy oar.

We drifted up the tree-lined river, Larry occasionally taking a pull on one oar or the other, the tide doing the rest of the work. Two miles later, we landed at Jack Whitehead's stretch of beach. A garden full of spring vegetables lined the gravel path that led toward a wooden

After this figurehead was completed, Jack and Doris Whitehead were invited to supervise its installation on the *Falls of Clyde* in Honolulu, Hawaii.

cottage. A stocky, thick-armed carver worked in a rough, open-fronted shelter built under a tree in front of the cottage. His hammer and chisel gouged large chips of elm from the nine-foot-high block that was just beginning to take the shape of a buxom woman. We produced our letter of introduction from Monk Farnham, a New York sailor, and it brought forth a warm invitation from Jack—"You're just in time for tea." He yelled up toward the cottage "Two more for tea," then took us to see the fifteen figureheads he was restoring for the Cutty Sark museum with the help of a partner and one son. Jack had lived on the Isle of Wight most of his life and had started work as a shipwright with Uffa Fox in Cowes. One day there had been a call for scrolled trailboards and Jack had done the carving. One thing led to another and within two years Jack was so busy he had to turn down jobs even though he had two people working with him. "The only other full-time figurehead carver I know of lives near Mystic Seaport, Connecticut," Jack told us while his wife Doris served fresh scones and homemade preserves. The nine-foot figurehead he was now carving would eventually grace the *Falls of Clyde,* a iron square-rigger being restored in Honolulu.

74

Jack urged us to stay another day as he walked with us down to our dinghy. When we told him about *Seraffyn* lying on her side in the mud, he said, "There's real soft mud in front of the yacht club. Move over there and she'll settle upright when the tide's out." Since the man Larry had met at the yacht club when he rowed Alf ashore had said the same thing, we decided it was worth a try and invited Jack and his wife to join us for breakfast.

We rowed *Seraffyn* across to a club mooring before we went to bed. I woke up slowly, dreaming I was falling. Larry came awake almost at the same moment. I clung to him as he grabbed the edge of the bunk. *Seraffyn* tilted first ten degrees, then fifteen, and within ten minutes, forty-five degrees. We tumbled unceremoniously out of the bunk and onto the sextant locker, Larry on top, me hysterical with giggles. "Guess local advice doesn't work when you've got a twelve-inch-wide keel," Larry said as he helped unzip our double sleeping bags. We climbed into the two quarter berths, laughing over the problems of living at such an extreme list, then slept separately for the rest of the night.

We sailed out of the river into the Solent after a lazy company breakfast of pancakes, maple syrup, and eggs. Portsmouth lay only eight or ten miles ahead. Sun warmed our decks, the stereo played soft music, our genoa and mainsail panted slightly in the five-knot breeze. *Rinky* chuckled along behind, tugging at the end of her twenty-five-foot, three-eighths-inch nylon painter.

We reached Portsmouth as the tide was rushing out the narrow entrance. We tried beating in, but the northerly wind slowly grew lighter. "Let's sail out of the channel and anchor on the shoals till the tide turns," Larry suggested. The chart showed eight feet of water at low tide on the large area just outside the big ships' channel, so I readily agreed. We reached off and the tide swept us seaward as we slowly edged out of the three-mile-long big ships' channel. The wind began to die, *Seraffyn*'s forward motion slowed to a trickle, and the tide carried us sideways at three knots.

Larry looked downtide and saw a buoy directly on our beam. "We're going to hit that buoy," he said, working to catch a breeze. "No," I said, "we'll clear it." A stray puff filled our genoa. "You're probably right, Lin, we'll miss it," he said as *Seraffyn* trickled forward. That buoy grew from toy size until it rushed toward us, nine feet high and eight feet around, red and rusty. All the time we kept debating,

"We're going to hit it, we're not, we are." Then, all of a sudden, we looked at each other and said, "We're going to hit it." Larry had the presence of mind to grab the two fenders that lay on the cockpit floor. He dropped them between *Seraffyn*'s topsides and that ugly fairway buoy just as we hit it beam-on at over three knots. *Seraffyn* shuddered to a stop. I was thrown off my feet as the tiller swept wildly across the cockpit. Larry yelled, "Grab the dinghy painter!" But it was too late. *Seraffyn* slid slowly off one side of the buoy and floated downtide. The dinghy went around the other way. For a split second we stopped, dinghy on one side of the buoy, *Seraffyn* on the other. The painter stretched until it was half its normal size. Then *Seraffyn* won the tug of war. The dinghy flew around the buoy, flipped five feet into the air, landed upside down, then followed *Seraffyn* downstream. "Get ready to drop the anchor," Larry said as he pulled the dinghy alongside and lifted her gunwale high enough to reach the oars that, fortunately, were still inside. At his shout I let the anchor go. It found bottom at twenty feet and *Seraffyn* quickly turned to face the rushing tide. *Rinky*'s upside-down pram bow caught the tide full on and acted like a paravane. The dinghy submerged and tugged fiercely six inches below the surface, trapped air and buoyancy tanks fighting to float her up. We

It was three hours before the tide slacked enough for us to right *Rinky Dink*.

tried to winch the dinghy alongside, but couldn't against the force of that tide. Larry carefully inspected *Seraffyn*, expecting to find at least a cracked plank or split frame. He looked wonderfully relieved when he announced, "Only damage is cosmetic." So there we sat for two hours, trying to look nonchalant as afternoon fishermen and sailors powered past us staring at *Rinky*'s white submerged bottom and the three-foot strip of red paint *Seraffyn* carried as a souvenir of our encounter with a fairway buoy.

Portsmouth is a naval harbor. You can tell that from the moment you work through the narrow fortress-guarded entrance. Gray-painted vessels from the size of rowboats to four-hundred-foot-long supply ships line its shores and anchorages. But nestled among the drydocks and warehouses we could see the masts of *Victory*, Nelson's flagship during the Napoleonic wars. She was the reason we'd come. Now we'd have a chance to see how Horatio Hornblower had lived as a midshipman. We'd be able to understand what C. S. Forester had written about how six-inch-thick hemp anchor cables took up half of one deck on a ship of the line. But first we had to find a place to moor. We looked over our detail chart. Every spare space seemed to be marked "Anchorage Forbidden." We spotted Camper and Nicholson marina and sailed alongside only to be told that one night would cost us twelve dollars. "No thanks," we replied, sailing off. The next marina had a mooring for the night at only two dollars, but said we had to clear off by 0800 as they were launching several boats then and needed the mooring. It was late so we tied up for the night and were under way at 0800. We sailed alongside a line of empty mooring stakes in an area that our charts marked as "numerous yacht moorings." Just as we were about to moor up, a launch rushed out from shore and the man on board yelled, "Can't tie there, navy only." We luffed *Seraffyn*'s jib and waited for him to come closer. "Where can we moor?" He pulled his naval cap down more securely, shrugged his shoulders, and said, "How should I know? But you can't moor here." Then he turned his launch toward shore.

"Come on, let's go to sea. No tourist attraction is worth all this hassle," I said to Larry and he agreed. We noticed a semi-empty marina up a small creek just inside the entrance to the harbor. "One more try?" Larry asked, glancing over at the yards and topmasts of *Victory*. "Okay, but if that one's a hassle too, let's call it quits."

There were only twenty boats tied in a marina built for a hundred fifty. We moored alongside the first float we came to, loosely furled our sails, then I set off to meet the uniformed man who was approaching us. I met him halfway. "Can't moor here," he said. Then I asked, "Can we at least use your phone to call the harbormaster and ask where we can anchor?"

"No problem," he said. "Come along." After fifteen minutes of phoning, he turned to me and said, "No place you can anchor; can't tie here either."

I stomped back toward the boat. Larry was talking to a tall, husky man who'd just sailed in astern of us. He introduced me to David Williams, then asked, "What did you find out?"

"Same old nonsense," I started. "Can't stay, no anchoring allowed in the harbor area. Might be room at the yacht club seven miles from here." David interrupted. "What's the problem?" Tears came to my eyes as I described the trouble we were having finding a place to moor so we could see the *Victory.* "Just wait here," David said. Then he turned and walked off toward the offices. His wife Pippa invited us on board for a cup of tea and shortbread cookies, then told us, "I'm from Canada, too. I hope David can help you." David was back before we'd finished one cup. He asked for our harbor chart, made an X on it, and said, "As soon as we've finished tea, you'd best sail over. You're expected. Good safe moorage, stay as long as you like."

We thanked David profusely as he helped us cast off our lines, then we sailed two miles up the harbor, past mothballed naval ships and the two-hundred-year-old teak ship of the line *Foudroyant.* Three uniformed men gave us salutes as we approached the floating docks X'd on our chart. As they took our mooring lines, the most gold-encrusted of the three told us, "Welcome to Whale Island Naval Artillery School. Come up to my office and I'll give you a pass for the main gate. Showers over here, make yourself at home."

We set sail four days later after a day-long visit to *Victory.* The hospitality at Whale Island had been in top British tradition. We'd had to fight hard to keep the bosun from dressing *Seraffyn*'s boom gallows completely in ropework, and we'd learned how to make a proper turks head. As we cleared the harbor Larry said to me, "I don't like your complaining to other people, especially with tears running down your face. But I must admit you chose the right man to gripe to. I was talking to the officer who took our lines that first day and he asked me, 'How long have you known Admiral Williams?' "

CHAPTER 8

Of Fogs and Fires

We wandered eastward, sailing into each harbor on England's south coast. Spring's changeable weather was a trial for the best of BBC's weather forecasters, so we weren't too surprised when we sailed into a heavy fog just off Dungeness, the narrowest, most crowded part of the English Channel. But we were worried. We'd left Newhaven at 1600 with a fair wind, fair tide, and fair-weather forecast bound directly for Lowestoft, one hundred seventy miles northeast. A light but steady southeasterly breeze had carried us along past Beachy Head and the marker on the shore that indicated exactly zero longitude. As dark fell we could easily see the powerful navigation lights set along the shores and on light ships throughout the funnel-shaped, shoal-encumbered Channel. We'd stayed close to shore to avoid the constant stream of shipping that throbbed steadily through the twenty-mile wide Straits of Dover. The wind increased slowly and drew ahead until we were working northeast, almost close-hauled with only the staysail and mainsail pulling us at four knots. I'd stood the midnight to 0300 watch. A sailing jacket and one sweater had been enough to keep me warm and comfortable. My watch had flown as I took bearings on various lights, confirming our position each hour. Twenty minutes before the end of the watch I'd decided to tack off-shore so we'd have more clearance rounding Dungeness. I brought *Seraffyn* onto the other tack, set Helmer, and after taking a careful look around, went below to start some water warming for hot tea.

I woke Larry at 0255, then went on deck to take a final check. A mile ahead a line of green navigation lights marched southward. I went below and, since Larry was almost dressed, began to strip. "Hot chocolate waiting for you on the stove. You'll have to tack within five or ten minutes," I said, climbing into the still-warm sleeping bag.

Larry clambered sleepily through the companionway, a mug of hot chocolate in his hand. "My God," he shouted, "we're going to hit that ship!" I felt him shove the helm to leeward. *Seraffyn* came about so quickly I almost fell out of the bunk as she heeled away on the new tack. I scrambled free of the bedclothes and looked toward the row of ships that now marched along on our beam. Larry was shaken and angrily said, "You let us get too damn close to the shipping lane."

It took a few minutes before Larry calmed down. "Lin, you didn't say 'We're heading toward the shipping lanes and need to tack within ten minutes or we'll hit a ship.' I climbed on deck completely unaware and there were ships' lights, looking as if they were only yards away."

We talked about changing watches as I brewed a cup of hot chocolate to replace the one Larry had spilled in his rush to tack. On a racing boat or any sailboat without self-steering, there's no problem. The helmsman waits at the tiller for the next watch to arrive, then he points out the situation before going below. But with a windvane on a cruising boat, the man on watch usually comes below to wake someone who is fresh out of a warm sleeping bag, groggy and trying to force himself awake. Then it becomes necessary to explain the complete situation to the new watchkeeper before he climbs on deck and is startled by the unexpected.

Larry, placated by the steaming, fragrant cup of chocolate, kissed me goodnight. I climbed into the sleeping bag in the windward quarter berth and secured the lee cloth in place. When he called me at 0600 we were shrouded in fog. A stiff easterly breeze kicked up a short chop but didn't seem to move the heavy damp whiteness. "Nothing I hate worse than fog," Larry told me while he studied the chart. Although Larry had sailed in the Pacific Northwest for several years and knew something about fog conditions, this was my first experience. I could hear the horns of shipping around us. I could imagine the surf on the shore we were steadily approaching. I stood on deck trying to will the fog away. Then Larry came up and said, "Chart shows two fathoms of water within a hundred yards of the shore, six fathoms a quarter mile off. I suggest we ease sheets just a bit and slant in toward the south side of Dungeness. Once we see the land, we'll know what the visibility really is. If it's less than a quarter mile, we'll anchor till the fog clears. It's a sand bottom so the anchor will hold in spite of the seas.

We'll be uncomfortable if we have to anchor, but it'll be safer than bumbling around out here without being able to see anything."

I looked around at the four-foot chop as I helped ease the sheets. "How about getting the lead line ready to use?" Larry suggested as he took a reading off our dependable little Negus taffrail log, then went below to advance our position. Ten minutes later we spotted the beach and identified a huge gray building that corresponded with the hydroelectric plant shown in our *Shell Guide.* I took a sounding, swinging the lead line as far ahead as I could; "Four and a half fathoms." Larry went below for the chart and plotted our position. "Here's where we are. Visibility is a bit over a quarter mile. Nearest deepwater harbor is Dover, about twenty miles north. There are three big pilot buoys with bells marked on the chart between here and Dover. So if we tack along this point till we spot the Dungeness lighthouse, then reach off and keep a careful DR, we should be able to pick our way from buoy to buoy. If we miss one, there's less than eight fathoms of water everywhere, so we can anchor."

I studied the chart with Larry and what had looked like a frightening situation turned into an adventure. His plan kept us well away from the worst danger, the shipping lanes. So we tacked eastward and found the end of Dungeness with its lighthouse. I set a course for the first buoy then pored over the tide charts and tables. Larry called down a log reading when he had the lighthouse abeam. He steered by hand to keep *Seraffyn* exactly on course. I carefully figured an average speed for the tide, allowing for a bit of leeway, then showed Larry the chart with my figures to double-check our navigation. After fifteen minutes I asked for a log reading. "We're making five knots through the water, tide is pushing us at around two knots, so watch for the buoy in twenty minutes," I told Larry as I heated a pot of coffee and some toast.

We were almost abeam of the buoy before we spotted its dim gray outline through the whirling fog. We could have missed it. We were almost a quarter mile to windward of the black-and-white-striped buoy. We had allowed too much for leeway. We eased our sheets still more and ran down to within fifty feet of the buoy, read the name stenciled on its side, took a new log reading, and set off on our treasure hunt for the next buoy. Two hours and two buoys later, the huge walls of Dover's breakwater broke through the fog, right when they should have. I gave Larry a hug and kiss, saluted our tiny spinning taffrail log, then climbed below and lit the stove, dreaming up a tasty lunch menu to serve as soon as we set our anchor. Larry eased our sheets to run into the harbor and *Seraffyn* flew through the water at over five knots. But a four-knot current and heavy overfalls slowed our progress to a crawl. Larry called down to me, "Man in the signal station on the breakwater end has just changed the black cones. What's this new pattern mean?" I brought the *Pilot* book on deck and we thumbed through it until we found the signal: "Do not leave harbor." Larry looked pleased when he said, "Must be warning shipping about us." I laughed at the idea of our twenty-four-footer stopping the traffic out of Dover's harbor.

Then we both heard it at the same time, pushing up behind us. Something sounded like a cross between an airplane, a vacuum cleaner, and a waterfall. Seconds after we first heard the roar, a huge hovercraft burst through the fog, radar scanner scanning, water foaming at its base. It was past us in seconds and disappeared through the fog at the mouth of the harbor. We followed it at our infinitely slower pace, bucking and weaving through the overfalls.

We blessed the quiet and safety we found inside the foggy harbor. A pilot boat directed us to the small-craft anchorage, an area that was unfortunately exposed to the swell caused by the easterly wind. We anchored, furled our sails, and climbed below out of the fog and drizzle, then closed our canvas companionway cover and settled into the warm cabin to eat lunch. Although *Seraffyn* rolled a bit, we were safe and I agreed when Larry said, "If I had to do all my sailing in the English Channel, I'd give up the sport. Always a threat of fog, extremely heavy shipping, strong tides, choppy sea, changeable weather, cold winds, cold water. No wonder so few English wives enjoy sailing."

Spring came back the next day and we used a light westerly breeze and the strong tide to continue north across the shoals of the sunlit Thames estuary. We often had so little wind that only the tide moved us along. As soon as the tide started to turn against us, we'd work over to a shoal patch and anchor. Since the shoal we chose at 2100 had only six feet of water over it at low tide, we felt safe from shipping with our kerosene anchor lamp burning, although we were anchored ten miles from the nearest land. The wind stayed light, the sea was smooth. We spent a quiet night and were under way with the first of the fair tide before daybreak. By midmorning a fresh warm southerly breeze set us running past the low sandy Suffolk coastline, and we tied in front of the Royal Norfolk and Suffolk Yacht Club at Lowestoft before dark.

The next morning we placed a call to the Russian Embassy in London. Every time we'd entered a port during the previous weeks we'd called to ask, "Are our passports stamped with the visas we need to sail *Seraffyn* into a Russian port?" The secretary had come to recognize our voices. As soon as we rang through this time he said, "Yes, you've finally succeeded. If you come to our embassy at ten o'clock two mornings from now, the consul will sign your permits and return your passports."

We took a train to London the next morning, spending the afternoon exploring the mammoth halls of the British Museum. After an evening of wandering around London, we took a room at an inexpensive hotel and the next morning set off for the Russian Embassy. As we walked past a newstand, I noticed huge headlines on the morning papers: "Espionage, Russian Diplomats Expelled from Britain." When we reached the embassy, everything was in confusion. The only face we recognized from our six previous visits was that of the secretary. He looked up from a mass of papers he was sorting and muttered, "Yes, you must be here for your visas." Then he turned and went into an adjoining office. We were motioned in almost immediately. Papers and boxes cluttered the usually neat consular room. A strange man sat behind the desk waiting for us. After introductions he said, "I'm sorry, but the signatures on your permit to enter the Soviet Union are no longer valid. I must write to Moscow to get a decision as to whether I should authorize your visas. Please return in three weeks." Larry and I both protested, "But we plan to sail from England this week." The new consular official shook his head. "It is beyond my power to authorize people to enter my country by any means other than on a recognized carrier. I'm sorry Mr. —— is no longer with us. Only he had permission to sign your visas."

We watched our hopes of being the first yachtsmen to sail into Russia fade away. After ten minutes of discussion we took our passports and asked to have all of our visa documents forwarded to the Russian Embassy in Helsinki.

We took the afternoon train back to Lowestoft, lamenting all the way about our lost chance. "What if Mr. —— had decided to sign those permits last week. Wouldn't it have been fantastic to sail up the Neva River right into the heart of Leningrad?" But we consoled ourselves with thoughts of the five other countries that would fill our summer.

We had heard rumors about the extremely high cost of food in Scandinavian countries. Members of the Royal Norfolk and Suffolk Yacht Club who had been to Denmark in the recent past confirmed the rumors. So we spent several days buying all of the stores we could fit on board. I filled my lockers with extra quantities of canned meats, especially steak-and-kidney pies, stewing steak with gravy, and chunky chicken in cream sauce, useful specialty items we've found only in English countries. We ordered two cases of duty-free liquor at the usual low price of about two dollars a bottle for Scotch, and we filled our butane tank. Then we wandered around the waterfront and rivers of Lowestoft waiting for an easterly gale to blow itself out.

A mile from the sea, on a deepwater canal lined with timber yards and warehouses, we found the once magnificent one-hundred-forty-foot schooner *Heartsease.* She had been built at the turn of the century as a racing yacht to compete for the Kaiser's Cup. Her newest owners, Caroline and Gordon, from Australia, welcomed us on board. We toured the luxurious staterooms designed during an era when labor was cheap and yachts like this had full-time crews of eight or ten

Our major storage lockers are under the two quarter berths with a third one under the head of the forward bunk. Together they hold almost thirty cases of canned goods.

professionals. Each stateroom was paneled in a different wood. The main bathroom had a full-size, three-foot-deep porcelain bathtub surrounded by African mahogany. The main saloon was paneled in bird's-eye maple from parqueted floors to shoulder height. From there up, the bulkheads were covered in pink striped satin. Unfortunately, the spars and rigging from *Heartsease* had been sold off during the years. Her huge lead ballast keel had been removed during World War II and made into bullets. She had been tied to the canal side and used as a floating houseboat. Now Gordon and Caroline dreamed of restoring *Heartsease* to her former glory. They had bought her for less than twenty thousand dollars, but were beginning to realize the immensity of the task ahead. Although the teak hull was basically sound, she needed a ballast keel, spars, and rigging. Also, the decks leaked, the houses leaked, the engines were inoperable, and the costs for the simplest items for a boat of such size were far beyond what Gordon had imagined when he first became involved. "Just to haul and scrape her, the cheapest shipyard around here wants eight hundred pounds," he told us during one of several visits we exchanged. Before we sailed from Lowestoft, Gordon and Caroline told us they had decided to go back to Australia and sell some more of their property to continue their project. We really sympathized with their problem. They had fallen for a romantic, but impractical, dream.

We came back from spending yet another afternoon in the cozy overstuffed chairs of the reading room in the friendly yacht club. The easterly wind whistled through our rigging for the fifth day and rain spattered on our decks. Larry lit the small butane heater, then trimmed the wicks on our three oil lamps, filled them, and polished the lenses while I cooked dinner. After eating, we lounged back on the two settees, feet up, listening to the rain on deck while we had a last cup of tea. "How about a game of cribbage?" Larry asked. I got the board and cards and, for once, came out on top in the three-game series. While we were playing, the rain increased to a downpour. It bounced off the cabin top so hard that large drops of it pushed through the half-inch opening under our skylight hatch. So Larry got up and closed the skylight.

We shed our clothes in *Seraffyn*'s warm main cabin, then I followed Larry into our forepeak bunk. When Larry blew out the oil lamp, we noticed the red glow from our heater. Larry molded himself warmly to my body. "Should shut the heater, uses a lot of butane." I couldn't bear the thought of climbing out of his arms. "It won't hurt to leave it burn just this one time."

We both woke up with headaches at dawn. Larry climbed over me and got aspirins and water for us. He used the loo bucket, standing up, then came back into the bunk. A few minutes later I climbed out and went into the main cabin where I sat down on the loo. I remember standing up and closing the bucket lid, but that's all. Larry heard me fall on the cabin sole. He rushed out of the bunk, shoved the sliding hatch open in spite of the drizzle, then lifted me off the floor. "You were like a limp sack of potatoes when I tried to carry you into the forward bunk. Your face was gray," he told me as soon as I regained conciousness. I only remember the dreadful worried feeling I had when I came to.

Both of us felt terrible, nauseous and headachy. I had a bad bruise on my chin. We realized we'd almost poisoned ourselves by having an unvented fire on board with too little air circulation. I'd been affected more drastically because carbon monoxide sinks and I'd sat down in the main cabin while Larry hadn't. We'd been okay in the forepeak because we were near the chain locker with its three-inch ventilator and open chain pipe.

We rowed into the clubhouse to have lunch and mentioned our episode to one of the members. "Even if your gas heater had been vented, you could have been in trouble. Last year, someone heard a baby crying on board one of the twenty-six-foot charter boats tied at the side of the canal. They went to investigate. The boat was all closed up, but not locked. When they opened the hatch, the investigators found four dead people sitting around the table with a half-eaten dinner set out. The remains of a charcoal fire smouldered in the stove with its one-and-a-half-inch flue. The baby was in the forepeak, right next to the open chain pipe. That's why it was still alive."

Our frightening experience and this sobering story made us realize that any fire in a closed area such as a boat is dangerous. To prevent loss of oxygen and the buildup of carbon monoxide, you need cross ventilation even if you have a smoke stack. After this, we kept a quarter berth ventilator and the skylight open every time we used our cabin heater.

The day we finally set off to cross the North Sea it was raining. Reports were for the wind to veer from the east to the southeast. Our course to the Limfjord in Denmark was northeast. "Come on, Lin. If

Once the wind is over Force 5, *Seraffyn*'s sail plan moves all inboard. Here we are on a close reach in winds of Force 9, carrying reefed staysail and double-reefed main.

we wait for perfect conditions we'll spend the whole summer here in Lowestoft." So we set off on the first of May 1973, after one last dash to town for ice and fresh vegetables. We had a fair tide under us as we cleared the high breakwaters. The wind was just north of east. We set our yankee, staysail, and mainsail to work north-northeast, hard on the wind. By nightfall, we had the lights of Great Yarmouth far astern. The wind increased until we took the yankee in and tied two reefs in the mainsail. Despite the Force 6 or 7 winds our motion was comfortable enough so that even I enjoyed the thick stew I had remembered to prepare before we left port. I'm sure if I'd had to prepare a meal from scratch, my perennial seasickness would have reared its ugly head. I dug out our North Sea charts before climbing into the bunk and raising the lee cloth. Then I watched Larry transferring our position from the coastal chart to the much smaller scale one we'd use for our four-hundred-fifty-mile North Sea crossing.

All that night and the next day we beat onward, making almost four knots through the water on a course that pointed just east of north on our chart. By dark our second night at sea we could see lights where nothing showed on our charts but deep water. Larry kept a careful watch as we neared the lights, and when he woke me for my watch, told me, "I sure made a stupid mistake. Those are oil-rig lights. Yet when I studied our DR track it showed us twenty miles to windward of the nearest rig. So I went over all our DR, then checked the tide charts. Finally figured out I've been subtracting the variation instead of adding it." Larry was pretty unhappy about his mistake and went on to tell me about a professional delivery skipper, a man with hundreds of thousands of miles under his belt, who'd made the same mistake. Unfortunately, the delivery skipper hadn't realized his error until he'd run the heavy-displacement, sixty-five-foot power yacht up on a sand shoal at ten knots.

Larry rummaged under our forward bunk cushion until he found an old chart. He cut the small inner compass rose off it. "From now on, if there is no magnetic rose inside the compass rose on a chart, we'll place this one at the correct variation. Then we'll check our course. When you can actually see the variation, there's much less chance of making an error." We later covered a small compass rose with clear plastic and put it right next to our dividers ready for instant use.

We carried on north through the oil rigs, and during Larry's second night watch, when *Seraffyn* was close to one of the huge platforms, we almost hit an unlit six-foot-high black buoy. Larry called me from my bunk and pointed at the heavy buoy pumping in the six-foot seas. The buoy was obviously used for mooring supply ships that came to service the rigs, and Larry commented, "I'm surprised the oil people are allowed to set unlit buoys. The rig is shown on the chart, but no mention is made of buoys or dangers. Could have taken our bowsprit off if we'd hit it."

By morning the wind lightened and veered. We were able to set our whole mainsail. After we'd untied the reefpoints, Larry hoisted the sail and I couldn't believe my eyes. From the reefpoints up our brand-new sail was grimy gray. We've since washed that sail in hot soapy water, but nothing has taken the stains out. Friends have suggested that the stains were caused by industrial pollution carried from the Ruhr Valley in Germany by the strong easterly winds. Others say the stains are from diesel exhaust fumes off the oil-rig generators. But we'll never know.

By afternoon our third day out, we were close-reaching slowly along on an almost flat sea with fog surrounding us. A few times that night we saw ships' lights and were able to estimate that we had one-mile visibility. We have aluminum foil rolled inside all the hollow sections of *Seraffyn*'s thirty-eight-foot-high wooden mast and the captains of two ships have told us that our picture on a radar screen looks like that of an eighty-five-footer. That's probably why ships never came near us during any foggy periods.

For three days we drifted through the fog toward Denmark, the wind slowly veering to the west. On the fourth morning, a large trawler broke through the fog and came within a hundred yards of us, then slowed down to match our speed. "Want a fish?" the captain called over the loud hailer. One of the crew held up a fish that was as long as me. I laughed and shook my head no. The captain called back, "Want anything else?" Larry shouted at the top of his lungs, "Can you confirm our position?" The men on the trawler tried to hear him over the throb of their engines, but couldn't. Larry went below and got a chart. He wrote POSITION on the back of it in big letters with a marking pencil. Then he came on deck and held up our "live reckoning" sign. The trawler's radar scanner started to rotate and minutes later the captain called back our latitude and longitude. Then the captain yelled, "Good sailing," and the *Boston Invader* steamed off into the fog.

We were fifteen miles north of our DR after three and a half days with no sights. The nearest land was still over a hundred miles from us. But with a confirmed position we were able to ease sheets even more, and by the next morning as we sailed out of the fog bank into the sun, Denmark's low sandy shore lay before us. Larry shot the sun and his LOP confirmed our latitude. We were ten miles north of the entrance to the Limfjord. We set the lapper on our sixteen-foot-long whisker pole and skimmed toward the harbor at the fjord's entrance, never once expecting the wonderous cruising that lay ahead.

September 15, 1972
June 4, 1974

CHAPTER 9

Sailing
Through a Farm

No matter how many times we make a landfall, I still have the same reaction. I get impatient to enter harbor, to go ashore and meet our first locals. So I set to work cleaning *Seraffyn*'s cabin, storing away charts and wet gear, polishing the stove top, wiping down the bunks and varnish work. Larry generally teases me about my sudden burst of energy. "You sure aren't like this when we can't see land!"

Larry seems to have different thoughts on his mind as we near port after each passage. He seems to look at the brave little boat under our feet with keen appreciation, marveling that our handiwork has carried us to the brink of yet another adventure.

I came on deck ready to help with the more demanding sail handling required to enter a harbor without an engine. We were rapidly approaching Tiburon's breakwater and both of us studied the detail chart of the old fishing port. Then Larry said, "Well, Lin, what's your plan?" All of a sudden I realized *I* had to maneuver *Seraffyn* into Tiburon. Larry had often urged me to improve my sailing skills by taking charge in close quarters, but previously I'd just let him make the decisions, then followed orders. After our tiff in Dartmouth, we'd agreed to take turns as captain. I'd forgotten this decision, but Larry hadn't. "The only way you'll get the confidence to bring *Seraffyn* alongside a crowded dock is by doing it. You can sail your dinghy anywhere. *Seraffyn* is just bigger and heavier. She'll scratch more paint off anything she hits if you don't plan right."

Now I became aware of the responsibilities of being skipper. *I* had to decide what the wind strength would be once we rounded the corner of the breakwater. *I* had to be sure we had the right sails set, that the anchor would be ready to let go if necessary, that mooring lines and fenders would be available in plenty of time.

I looked at our Canadian flag lifting to the following wind. We were running east; to get into the harbor we'd have to beat west. "Okay, Larry, let's drop the jib and set the staysail instead. This wind will feel a lot stronger when we have to beat. Besides, the staysail is easier to tack than the big jib." I issued my first command and with that decision made the whole task began to look easier. I took the helm while Larry made the sail change, then I steered for the far side of the channel in front of the breakwater so we could look inside the entrance and avoid colliding with any outgoing vessels. Then Larry hardened in the staysail while, tiller between my knees, I hauled the mainsheet in to start our beat. The harbor looked smaller than I'd anticipated, its wharfs and docks encrusted with fishing boats. But *Seraffyn* came about easily and gained on each lift of the wind. We short-tacked around several piers, through the outer harbor to the big inner harbor. Then I saw the small-boat harbor at the windward end of the mile-long maze of wharfs and piers, and chose the spot where I wanted to tie up. "We'll need mooring lines and fenders on our starboard side," I told Larry, remembering the countless times similar things he'd said to me.

Then I remembered to tell him my plan. "I'll come along that second fishing boat after I take one more tack. You be ready to take the breast line and slow us down if necessary. I'll handle the stern line. We'll be heading almost dead into the wind, so just let the sheets loose when I say." Larry teased me, "Okay, captain," then prepared the mooring lines and fenders. My plan worked. I took one long tack to the far side of the two-hundred-foot-wide harbor, then tacked over toward my chosen spot. "Let the staysail sheet go," I told Larry as I eased the mainsail sheet. The sails luffed and lost their power. *Seraffyn* began to lose her way a little too quickly, so I sheeted in the mainsail to give her just a bit more speed. Then I pulled the tiller to leeward, let the mainsheet fly, and *Seraffyn* slowly came to a stop, abeam of and one foot from that fishing boat. Larry only said two words as he stepped off to secure our mooring lines—"Nicely done." And that was more than enough for me.

Tiburon stands on a windswept beach. Brick houses huddle against the violent North Sea winds. There are no gardens or trees, only eight or ten sandy streets. The fish plant and trawlers provide Tiburon's only reason for existing, and even on this bright sunny day the village looked depressing. But the people made up for it. The harbormaster arrived as we were furling our sails and spoke enough English to explain that we needed no stamp in our passport, no cruising permit, no clearance since we'd come directly from England. He also knew the heart of a sailor because he told us, "Hot showers at the seaman's club," then pointed to a building nearby. We took our clean clothes and kits and went ashore.

A bank hugged the side of the seaman's club so we changed a travelers check before going for showers. The door of the club opened into an immaculate tiled foyer, which in turn led into a small cafe. A row of hooks lined the foyer wall. Sea jackets hung from half the hooks and below each jacket was a pair of shoes. We looked in the cafe and saw ten or twelve fishermen drinking beer in stocking feet. So we shed our shoes and set them in the line-up. We walked into the spotless cafe to find that the girl at the counter spoke some English, too. She directed us to the showers, which were as immaculate as the rest of the club. Throughout our stay in Denmark we found the same traditions. Shoes came off at the entrance. Homes, restaurants, bars, offices—all were immaculate. Even the roadsides were clean and free of the beercans and cigarette butts that adorn roads and paths of other countries.

We walked back toward the boat after showers and coffee. I glanced into a small butcher shop and couldn't believe the prices marked. I refigured the exchange rates and, sure enough, the pound of Plumrose brand Danish bacon that sold for eighty-five cents in England cost two dollars in Denmark (1973).

We left Tiburon the next day. The wind still came from the west and sailing out was easy. Then we began our meander through the beautiful Limfjord. About a hundred miles south of the Kattegat there is a chain of lakes connected by rivers and channels kept dredged to a depth of at least twelve feet cutting right across the Jutland peninsula. Prime farming lands line the shores of the sheltered passage. Forty or fifty small man-made harbors are scattered throughout its ninety-mile length. Red brick houses and small tidy towns nestle among the trees on shore. Cows and sheep come right to the water's edge to graze. A constant breeze filters over the low rolling hills. There are numerous shoal areas, but the only really narrow part of the whole system is one two-hundred-foot-long, hundred-foot-wide passage that is carefully marked by stakes. We could have spent a whole summer wandering from one spot to another in the Limfjord, and our first port after Tiburon made us want to.

We reached into the small yacht and fishing boat harbor of Lemvig at about 1630 on Saturday the twenty-sixth of May, 1973. People were working on their boats or fishing off the pier, enjoying the warm sun and light breeze. Larry spotted one empty mooring between two small yachts. "May we tie alongside the blue sloop?" he called, hoping the man on the dock spoke English. "Yes, please do," the young, curly-haired blond called back. We sailed carefully in and were told, "Hand me your bow line. I'm Charles Madsen. You're coming to our yacht club party tonight, aren't you?" We tied our lines and Larry said, "Thank you, but we don't speak any Danish." Charles didn't hesitate, "Don't worry, after six schnapps, that won't matter. But I must rush now. I'll be back for you at seven. There will be dancing and dinner, but sailing clothes only."

Charles was right on time. The yacht club party was in full progress when we arrived. We soon discovered that almost every person under thirty in Denmark spoke enough English to carry on a comfortable conversation—after the loosening effects of a few schnapps (aquavit).

It is a Danish custom to have a shotglass filled with the colorless but potent liquor next to each guest at dinner. Throughout the meal, people catch your eye, lift their glass, and say "Skol." Then everyone at the table downs the contents of his or her schnapps glass. I'm sure a person's tolerance grows with practice, but I stumbled when I was asked to dance after only two "Skols." That's when my shrewd neighbor came to the rescue. He filled a schnapps bottle with water and shared that with me.

Charles asked me to dance. "Why did you ask two complete strangers to your great party?" I wanted to know. We whirled to the international music of the Beatles and he answered, "I figured that anyone who'd sail from Canada on a boat as small as yours had to be interesting."

It was 0200 before the party started to break up. Good-byes took another half hour. We weaved outside for the ride back to the harbor. The sky was a pink and blue glow. Although it was only 0300 when we reached *Seraffyn*, we sat and watched the sun rise before we went to bed.

Charles came sailing with us the next day as we voyaged eastward between the low green banks of the fjord. He had been an Olympic Dragon sailor until he had had a frightening accident the previous year. He'd trucked his Borenson Dragon to the site of the final Olympic trials at Kiel and set to work on the deck of his boat, preparing it for the crane that was to lift it off the trailer and put it in the water. Then Charles had made one misstep and fallen to the ground, his ankle fractured in seven places. Now he'd given up international racing but his instincts for speed were still keen. "Got a spinnaker?" he asked. Soon we were tearing down the river, spinnaker flying, our lapper set like a tall boy halfway out the bowsprit. Larry put Helmer to work when we reached the final leg of our day's sail. We skimmed over the smooth water at almost full speed, the sun glowing on our decks. I spread tuna salad on crackers to serve as hors d'oeuvres, then looked out at the two absolutely contented-looking, handsome, sun-browned

Palle and Gerda sailing in company with us.

men. "I've got the world by the tail" was my only thought.

In 1967, Larry had been involved in a crazy, fun project. He'd organized the North American team for the first attempt to sail across the Sahara Desert. Seventeen men from six countries sailed landyachts seventeen hundred miles from Colom Bechar in Algeria to Nouakchott in Mauritania, accompanied by several Landrovers (see *National Geographic Magazine*, November 1967). During this expedition, Larry had become close friends with Leif Møller, one of the Danish landyachters, and we'd kept in touch through the years. And as soon as we tied in Charles's home port of Holstebro-Struer, we called Leif in Copenhagen. He was thrilled to hear from us. "You wrote me when you left California and said you'd be in Denmark in a year. It has been five. What have you been doing all that time?" Larry answered easily, "Having fun!" By good fortune we'd called Leif two days before the European Landyacht Championships. "I'll come and get you," Leif insisted. "You'll love the DN machines we use. They make the desert machines look like Landrovers compared to an XKE Jaguar."

Charles and his friends Palle and Gerda Carlsen, who had a beautiful varnished 5.5 sloop moored next to us, readily agreed to watch *Seraffyn*. So off we drove, crowded into Leif's sport sedan along with his girlfriend, her two young boys, sailing gear, and parts of the two disassembled landyachts that were lashed on the rooftop.

The European Championships were being held at Leif's boyhood home of Rømo, a Danish island right next to the German border. Leif was in charge of the 1973 championships, and as soon as we drove across the long causeway leading to the island, we agreed with his choice of sites. Rømo had miles of hard-packed, flat sand beaches stretching toward the North Sea. Five feet four inches tall, goateed and sandy-haired, Leif was a ball of fire and we came to call him the "Great Dane" as we watched him organizing the rest of the regatta. With his inexhaustable supply of energy he even managed to locate and help assemble a spare DN for Larry to sail.

German. French, Belgian, and Dutch landyachters, some of whom Larry had sailed with seven years before, arrived and soon the small inn reserved for the competitors buzzed with sailing talk.

Land yachts can make up to seventy knots with a good breeze. Because of their low resistance, they can go four or five times the wind's speed, only slightly slower than ice yachts. Sailing on one is a new experience to a water man. Landyachters learn to keep hardening

Leif Møller explains that it's best to loosen the wheel bearings on a landyacht to get the least friction.

The landyachts hit the puddle on the homestretch at over fifty miles per hour in the twenty-knot winds.

in their sheets as their machines gather speed because the apparent wind rapidly moves forward until the sail must be kept flat amidships even on a broad reach. Once the machine reaches the speed of the wind, the sail flutters through the wind at each jibe with none of the force it would have on the much slower water-bound sailboat.

On the day of the main races, a cool fifteen-knot wind swept the beach. Rain during the night had left puddles, and despite planning the course to avoid them, one puddle lay like an obstacle on the home-stretch. Thirty-five machines spread out over the five-mile-long course moving at close to fifty miles an hour. Each one would hit the thin sheet of water and skid through, barely under control, spray and sand flying twenty feet in the air. The colorful sails of the landyachts and the flags for each competitor's homeland added to the wonderful spectator sport of the day. One person seemed to be enjoying it more than the rest. Tom Nibbea, an American photographer doing a story on Denmark for *National Geographic* magazine, calmly shot roll after roll of film. We came to know him well during the four-day regatta.

Tough, handsome, and dark-haired, born in New York of Italian parents, Tom had been an army photographer during the Korean War. He'd then worked with newspapers until he caught the eye of *National Geographic*. He shared his knowledge of photography with us over meals of meatballs, smoked fish, and overabundant boiled potatoes. "The only way to get good photos is to use your camera," he said. "Won't do you any good sitting in its box. Have it ready all the time. Shoot lots of film. I figure I'm doing my job if I get one good transparency out of a roll of thirty-six exposures—other professional photographers use up to six rolls of film to get one good shot. Take photos of people. People love to see people. What fun is a photo of sailing unless you see the people on the boat. Figure a way to get in close to your subject, and when you are taking action shots, bracket. That is, shoot three different exposures because, especially on the water where you get lots of reflected light, it's almost impossible to get a perfect meter reading every time." Tom kept us fascinated by tales of photographic safaris to Africa, meanders through the islands of Georgia looking for the spirit of the American South, voyages to Greenland. Now he kept a home in Copenhagen. "Come see me when you get there. I think a photo of your boat sailing past Helsingor Castle would look great for a Denmark story. Got a spinnaker? What's its color?" We told him that, yes, we had a blue-and-white-striped one. "Great," Tom said as he prepared to drive home. "It's a date. We'll take a photo of you two sailing past Helsingor with your spinnaker set, in a week or two."

We promised to call Tom and Leif as soon as we reached the island of Zealand where Copenhagen is located. Then we rode back to *Seraffyn* with new Danish landyachting friends who were going right past Holstebro-Struer.

The Limfjord provided us with one of those days of sailing that make up for all the discomforts of life on a small boat. The sun was warm enough so that in spite of the fifteen-knot northerly wind we didn't need sailing jackets even while beating to windward on the first leg of our day's run. *Seraffyn* heeled to the brisk wind, challenging the tiny white horses that had only a four-mile fetch to grow in. We'd chosen the perfect sail combination for the day, a reef in our mainsail

Sailing on the Limfjord.

and the yankee jib. Water gurgled along the channels, occasional spray flew across the foredeck, but the cockpit stayed absolutely dry. I left the housework undone and joined Larry in the cockpit. We took turns working *Seraffyn* to windward, catching each puff of wind that would give us a lift toward the channel markers leading to Aalborg. Before we became hungry for lunch we reached the beacon that marked the narrow channel and were able to ease our sheets until we were on a beam reach. I went below and boiled up coffee, mixed a tossed salad, and straightened up the boat, watching the green shores slide quickly by the port lights. We ate lunch in the cockpit, wearing swimsuits, taking turns steering through the maze of stakes marking our route. Larry reminded me about Peter Pye and his voyage on *Moonraker* through these same narrow channels. Peter had said that everyone told him it was impossible to sail through the Limfjord without going aground. After three groundings, Peter had agreed. But we were forewarned. And the stakes with broom heads of twigs were laid out more carefully than in previous years, and luckily we never touched.

A few small cargo boats passed us during the afternoon. As we neared Aalborg, some local sailboats joined us on the shining river. Despite four inches of weeds growing on her bottom *Seraffyn* kept up a speed of almost six knots, and when we reached the port at Aalborg we were reluctant to stop. But that weed was a bother.

We moored in the small harbor and, as instructed by Palle Carlsen, went into the old ship's wheelhouse that sat on the breakwater acting as restaurant and yacht club. The young bartender, also the yacht club secretary, spoke perfect English and was obviously expecting us. "Palle called. We've located a club member whose boat is a similar size to yours. His cradle is free and he's offered to come down and show you how to operate the ways car." The bartender made a phone call and an hour later a friendly man in a business suit came for us. He explained how the yachtsmen from several clubs on the Limfjord had gotten together and built a do-it-yourself shipyard. Each donated a few days a year to keep the equipment in good condition and paid a very small fee. Then each member could haul his own boat in and out of the water as often as he liked at no cost.

The equipment we saw was first-rate. The car and winch were strong enough to haul the largest yacht in the Limfjord with ease. Individual metal cradles built by members to hold their boats in the winter lined the sides of the clean yard. The cradle we'd been offered needed only a small bit of blocking to accommodate *Seraffyn*'s bottom. So the next morning we set her on the cradle and hauled her out—all by ourselves. We used sand and big brushes to remove the weed that had grown after only two months on the English antifouling paint we'd used. Then we applied a coat of the cheap paint used by the fishermen in Aalborg. And early the next morning we relaunched *Seraffyn* and stored the cradle back where it had come from. We offered the waiter at the clubhouse some money toward the upkeep of the wonderfully convenient self-run shipyard. "No thanks!" he said. "Free to guests. Only members pay." We offered him a drink, but he poured us one instead.

Two days later, when we sailed clear of the Limfjord into the sound between Denmark and Sweden, Larry and I looked back wistfully. "It's like we just sailed through a farm," Larry commented. "The same tranquility, the same warm hospitality we were treated to in Virginia."

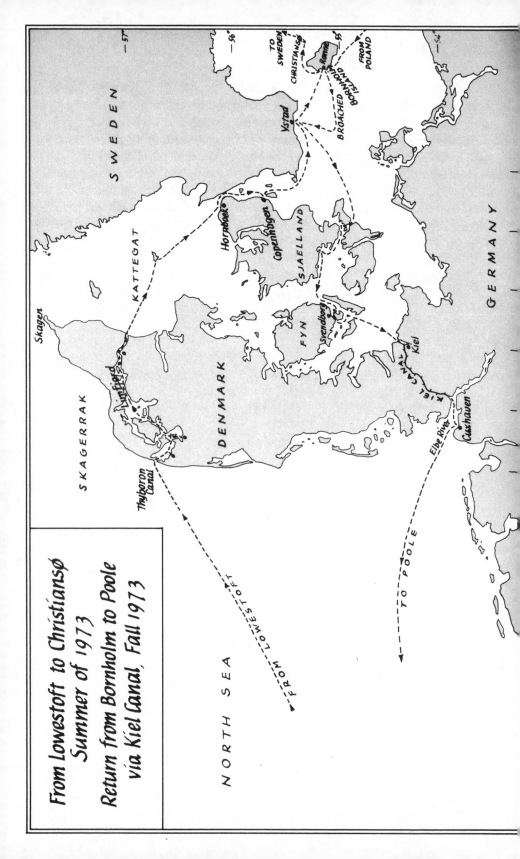

From Lowestoft to Christiansø
Summer of 1973

Return from Bornholm to Poole
via Kiel Canal, Fall 1973

NORTH SEA

SKAGERRAK

SWEDEN

KATTEGAT

Skagen

Limfjord

Thyborøn
Canal

DENMARK

FYN

Horbaek

Copenhagen

SJAELLAND

Svendborg

GERMANY

Kiel

KIEL CANAL

Cuxhaven

Elbe River

TO POOLE

FROM LOWESTOFT

Ystad

Rønne

Bornholm

BORNHOLM
BROACHED

CHRISTIANSØ

TO
SWEDEN

FROM
POLAND

— 57

— 56

— 55

— 54

CHAPTER 10

~~~~~

Adventures
on the Sound

We roared south through the Kattegat, all sails set. The gray
clouds sifted slowly away as we approached Zealand on a broad
reach. But as we drew nearer the land, the wind slowly died until we
were becalmed three-quarters of a mile from the small resort harbor
of Hornebek. We waited patiently for a wind, enjoying dinner in the
warm flat calm. When I'd finished washing the dishes there was still
no sign of a breeze. It was almost 2000 but the sun was high above the
horizon.

Larry finished his brandy, decided to row in and went forward to
unlash our fourteen-foot oar. I dropped the mainsail and furled it
loosely in the lazy jacks, ready to use if necessary, then settled the
boom in the starboard notch of the boom gallows. Larry put the
oarlock and oar in the socket on the port bulwark and started rowing
with a slow but steady motion, feathering the oar on the backstroke
so he didn't have to lift it clear of the water. *Seraffyn* started forward.
At first she tended to round toward starboard, away from the thrust
of the oar, so I held the helm almost hard over. But after ten or fifteen
strokes she gathered way and held a straight course with the tiller less
than five degrees off center. She moved over the flat water at about a
knot.

Evening strollers watched us as we moved slowly toward the high
stone seawall. Our chart showed little clearance on either side of the
sixty-foot-wide dredged channel for *Seraffyn*'s four-foot eight-inch
draft, so Larry switched the oar from the rowing position to the
sculling lock on the taffrail. We lost a bit of speed as Larry sculled
instead of rowed, but *Seraffyn* became much more maneuverable.

When we could see inside the harbor, I did a double take. The three-hundred-yard-wide, five-hundred-yard-long harbor was almost filled to the brim. Larry began pulling in one direction with the sculling oar and *Seraffyn* turned in a tight 360-degree arc. This gave me time to prepare our mooring lines. When I was ready, Larry began sculling like the French fishermen do and *Seraffyn* moved forward into the crowded harbor.

We came to a stop, *Seraffyn'*s boomkin was only about twenty feet inside the entrance. But that was as far as we could go. Boats were tied five and six deep along the walls. The only open space in the whole harbor was a fifteen- or twenty-foot-wide passage from the pilot boat's mooring to the entrance.

The man on the thirty-foot motor sailer nearest the entrance helped us tie up alongside and said, "This is nothing. Wait till June twentieth when the schools let out. Then there won't be room even for you in any harbor on Zealand if you arrive after 1700." When the harbormaster came five minutes later, he also told us of the crowds he expected in two or three weeks' time. "Every yachtsman in Germany seems to head over here for the summer. So the Danes all head north to Swedish waters, the Swedes head north to Finland, and I don't know where the Finns go." This was the first harbor we'd visited in Denmark that charged us harbor dues, the equivalent of $1.50 for the night. During the rest of our Baltic cruise, only three other harbors charged us fees.

Leif Møller joined us the next morning. His unsuppressed eagerness opened our eyes. *Seraffyn* had been our home for over three years. I'd never say we'd become blasé about the world she opened to us, but it was interesting to look at our lifestyle through someone else's eyes. Although Leif was a naval architect and the head of the Danish division of Lloyd's ship surveyors, up until this time his sailing, other than land yachting, had been limited to afternoon excursions in dinghies or on friends' small weekend cruisers.

We had to be out of Hornebek harbor by 0800 so boats tied inboard of us could keep their rendezvous. Leif pitched right in, learning the ropes quickly as we reached out of the crowded harbor. Once we were under way he seemed to step back and realize that he was actually in our home. A fresh breeze filled in from the north and we set the lapper and mainsail. Then Larry put Helmer to work. I poured hot coffee and set out a plate of fresh buttered toast. Leif settled back in the cockpit and began to fire questions at us.

"Where are you headed now?"

Larry answered, "Generally north, wherever things look interesting."

"What's your schedule?"

"Haven't got any," I replied. "We have money enough to cruise until next December. Our only date before then is Tallinn in Estonia, August 10, if we can get our Russian visas finalized."

Leif thought about the idea of no schedule for a few minutes and then said, "Surely you have plans for winter? You have a job planned somewhere."

Larry told him, "We've got some ideas, no plans. I'd like to find a really first-rate shipyard somewhere here in Denmark and work building new wooden boats. I know I'd learn a lot and the Danish consulate told me Canadians can work in Denmark easily. But we'll worry about that when winter comes. Right now we've got the whole Baltic to explore." We could see that we'd given Leif something new to think about.

We took a roundabout route through the sound, skimming past the small island of Ven, an often-disputed piece of land exactly halfway between Sweden and Denmark. Then Leif pointed south to an island barely showing above water. "That's where the two countries have been considering building a bridge. All sorts of studies have been going on. Of course, the shipping lines are against the bridge—their ferries would become obsolete. But the funniest thing about it was the fight in Parliament. One M.P. said, 'I know how to save Denmark millions of kronor during the next years. We'll cancel all plans for a bridge to Sweden.' Our renegade Parliament member, Glistrup, a man who always embarrasses the government, piped up, "I know how to save even more millions. We'll plan a bridge all the way to Germany. That will cost ten times more than a bridge to Sweden. Then, to save money, we'll cancel it!'"

As we reached into the main harbor at Copenhagen, past the diminutive bronze mermaid made famous by Hans Christian Anderson and Danny Kaye, Leif told us more about living in Denmark. "We Danes pay forty-seven percent of our income in direct taxes and fifteen percent more in indirect taxes. So almost all of us have started trading labor to avoid the tax man. Carpenters build new rooms for farmers in exchange for fresh meat or produce. Everyone has a deal. That's the only way we can live so well. Denmark, Sweden, it's almost the same. Wonderfully safe places to live, but not much adventure left. Our generation is doing well. It's the people still in school I worry about. There just aren't enough challenging skilled jobs for them when they graduate. More and more young people are becoming craftsmen and artisans instead of becoming doctors and lawyers."

Our discussion of politics flourished as we ran out of Copenhagen's harbor. Leif pointed toward two huge storage tanks about four miles past the entrance. "That's the yacht club harbor. My friends are expecting you."

We could see dinghies and small cruisers sailing into the yacht club. From a distance they looked like Folkboats and Spitsgatters. Larry had often told me about the Spitsgatters of Denmark, chubby double-ended boats designed with clean simple rigs that had no backstays at all. Their rigs consisted of three wires, a forestay and two shrouds attached three-quarters of the way up the extra-stout mast. The shrouds were carried to a position about two feet aft of the mast. Larry said, "I raced against some Spitsgatters in Vancouver. They used to carry spinnakers in pretty heavy winds, but I never saw one loose its rig."

The race boats were inside the harbor before we reached the entrance, but seven boats came pouring out through the narrow entrance as we approached and rushed to meet us, foghorns blaring, shouts of "Welcome to Sundby Yacht Club" coming from Clockamaker, one of Leif's friends we'd met at the landyacht championships (and a clockmaker by profession).

We turned to Leif in surprise. "Super reception, but how did they know when to expect us?" Leif looked smug when he said, "Danish efficiency! We gave the coast guard a description of your boat and they reported each time we passed one of their observation posts—Helsingor Castle, Ven Island, each entrance to Copenhagen."

Clockamaker yelled, "I'll tow you in. Here's a line."

But the fun, confusion, and excitement made Larry rise to the occasion. "We've sailed this far, we'll sail her in. Thanks anyway."

Leif looked at Larry. "Can you? It's a terribly small entrance." Larry glanced at our chart, then at the narrow hundred-foot-long channel leading to a forty-foot-wide opening between two low stone breakwaters. Inside we could see a crowd of yachts lying stern-to at low wooden piers, bows to mooring buoys and pilings. The entrance was dead to windward. "Well," Larry commented, "if a Folkboat can do it, so can we. Besides, we've said we'll do it, so we will. Might need a few practice runs, though."

Leif shouted to his friends in Danish. Larry and I listened to some sort of argument as we reached back and forth in front of the entrance. Finally Leif laughed and translated, "Half say you can't do it. Half say you can. All of them are worried about how long you look with your bowsprit. They can't believe your hull is as short as a Folkboat." The wonderful crowd of spectators moved to the side of the channel and Larry told us, "Don't worry, absolutely no swell or sea. Worst thing that could happen is to run aground and be embarrassed." We took a practice run, short-tacking up the sixty-foot-wide channel. "The wind is slightly more favorable on the starboard tack," Larry said as we came near the rocks of the breakwater. "Let's bail out and try it again so we're on the starboard tack when we're next to the entrance. Leif, you let the mainsheet loose. Lin, you back the jib." Larry pushed the helm to windward and the backed jib quickly spun *Seraffyn*'s bow around for the run out the channel. "Come on, Larry, let's take a tow," I pleaded. "It won't hurt just this one time." But Leif was caught up in Larry's little game because he answered, "Why not try it? If Larry isn't worried, why should we be?"

We winched in the sails and took three tacks. Then came the moment of truth. Larry tacked within ten feet of the starboard breakwater end. He gave *Seraffyn* lots of time to gather way, then pulled her as close to the wind as she could go. "Leif, stand on the leeward deck and be ready to fend off that piling," Larry called as he pulled the tiller to leeward quickly. *Seraffyn*'s mainsail luffed for just thirty seconds and her five and a half tons of weight helped carry us through the breakwater's entrance. *Seraffyn* heeled to the twelve-knot breeze and Leif, with his usual sense of the ridiculous, kissed his fingertips, then tapped the top of the closest piling lightly as it slid by less than nine inches from our shrouds. "We made it!" I yelled as a blast went up from our escorts. We tacked again into the open area in front of the club and headed toward the space Leif had reserved for us. Then we ran into one of the underwater lines leading to the main mooring chains. *Seraffyn* stopped short. Larry rushed forward and let go the anchor before we drifted into any other boats. Then we launched the dinghy and warped into the pier. "Not bad," Leif said as we tied our lines. I repeated his comment, but Larry was busy analyzing how we could have sailed all the way in if only we'd tacked sooner after we'd cleared the entrance.

He didn't have long to speculate. Our reception committee moored their boats and descended on us. I exhausted our supply of eight wine glasses and eight coffee mugs, and more were borrowed from the clubhouse so we could share our duty-free whiskey with Leif's wonderful collection of yachting friends. The party moved to the buffet in the clubhouse and lasted until midnight. Danish and English mingled in the warm atmosphere, and I took time off before climbing wearily into the bunk to record my favorite comment of the evening in our logbook. I laughed to myself as I remember being told, "One of our members *circumsized* the world."

Leif spent the night at home and arrived late the next day with Tom Nibbea. Tom's reaction was typical of most people who have never been on a sailboat. He stood on the pier, stared, and then said, "You live inside that? Your boat isn't much bigger than a rowboat." We persuaded him to come on board. After he was seated in the cockpit enjoying the warm sun, a rum punch in one hand, fresh hot bread in the other, Tom began to believe we did indeed live on *Seraffyn*. "Arrangements are all made," Tom told us. "Leif has made it possible to hire a pilot boat tomorrow morning and will act as translator. Can you have your spinnaker up?" Larry glanced at the telltales lifting to a caressing breeze. "No problem. Where will we meet you?"

Tom told us to rendezvous in the pilot harbor just south of Helsingor at 0900, then left to rush and take photos of a Great Dane kennel for his Denmark story.

We didn't leave Sundby Yacht Club until almost 2100 because of one last drink with twenty different new friends. So by the time we'd cleared the harbor and headed north, it was growing dark. Leif was firmly entrenched at the helm as a soft offshore breeze carried us along on a reach. "Go catch some sleep," Larry suggested to both Lief and me. But Leif replied, "This is the first time I've ever been sailing at night." So Larry said, "Okay, call me in two hours and I'll take over."

Five hours and twenty miles later, Leif woke us both. "Helsingor Harbor just ahead." Larry glanced at his watch and told me to stay in bed if I wanted to. He climbed out of the bunk, then asked Leif, "Why didn't you call me sooner?" Leif sounded tired but content when he said, "I didn't want to miss one minute of this. It was like being in command of a magic carpet."

It was just daybreak when Larry and Leif finished furling the sails.

But it was only 0230 so everyone turned in for some sleep. The only sound in the quiet harbor came from a pair of garrulous seagulls.

I dreamed someone was throwing rocks on our decks. Larry turned in his sleep and my mind scrambled into reality. Someone *was* throwing rocks on our deck. Not only that, but our rigging was shrieking to a heavy wind. I rushed into the main cabin and pulled on my sweater and jeans. Larry was close behind me. Leif yawned in the quarter berth. The sound of rocks hitting the decks persisted and I flung open the sliding hatch and couldn't believe the strength of the wind—it was lifting dust, sand, and half-inch pebbles from the street we were tied next to. *Seraffyn's* decks were almost covered. Each gust of wind caused a new barrage of pebbles to hit the cabin sides. I pulled the hatch closed quickly to keep as much of the debris out of the cabin as possible, but as I did Larry noticed six armed policemen approaching.

"Leif, are you sure we're supposed to be here?" Larry asked after describing the officials.

Leif climbed out of his berth and opened the canvas companionway covering. The official in the lead set off in a barrage of Danish. Within minutes all of the policemen were laughing. Leif asked us to come on deck. We shook hands with each police officer before they walked off. Leif was chuckling as he pointed to what remained of our old Canadian ensign. We'd accidently left it up during the night and the unexpected gale-force winds had torn almost two-thirds of the flag to bits. All that remained was the red inner portion and about an inch of white. Leif told us, "The NATO post saw your flag and thought you were Polish defectors looking for asylum."

Larry and I laughed at that. But all of a sudden I remembered Tom Nibbea. "We can't possibly go out in this wind to take photos," I said as I poured coffee and tea. Larry listened as more pebbles hit the deck. "If Tom shows up, we'll have to. He's gone to a lot of trouble making arrangements."

As soon as breakfast was over, we went on deck just in time to see Tom come running down the street, camera case in one hand, light meter in the other, two cameras around his neck. He was grinning from ear to ear. "Fantastic, look at those clouds, look at the color of Kronenberg Castle's roof!" We had to agree with him, but Larry did say "No spinnakers today."

So Leif and Tom departed and, as we put two reefs in our mainsail and prepared to run out of the small basin, we heard a forty-five-foot pilot boat start its diesel engine. We cleared the entrance and flew onto a white-capped sea, then hove to. The pilot boat came alongside and Leif translated back and forth for Tom, the pilot, and us. He yelled over the wind's whistle, "Deep water within eight meters of the shore in front of the castle. Wind is Force 9, current is running south about one knot. But it won't set you onshore. You sail, the pilot will stay out of your way."

So, as soon as Larry and I had finished sweeping the sand and pebbles from our cockpit, we ran south one mile past Helsingor Castle, the pilot boat clinging to our wake. Tom climbed all over the pilot boat, pointing first his camera at us, then his light meter. Then he yelled, "Okay, go the other way."

We came about and sheeted *Seraffyn*'s staysail and reefed main in until we were just five degrees off a beat and all of a sudden felt the full force of the wind. Sheets of spray flew across our sharply heeled deck. All of the sand flushed away within minutes and *Seraffyn* flew through the water with a huge bone in her teeth. Five times we beat past that castle only to turn and run back again. The pilot boat was handled superbly, sometimes ranging within ten feet of our beam but never disturbing us. Tom shot off two rolls of film, looking quite

The cover shot of *Seraffyn* passing Helsingor Castle. This was the setting for Shakespeare's *Hamlet*.

satisfied. Then an hour later Leif yelled, "Meet you in the yacht harbor north of the castle. Tom wants to buy you lunch."

The pilot boat peeled away and we started the two-mile beat to the shelter of the yacht haven. It took us over an hour to beat the tide. We were soaked and tired from the hard work of sailing with such a strong wind. But Tom made up for that during a good lunch of frikadeller (meatballs) by saying, "Even if *National Geographic* uses one of these transparencies, I took enough really good ones to give you something exciting for your own use." He went on to tell us, "All of the best sailing photos are set-ups like we did today. The only way to get a good picture of a boat is to have a maneuverable stable motorboat to shoot from." We'd learned a tremendous amount from Tom, and he kept his promise by providing us with the photo that eventually graced the cover of *SAIL* Magazine in the United States and *Yachting Monthly* in the United Kingdom.

That evening the wind dropped and in the morning we set our biggest sails to head toward Sweden. Halfway there we ran completely out of wind. "Now what do you do?" Leif asked, looking toward the land, which lay at least six miles away.

"Relax and enjoy it," Larry told him. And soon Leif did. Larry showed him a favorite spot of ours, lounging against a sailbag on the sunny foredeck. We produced some of our favorite sailing books. Then I set to work doing some mending while Larry answered letters. We had dinner in the cockpit, *Seraffyn* motionless on the flat warm sea.

We thought about our three-and-a-half years of sailing and concluded that we'd had about a hundred hours of absolutely no wind. Leif put it right when he answered, "When you've got your home with you, a day becalmed is just like a lazy Sunday ashore."

We took a sounding at dark and found bottom at thirty-five feet. We were well clear of shipping. So we set our anchor, lit our anchor light, and set a bunk out in the cockpit for Leif. When we awoke, a light breeze was blowing across the sound and we sailed into a tiny port where Leif could catch a ferry for home and his busy work schedule. As he left, Leif called back to us, "I'm going to get a boat like yours someday. The past five days of sailing have been better for me than a month's holiday."

After he left we sat back and talked about how fortunate we were. Leif's enthusiasm had made us doubly appreciative of the joys of our floating life.

CHAPTER 11

Into the Baltic

There wasn't a ship on the horizon when we sailed from the small Swedish harbor of Ysted about three days later. Bornholm Island lay dead to windward, forty miles northeast of us. But with an absolutely flat sea and five or six knots of wind, beating was a pleasure. This was what *Seraffyn* was designed for. We set our 180-square-foot mainsail and our 369-square-foot number-one genoa. *Seraffyn* heeled about eight or ten degrees and made the sunlit sea chuckle past her sharp bow.

We headed north along Sweden's green-cliffed shore, Helmer steering, the two of us comfortably reading in the cockpit. The roar of large high-speed engines carried toward us from upwind and Larry got up and looked around. A gray launch was headed directly toward us. As it came closer, we could see seven or eight uniformed men on board. The launch carried no flag. I put up our Canadian ensign, remembering the flag incident in Helsingor. But the launch roared determinedly toward us. When it was about forty feet away, the helmsman shut down his engines and yelled in accented English, "Where are you headed?"

Larry called back, "Ronne Harbor, on Bornholm."

The helmsman answered, "Please keep moving and clear the area as soon as possible. There is a NATO exercise on and we wish to use the cliffs behind you for target practice."

We waved to let them know that we understood. Then the helmsman pulled his throttles full on and roared off seaward.

As *Seraffyn* continued chuckling along at about four knots we noticed a whole flotilla of warships massing on the horizon. Fifteen minutes later the same launch charged at us again. "Can't you get a move on?" an English naval officer yelled. "You're costing NATO thousands of pounds an hour!"

We tried to oblige by putting up our staysail. Three hundred yards away from us the NATO launch idled and gurgled as *Seraffyn* beat determinedly past the cliffs. Thirty minutes later the launch turned dead to seaward and its engines came alive as it roared off at full throttle. Then we heard the first thud of heavy artillery and felt shock-waves through the cockpit sole as each shell exploded against the peaceful green cliffs we'd passed.

We beat into Ronne, the main harbor on the Danish island of Bornholm at 0230 the next morning. The sun was up and so was the harbormaster. He helped us secure *Seraffyn* in a corner of the fishing port, then told us, "In twenty-four hours this harbor will be full because the fishing fleet will all come in for the Midsummer's Night festivities. Come see me in the morning and I'll tell you where the best things happen."

When he left, Larry and I climbed into our bunk. We tossed and turned, trying to fall asleep in the bright sunshine at 0300. Finally Larry went on deck and covered the two deadlights with a sailbag. He set another sailbag on the deadlight in the hatch. We both quickly fell asleep in the dark forepeak.

The harbormaster met us at the seaman's club at noon and bombarded us with descriptions of Midsummer's Night. Since the very best festival would be at the northeast end of the island, and since no buses ran on holidays, we decided to splurge and rent a car. When the harbormaster heard this, he insisted on calling a friend at Sveneke where the festivities would be held. "Go up there today," the harbormaster told us. "My friend is expecting you and will include you in on all activities."

We stopped at least five different times during our fifteen-mile drive across the soft green plains of Bornholm. We'd only been under way ten minutes when Larry slammed on the brakes. "Did you see that?" he asked as he put the car in reverse. I had been engrossed, watching birds flying from a reed-covered lake on my side of the car. As soon as we'd backed up a hundred or so yards I saw what Larry was so interested in. A red thatch-roofed farmhouse stood by the road, shaded by dark pine trees. Behind the house was a large red barn surrounded by piles of straw-covered thatch. Three men were busy sewing bundles of thatch on the wooden latticework that rested on the rafters of the barn's roof.

The barn's owner saw us watching from the car and came over. We greeted him, using one of the five Danish words that made up our vocabulary. But he immediately sensed that our native language was English and invited us to take a closer look. "The last time that roof was rethatched was twenty years ago," the owner told us. He went on to explain that the thatch they were using was actually reeds cut from frozen lakes during the winter. "It's hard to find men who have the skill to do a good job of thatching," he told us. "I had to engage this group a year in advance."

We kept the rented car for five days, driving from one end of Bornholm to the other. Tiny man-made fishing boat harbors dotted its shore, some of them with entrances less than forty feet wide. We made friends with two of Sveneke's fishermen, using the kind introduction of Ronne's harbormaster. And after the dancing, singing, and huge bonfire of the Midsummer's Night festival, Larry set off to watch as they hauled in their herring nets. I flopped on the backseat of the car and slept.

The next morning we drove back past the red barn and admired its new twelve-inch-thick, carefully trimmed, gold-colored thatched roof. Then we returned to Ronne and turned in our rented car. We were shocked at the sixty dollars it had cost until we considered the benefits. In a place where the cruising season is as limited as the Baltic, we had to use the time we had carefully. We would never have been able to join in the fun of Midsummer's Night, nor have come to know the central lakes and beautiful farmlands of Bornholm any other way. But if we had a larger boat, a small motorcycle or two bicycles would have been a treat and a money-saver.

Before we left Ronne harbor on June 24, 1973, everyone was telling us, "This weather is some of the best we've had in years!" We skimmed northeast along Bornholm's cliffy shores wearing only bathing suits as we passed a ruined castle clinging to the cliff tops. Then we turned and reached into the neat, grass-fringed harbor of Hammershus. Three Danish yachts and one German one lay against the seawall. We had barely secured our mooring lines and fenders when the harbormaster arrived. "Beautiful harbor you have," Larry said by the way of a greeting. The harbormaster smiled as he glanced around the peaceful scene. "Yes," he chuckled "but in every paradise there

Though we'd seen many thatched roofs in England and Denmark, this was the first time we'd had a chance to see how they were made.

These herrings would be smoked and served as Bornholmers, a fish delicacy known throughout Scandinavia.

is a snake. I have come to collect your harbor dues."

The people off the German ketch came by and, after looking through *Seraffyn,* invited us to come and share some schnapps. Werner gave us a tour of the forty-five-foot ketch he used as sailing school boat for people wanting to get their offshore sailors license. He was surprised to hear that no licensing of any kind was required of North American pleasure sailors. We discussed the relative merits of the voluntary system of sailing education available to Canadians and Americans compared with the compulsary licensing enforced in most of Europe.

One of Werner's students broke up the conversation by saying, "Enough serious talk. How about playing some music?" So Werner grabbed his accordion and a crewman came back from the galley carrying a broomstick with two pie plates nailed loosely to one end, a washbasin tacked on the side of the stick, and two nylon strings secured from the stick ends across the basin. Werner squeezed his accordion until the boat rang with the strains of a familiar-sounding polka. The crewman thumped his "devil's violin" on the cabin sole, plucking its two strings. The tins rattled and clanged in rhythm and ten of us swayed to the music. My feet itched for room to dance and I knew Larry felt the same as he put his arm around my shoulders and squeezed. We sang and listened as the sun set and rose again. Once more we had to cover our forepeak deadlights when we finally went home to get some sleep.

"Who controls Christiansø, controls the Baltic," eighteenth-century naval experts said of the two tiny islands north of Bornholm. We couldn't quite believe these miniscule dots of land had such an important place in history until we sailed into the tiny but very protected natural harbor that lay between them. The islands consisted of less than fifteen acres of land but had always been the home of fishermen, merchant sailors, and smugglers. Several years ago the Danish government declared the islands a national museum, so the beautiful yellow stone buildings with red tile roofs looked as they must have three or four hundred years ago. The 112 fishermen who now live on Christiansø are often ice- or weather-bound for three or four weeks in the winter. But in the summer their quiet island population is increased by artists who come from the mainland, attracted by the island's crystal-clear light.

Once each day from June to September a ferry full of tourists arrives and stays for three hours. But when it leaves the quiet peaceful mood of the enchanted islands returns.

On the first evening of our stay, the mayor arrived to welcome us. Mr. Jacobsen shared a glass of whiskey in our cockpit as he told us about the islands. He'd been appointed mayor five years before, and explained, "I have thirteen titles besides: justice of the peace, head of sanitation, curator, . . . and the amazing thing is, the government sends me a separate check for each job! I get eighteen dollars a year as head of sanitation, thirty-five as justice of the peace."

Our second afternoon in Christiansø we watched a handsome forty-seven-foot yawl enter the harbor flying an American flag. This was the first non-Scandinavian, non-German yacht we'd seen since we'd entered the Limfjord. The harbormaster came running down the stone pier and told the American yacht to moor in the nonexistent

The only change on Christiansø Island that is visible from the sea is the light-house on top of the castle.

space between us and a thirty-foot Swedish sloop. With an anchor set astern, two lines ashore, and eight people tugging, shoving, and pulling, *Puffin* was squeezed into her designated spot. We tried to help, adjusting our fenders and fending off. But none of our efforts seemed to ease the look of horror on the face of the gray-haired lady who stood staring at our protruding five-sixteenths-inch-thick solid-bronze chain plates which threatened to gouge *Puffin*'s topsides if any fender popped out of place. We've been told before that our external chainplates—standing four inches out from *Seraffyn*'s hull on channels—are unsociable, and after learning that *Puffin* had just had a complete refit, during which hundreds of dollars had been spent to give her topsides a magnificent glowing white finish, we were extra sympathetic.

As soon as *Puffin* was squeezed in and well fendered, the introductions began. The gray-haired lady broke into a beautiful twinkling smile and said, "I'm Betty Greeff. This is my husband Ed and my ten-year-old grandson Geoffrey." We also met the rest of *Puffin*'s summer crew, all New Yorkers—Pam and Bill Kellett and their thirteen-year-old daughter Allison, and Harry Anderson. Every inch of *Puffin* proclaimed the art of wooden boat building, and when Ed invited us to have a look on board we gladly accepted. *Puffin* was a Sparkman and Stevens–designed CCA ocean racer/cruiser. She'd been built for the Greeffs in 1969 by the Walstead Yacht Yard in Thruro, Denmark.

After five years of extensive racing and cruising *Puffin* needed a refit, so Ed sailed her back from New York to the yard that had built her. Walstead's took care of her during the winter while the Greeffs flew home to New York. In the spring the Greeffs and their crew of friends arrived in Denmark to find a *Puffin* that looked almost like new.

Larry was into every nook and cranny of *Puffin*, firing questions at Ed about her construction. He pointed out her varnished frames and told me, "That's locust [acacia], just like the timber we cut and stored in Virginia last year. I knew it would make good frames if we built another boat." *Puffin* was beautifully constructed of teak, mahogany, locust, and oak, bronze fastened. After hearing about the special laminating methods used by Walstead's, Larry asked Ed, "Do you think Walstead could use an extra shipwright this winter?" Ed told us about the three boats Walstead's yard planned to start and said that Mr. Walstead, like most boat builders, complained about a shortage of skilled help.

When we went on board *Seraffyn* later that afternoon, Larry said,

Puffin, owned by Ed and Betty Greeff. Length overall, 47'; load waterline, 35'; beam, 12.5'; draft, 8'; sail area, 1,048 square feet.

"Lin, I know what I want to do this winter! I want to try and get a job at Walstead's. I know I'd learn a hell of a lot about boat building there. Ed says there are cottages for rent near the boatyard. We could get one and live ashore while we did up *Seraffyn's* interior varnish." I loved the enthusiastic look Larry had and readily agreed that a winter in Denmark might prove to be a lot of fun, as long as we had a warm, cozy place to live.

Puffin lay alongside us for two days and we found once again that youngsters belong on cruising boats. Geoffrey and Allison kept everyone delighted with their observations. The morning *Puffin* was preparing to sail, Betty Greeff told us, "Yesterday after dinner we had the kids sit down and draw pictures of boats they'd like to own. Allison drew a lovely picture of *Puffin*. But Geoffrey drew one of your boat, and not too diplomatically said, 'I like *Seraffyn* because she is just the right size for a boy like me to sail by myself.' "

We waved good-bye as *Puffin* and her friendly crew powered out the narrow entrance of Christiansø then we took our towels and a book each and found a spot where we could sunbath comfortably on the warm rocks. That afternoon Larry brought up one of the problems that faced us as we cruised the Baltic. "We'd better get moving if we want to see any of the Finnish islands," he said. "I know Christiansø is beautiful, but there are only two or three months of decent weather left." Our years of casual meandering in the tropics, during which we'd often stopped for a night and stayed a month, had spoiled us. But neither of us had any desire to spend six months iced into a winter in Finland, although in retrospect that might have proved interesting.

We had coffee and cakes that evening with Mr. Jacobsen, and Larry mentioned that we planned to set sail within an hour or two. He went on to ask, "The wind is from the south so it would be quite tricky to sail out the southern entrance. Is it possible to have the bridge opened so we can sail between the islands?"

"Of course it is," Mr. Jacobsen replied. "All you have to do is ask the mayor."

So after we'd finished our coffee, Larry and I went back on board and prepared *Seraffyn*. It was 2200 and the sun was almost on the horizon as we pulled *Seraffyn* back to her stern anchor.

Mr. Jacobsen waved from the winding wheel at the end of the bridge and started turning its handle. The bridge slowly swung open and Larry pulled up our lapper, then came aft and hauled our stern anchor on board. I sheeted the lapper in and steered as *Seraffyn* gathered way. Larry had the mainsail up and pulling wing and wing as we passed the open bridge. We called good-bye to our Christiansø friends and were out onto the open sea in less than five minutes.

We set the jib on the spinnaker pole, Helmer took command, and I drew the first watch. I wore shorts and a sweatshirt and read on the afterdeck as we ran north at about four knots. At 2330 the sun set, but I still had enough light to read by. At 0130 the sun rose, a glowing gold disk over a smooth gray sea. At 0155 I woke Larry with a cup of hot chocolate. Then I climbed into the bunk and quickly fell asleep as *Seraffyn* ran steadily on toward Sweden's twenty thousand islands.

CHAPTER 12

Twenty Thousand Islands

When Larry was nineteen he'd fallen in love with a twenty-seven-foot Tumlaren-class sloop designed by Knud Reimers and called *Annalisa*. She'd been built by the Kungsor yard near Stockholm in 1948 for the crown prince of Denmark. By taking a bank loan, countersigned by his father, Larry had been able to buy the completely varnished sloop and for five years he raced and cruised her around Vancouver. From the time I met him, two years after he sold *Annalisa*, Larry had raved about his magnificent sloop. I'd almost grown jealous for *Seraffyn* as he described the extreme lightweight, scientific construction of the narrow, delicate Tumlaren. *Seraffyn* is twenty-four feet four inches long with a beam of nine feet, and weighs close to eleven thousand pounds. *Annalisa*, at twenty-seven feet on deck, was only six feet wide and displaced only thirty-eight hundred pounds. As we cruised north through Sweden's multitude of islands I came to appreciate the ideas behind the Tumlaren's design. She, like the much better known Folkboat class (see Appendix B), had been created for families who had protected waters to sail in. From a hundred fifty miles south of Stockolm north to Finland and east to Helsinki, a stretch of over six hundred miles, there are so many islands and anchorages that there is never a need to be more than four or five miles from land. The islands keep the seas flat with only occasional chop. Tiny villages dot the archipelagos so a family cruiser need carry only a few days' worth of supplies. But the intricate passages among the rocks and islands require boats that are handy to tack and close-winded, boats that accelarate quickly to use each puff of wind that whispers around the points and trees. These boats are built light to save money since they can only be used three or four months out of the year. We saw hundreds of them throughout Sweden and Denmark, and many are sailed without engines.

On the other hand, Swedish yachtsmen were fastinated by husky, beamy *Seraffyn* with her high lifelines, bulwarks, self-draining cockpit, and heavily stayed rig. "We don't see many real oceangoing yachts here," several sailors told us when we tied in Borgholm on Kalmar Island en route to the Stockholm Archipelago. We were moored among at least three dozen small cruisers, and *Seraffyn* did look different. One Swedish couple came by three or four times and stood whispering to each other on the dockside. I was just serving Larry a drink and so I called to them, "Do you speak English?" As we had come to expect, they answered yes. So I said, "Come have a drink with us." Breta and Walter Nathansen came on board and we soon had all our Swedish charts out as they described their favorite anchorages from Oland north to Finland. They saw my dinner set out ready to cook and left after only one hour, but pointed to their large steel ketch, moored at the far side of the harbor. "Come over after you eat," Walter insisted. "I have something I want to give you."

Two hours later we were on board the Nathansens' specially built Baltic cruiser. Walter, a Stockholm architect, explained, "The season up here is just too short for me to have a normal boat. This one has one-inch steel plating on the keel and three-quarter-inch plating at the waterline so as soon as the ice breakers clean a channel in the spring, I can set off cruising." I noticed the huge hot-water radiators everywhere in the carefully insulated accommodations.

As the evening drew pleasantly on, Walter commented, "I want you to visit my archipelago," and then he brought out a chart with a circle around a group of forty or fifty tiny islands. He'd drawn a course along the path he felt was safe for us and then a pencil line we were to follow through the island group with an *X* where he felt we could anchor comfortably. "I've written a note to our caretaker telling him to give you fresh fish and strawberries. I'll use my radio to contact my son who should be on the islands holidaying with his family."

As we sailed north, closer to the Stockholm Archipelago, we started studying the detail charts. Although each chart only covered twenty to thirty miles, some showed as many as a hundred islands and islets. The charts clearly showed every possible danger in the main channels. Lights and beacons abounded in carefully thought-out positions. But large areas of each chart were lined off and the legend on the chart explained, "These areas are not fully charted for reasons of military security." Stora Nassa, the place Walter had called "my archipelago," was inside one of these "not fully charted" areas.

It was great sailing among the gray rocky outer islands of Sweden. Evergreen trees clung to each one. Most had no inhabitants at all except for an occasional camping family with a small runabout. Others had wooden summer cottages on them. We moored at Sandhamn, the Stockholm Sailing Club's out-station, and when we raved about the wonderful weather, light breezes, and warm sunshine, several Swedes informed us, "So far this is one of the best summers in recorded history." We were also told, "Wait till you get to the Oland Islands and Finland. There are so many islands and anchorages there that if you want company at night you leave your ensign up when you anchor. But if you want to be all alone so you can go nude, you take your ensign down and no one will stop within sight of you."

We set sail from Sandhamn on one of the few blustery, cool, cloudy days we had that summer. As we tacked east, deeper into the archipelago, a light spray flew across our decks. But we didn't consider putting on wet-weather gear since the spray was fresh water and dried within minutes. That's one of the treats of Baltic sailing. Once you are north of Bornholm Island, there is so little salt in the water you can wash your hair and clothes right off the boat and feel great. Near Finland the water is almost good enough to drink. From the beginning of July until the middle of September we were surprised to find that less than three hundred miles from Arctic Circle the water was warm enough for swimming, especially on sunny days.

We followed the main shipping route north, glad to have a definite goal. Otherwise we'd have never been able to choose which channels to sail through. We reached the striped lighthouse on the third island north of Moja after two pleasant day sails and turned onto a compass course of ninety-two degrees. A warm southerly wind gave us a perfect beam reach. As soon as we'd sailed half a mile we were into the "not fully charted" area.

I stood on the foredeck holding the chart, watching for rocks while Larry kept reassuring me, "The Nathansens have been taking this route several times a year for forty years, Lin. If there were any dangers, Walter would have told us. His boat draws two feet more than *Seraffyn*, so as long as we stick to his bearings there can't be much danger."

Within a few miles the islands began to be farther apart. Fewer and fewer had trees on them. Soon the only islands in view were bare granite rocks less than fifty feet high. Our taffrail log showed we'd gone seven miles when we spotted the "island with one short tree" that marked our first course change. We skirted the island, keeping a hundred yards off as Walter's pencil line indicated. When we could lay a course of seventy degrees with the tree dead on our stern, we eased our sheets and ran for the designated four miles. Each ten or fifteen minutes Larry took a bearing over our stern, sighting on the lone tree to make sure we weren't being set off our course by a current or inaccurate steering. I practically wore Walter's chart out taking cross bearings, marking our advancing position and calculating our speed.

Fifty minutes later we resumed a course of ninety-two degrees and dead ahead of us, five miles distant, lay a cluster of islands. As they grew closer we encountered one of the most difficult problems of navigation—judging distance and height. How long is two miles, how high is 135 feet, how wide is a ninety-foot channel? Walter's archipelago covered only about four square inches on our large-scale chart. I took our dividers out and scaled this off to find forty-seven islands and several hundred rocks squeezed into an area two miles by three miles. The channel we were to run through had a spot that was less than sixty feet wide.

Seraffyn was quickly closing on the islands so I brought the chart on deck. Larry looked over my notations and asked, "Which islands do we sail between?" I went on the foredeck to search the islands for a clue, then called back, "I just can't say for sure, they all look the same to me. What do we do?"

"I'll head into the wind, you drop the jib," Larry called. "Then we'll heave to and figure this out." With her mainsail sheeted in hard, jib down in the jib net, *Seraffyn* headed close to the wind and our speed dropped from five knots to almost nothing in the twelve-knot breeze. We lay the chart out on the cockpit floor and took bearings on each end of the archipelago. The cross put us half a mile off the entrance. The two 135-foot-high rocks with only a thin ribbon of water between them *were* the ones we were supposed to sail between.

"Okay, Lin, let's set the staysail instead of the lapper. No need to sail into a strange situation at full speed. If things don't look right, we can reach back out here." So I hoisted the 104-square-foot staysail, Larry sheeted it in and eased the mainsail, and we reached along Walter's pencil line. A passage ninety feet wide appeared before us and then we were among the gray rocks, counting each one off as we turned north and wound our way toward the one island that had cabins on it. I pulled in our taffrail log as Larry checked our course on the chart. We skirted a barely submerged rock and then spotted four wooden cabins. "We round up just past this next big rock and we should be right where Walter said to anchor," Larry told me. "You take the helm. I'll get ready to anchor. Looks like close work."

We put *Seraffyn* hard on the wind for the last two-hundred-yard leg of our exciting day. Larry went forward to the leeward shrouds and we waved back at the two people who were coming toward the shore. "Larry, there's a rock ahead of us, I think," I called from the tiller. I wasn't sure; the water just seemed a slightly different color. Larry glanced quickly at the folded chart in his hand and said, "None shown here." I steered toward the center of the tiny anchorage. *Seraffyn* heeled sharply to a gust of wind. Larry looked down at the water rushing by *Seraffyn*'s channels. His face went white. He couldn't speak; he only pointed—straight down. I leaned over the side to look and went white too as I saw a rockpile slide by our bilge less than two feet below the water. If *Seraffyn* hadn't been heeled we'd have hit it, and at the four knots we were making through the water, all five and a half tons of *Seraffyn* would have hit those rocks hard! "Head into the wind," Larry shouted. When we were a hundred yards past the rock, Larry let go our anchor and *Seraffyn* came to rest with just enough room to swing in ten feet of water with fifty feet of chain out.

Larry was still quite pale; I couldn't see myself so I don't know what color I was. We furled the mainsail, then sat down and looked at Walter's chart again. I got a sudden idea and went below for a pencil. I carefully erased Walter's pencil mark and there was our rock—right under one leg of his *X!*

The two men from shore came alongside in a runabout. "Welcome to Stora Nassa. Really exciting entrance you made. We didn't think you knew where our rock was at first. But obviously you did. At least ten boats a year end up on top of it," Walter's son Thomas said. He and his cousin Hans never believed we'd missed that rock only by luck.

Thomas and Hans towed us around to the tiny dock in an almost enclosed area in front of the four cabins. As soon as we'd secured alongside, their children and wives appeared and we learned more about Stora Nassa. From the first we'd assumed that Walter Nathansen had been using English improperly when he called the islands of Stora Nassa "my archipelago." But Thomas explained that Stora Nassa had been deeded to his grandfather by the king of Sweden on the condition that it be kept as a bird sanctuary, with any structures restricted to one island only. A fisherman and his wife had been found to live on the islands year round as caretakers. Then the Nathansens built him a home plus four summer cottages and a sauna. During the main bird-breeding months, from mid-April to mid-June, no one was allowed to land on the other islands of Stora Nassa. But the rest of the year visitors were welcome if they were careful. We could see the masts of three or four other yachts moored behind various islands. In the crevices and valleys of the rocky half-mile-square main island the caretaker's wife had planted a beautiful garden with hundreds of strawberry plants. Hans sent his son for some and soon we were all sitting around, dipping fresh rosy strawberries in sugar and eating them whole.

We were immediately adopted into the summer camp atmosphere of the island. Thomas acted as activity organizer, Hans as camp comic.

Just a few of Stora Nassa's two hundred islands.

At about nine o'clock our first evening, Thomas arrived, trailed by four children and Hans. "Come on, Larry," he shouted. "Every evening every man and child on Stora Nassa runs completely around the island then dives in the water for a swim. It is a tradition."

Larry pulled on his shoes while Hans commented wryly, "Ya, it is a tradition ever since two weeks ago when Thomas dreamed it up."

The next morning Thomas, the organizer, was down to see us within minutes after Larry stepped on deck with his first cup of coffee. "Shopping day. Launch leaves at 10:30. We'll give you a tour of the inner islands on the way," Thomas told us.

We climbed into the Stora Nassa launch with Thomas, his wife, and their two children, and roared off at twenty-five knots, retracing in less than thirty-five minutes the route *Seraffyn* had taken seven hours to sail the day before. As we reached the limit of the "not fully charted" area, I commented, "Nice not to have to worry about uncharted dangers if you stray a little off your course now." Thomas laughed at my concern. "Didn't anyone tell you? Every possible danger that is within three meters of the surface is listed. It is only deep-draft vessels those charts are supposed to fool."

I related this information to Larry who was seated on my opposite side and couldn't hear Thomas over the roar of the motor. Larry commented, "That's the logic of politicians. Now all an invader has to do is use shoal-draft boats. But it's good to know so we can stop worrying about running into phantom rocks."

The closer to Stockholm we got, the greener and denser the islands became. Tour boats, cargo boats, car ferries, and pleasure craft became more plentiful. We stopped at an island with a fuel dock and grocery store on it, and watched as a small cargo boat off-loaded plastic-lined five-gallon round metal containers and then took off the same containers, only sealed and obviously full. When we asked what the containers held, Thomas proudly explained, "Five years ago the pollution in these islands within ten miles of Stockholm was so bad that swimming had to be forbidden. There are no tides to help clean up debris, so the government got down to business and introduced a law forbidding the discharge of human waste from any inhabitants of these islands. Then they arranged for the regular distribution and pickup of these toilet buckets. Yachts that are not moored near clubs or camp grounds are exempt from rules because their total pollution can be absorbed by the ecology. But everyone else has to use these buckets. It's really been

Thomas in the *Optimist* and Larry in *Rinky* run neck and neck toward the finish line.

Hans, the comedian, and his wife Gretta and two children on board *Seraffyn* after a picnic lunch.

worthwhile. Now we have clean, clear water right in the middle of Stockholm itself."

I had quite a shock when I looked at the food prices. Danish prices had been high, but Swedish ones were higher. Thomas reassured me when he said, "Wait until you reach Finland to shop. Prices are a third of what they are here." I hoped he was right because our stock of English canned foods was being steadily depleted.

We were back in Stora Nassa for a late lunch. Thomas challenged Larry to a dinghy race around the island. Larry set off in *Rinky*, Thomas in his Optimist pram. An hour later they returned, dead-running within inches of each other, laughing and taunting each other like two schoolboys. Thomas came over the line first. "I'd have done better with some local knowledge," Larry commented as soon as he tied up. He was still chuckling as he explained, "I ran into a couple of rocks."

Thomas kept our days full to the brim. Saunas, walks, shared smorgasbord meals. The day before we departed, Hans and his family joined us on *Seraffyn*, Thomas took his family in their fifteen-foot sailboat, and we all sailed to the easternmost islands of Sweden for a picnic lunch, laughing most of the time.

All of us returned to find that Breta and Walter had arrived on their steel ketch. We made fresh bread, cabbage salad, and a big pot of spaghetti and invited everyone on Stora Nassa for dinner. Larry rigged our stereo speakers on deck. I used salad plates and spoons to serve the children, while adults got dinner plates and forks. Knives had to be shared.

Larry and I prepared to sail the next morning despite the hard-to-refuse suggestions for more outings and explorations with the delightful Stora Nassans. We had a fine sendoff after Walter lined a course northward toward Finland on our chart. "Turn at the oil drum with a cross on it," he shouted as we ran off under main and lapper. Soon we cleared the tiny islands and, sure enough, two miles ahead of us stood a rock surmounted by a fifty-five-gallon drum, a wooden cross on its top. We turned northwest toward the main shipping channel and Stora Nassa, the magical family-owned archipelago, slowly faded from our view.

~~~~~~

CHAPTER 13

Thirty Thousand Islands

As Larry steered north past the last of Sweden's islands, I went below to sort out charts. Just to cruise from the south coast of England to Finland, we'd needed over fifty charts plus two *Pilot* books. If we'd had to go out and buy these charts they'd have cost us over a hundred eighty dollars in 1973. But fortunately, we've found that cruising sailors worldwide are willing to trade or loan charts. When we'd set off cruising in 1969, we'd purchased two hundred dollars' worth of charts covering the area from Newport Beach, California, to Panama. In Panama we traded with a westbound yacht for all of the Caribbean charts. And so it went. During more than nine years of cruising, we've only spent eighty to a hundred dollars more for charts we couldn't acquire by trading. During our winter in Poole we'd mentioned our sailing plans to various people and soon heard of a large power yacht fresh from a cruise of the Baltic, and we soon had the loan of all the charts we needed, plus some excellent firsthand advice.

When I brought the first of the Finnish charts on deck, Larry set Helmer steering and joined me for a look. Finnish charts are really different. Not only do they use green and yellow to show shoal water and marshes instead of the blue or gray we were used to, but because there is such an unbelievable number of islands protecting the Finnish coast, the Finnish hydrographic office hasn't tried to chart each danger or even each island. Instead, there are a large number of selected, marked routes leading to all of the inhabited islands. These routes, thin black lines threading between beacons and lighthouses, have numbers next to them which indicate the deepest vessel that can safely use them. Some say fifteen meters and are routes used by the big car ferries we saw flashing by as regularly as buses. But most of the routes we took were marked 1.8 meters or 2 meters. Since *Seraffyn* draws 1.4 meters, we were reluctant to take any route marked 1.5 or less, but we later learned that we would have been safe since the depths figured are for extreme low water.

Light winds slowed our progress across the forty miles of open water between Sweden and Finland. Already in the middle of July there was a perceptible lengthening of the time between sunset and sunrise, although the sky never lost its dusk-like glow. Larry stood the first three-hour watch and when he woke me, suggested that I heave to and wait for full daylight if I didn't spot the lighthouse marking the entrance to Marianhamina. Several lights winked, but none of their characteristics seemed to make sense. I backed the jib, tied the tiller to leeward, and *Seraffyn* lay quietly in the six-knot breeze, making absolutely no way. It was fully daylight at 0300 when Larry came on watch. Dozens of islands lay less than five miles north of us. But not a ferry was in sight and we were even more confused than we'd been during the short night. Then I spotted what looked like a patrol boat coming toward us. "That's the answer. Let's wave him down and ask where we are."

Larry wasn't too keen on that idea and suggested, "Let's try and figure this out ourselves. It's not fair to disturb other people with our problems." He poured over our chart, scanned the horizon, and read the *Pilot* book, looking for some identifiable landmark. Each island looked the same—pink granite covered with trees.

The patrol boat came directly toward us and was within fifty feet of us when a man on deck called to us in Swedish. I put up our Canadian ensign while Larry yelled, "Do you speak English?" The patrol boatman yelled back, "Is everything all right?"

"Can you confirm our position?" Larry called at the same time as I yelled, "We're lost."

The big bald Finn laughed and called back, "I'm not surprised. We've added several new navigation lights and changed all the light sequences this spring. Hold on, I'll give you a course to steer. Where are you headed?"

When we plotted in the position he'd given us, we found we had been set five miles west during the night. This surprised us because the Baltic is supposed to be tideless. But we later learned that changes in barometric pressures caused by depressions moving across Europe can cause currents up to two knots to flow through the Baltic channels.

The yacht club at Marianhamina is a tiny, bright-red wooden house heavily trimmed with white gingerbread carvings. Green trees crowd over it and less than two hundred yards away the towering rig of the iron sailing ship *Pommern* dwarfed the otherwise lofty-looking spars of *Puffin,* which had arrived two days before us after taking a completely different route north by way of Goteland and Stockholm.

The friendly yacht club manager alloted us a mooring, then hoisted a Canadian flag on the last empty guest flagpole alongside those from Germany, Sweden, Poland, and the U.S.A. The beautifully protected harbor made us feel confident about our decision to leave *Seraffyn* for a few weeks while we took a long-anticipated trip inland.

Six months before, when we'd been in London visiting various embassies, the consul for Finland had given us a pile of travel brochures. He'd asked us when we'd be in his country and when we answered "June or July," told us, "You are lucky because that's when all the Finns celebrate the long evenings by having music festivals. There's a classical music festival, one for jazz buffs, another for folk music lovers, and one for opera fans. Wonderful festivals in the nicest villages of Finland."

As we entered Marianhamina, we saw the full-rigged ship *Pommern.*

His enthusiasm was contagious. "Which one is best?" Larry wanted to know. The consul answered, "I've been to them all. It depends on what you like. But the folk festival at Kaustinen gets bigger every year." He'd given us a festival brochure and wished us a good summer in Finland.

We'd arrived in Marianhamina three days before the Kaustinen Folk Festival was to begin. We asked the yacht club caretaker to check *Seraffyn's* doubled-up mooring lines, packed two small seabags, and discovered one of the delights of traveling in Finland. Because there are so many islands and lakes, and because roads are so hard to keep open during the long severe winters, the Finns have developed a wonderfully effective internal airline system. Low air fares, no reservations. We bought our tickets right on the plane. Flights were frequent. Our first flight to Helsinki, a distance of four hundred miles, cost us ten dollars each, and we carried out luggage on with us.

During our two-hour flight we once again debated the question of trying to get visas to visit Russia. "It's worth a try," Larry felt, so we went to the Soviet Embassy as soon as we arrived in Helsinki.

The Russian consul, a charming young man dressed in the most mod of suits, was extremely friendly. "I know we can arrange your visas. But we must rush because your port clearance is dated five weeks from today and that would be hard to change." We left feeling hopeful since the consul had been placing a call direct to Tallinn, our proposed first port of entry, when we left his office.

Once again we splurged and enjoyed the convenience of having a car for our trip to the Kaustinen festival. The drive across Finland, unhassled by concerns over bus schedules, taxi fares, and luggage, was a treat. When we arrived at the tiny farm community less than sixty miles from the Arctic Circle, the crowds that swamped the reception center glowed in their various national costumes. We located one of the thousand beds made available in the homes of local farmers. For a set fee of three dollars each we were provided with a bed, a delicious breakfast of fresh bread, fruit, and homemade cheese, and one sauna bath per day. Next to the farm we stayed at were the huge fields set aside for the thousands of people who had brought their caravans, tents, or just sleeping bags. We could hear the strains of a hundred different musicians warming up and practicing everywhere we turned.

The festival organizers had sent formal invitations to two hundred

Young and old, the music rang for sixteen hours a day

Erikke Shastamoinen, entertaining us first with his music (below) then with the music of his anvil (page 138).

folk musicians and dancers from eleven countries. Over two thousand arrived, plus fifteen thousand spectators. There were three regular exhibitions going on at all times—one in the school stadium, one in the auditorium, and one in the ski lodge, a quarter mile from the school. These cost twenty-five cents to enter. But it was the free, unscheduled sessions, put on in any convenient piece of shade or any open spot with enough room for the dancers to swing their partners, that kept our heads spinning. Larry's camera shutter seemed to click in tempo with polkas, reels, and schotisches. I wanted to rush from one end of the festival grounds to the other as I heard a new violin call out or caught the shouts of yet another Hungarian dancer. The tomtom beat of a group of young Canadian Crow Indians in full war dress was in sharp contrast to the bagpipes, flutes, and bass violins of European folksong. These wonderfully casual performances caused the shiest of performers to lose their inhibitions and sparkle as dancers and spectators from twelve or fifteen countries urged them on with whistles, shouts, and clapping.

I fell in love with accordion-playing Shastamoinen, a shaggy-haired sixty-seven-year-young Finn who was famous throughout Scandinavia for his renditions of songs and dances of northern Finland. We sat and listened, laughing at songs we couldn't understand, several times during the five-day festival. Shastamoinen noticed our obvious interest, stopped a young Finn, and, asking him to translate, questioned us for a few minutes. Then he told our friendly translator, "Tell them to come visit at my house when the festival is over. They need to see a real north man's home!"

The Polish dance group was another of our favorites. Larry happened to sit next to their translator during one performance and mentioned that my grandparents were from Poland. After the wildly beautiful performance, a musical pantomime of a fight between barbaric mountain outlaws and ax-swinging highlanders, she took us up to introduce us to the dancers. They were all amateurs from a mountain village in southern Poland. "What are you doing in Finland? How did you get here?" the Poles asked. Yet again we had the fun of watching amazed faces as we pulled out a somewhat tattered photo of *Seraffyn* and tried to explain our small magic carpet to people who had never heard of cruising.

The head of the Polish group, a tiny violin maker named Marion, thought for only a minute. "If you are sailing to Poland, you are going to come and stay with us," he said, then wrote his address on the back of a festival program.

Our heads were swimming with new sounds by the time the festival came to an end. Larry's camera had been used to the hilt. We walked around saying good-bye to friends we'd made during the five days of song and dance. Vesa-Pekka Takala, the young Finnish reporter who'd translated for Saastamoinen, searched us out only minutes before we were to climb into the car to return to *Seraffyn*. "When are you heading for Saastamoinen's?" he asked. "I'd like to ride there with you." We explained that we felt Saastamoinen's invitation had been only a spur-of-the-moment politeness. But Vesa-Pekka showed us a map drawn especially for us. So the three of us set off together over the dirt roads of northern Finland.

We had a terrible time remembering Vesa-Pekka's name, and as we came to know him better during the three-hour drive, I finally decided to tell him the nickname we had used for him during the festival. I pointed at his short leather pants, "We called you Peter Lederhausen." Vesa-Pekka nodded his tousled blond head, then repeated, "Peter Lederhausen, I like that." So the name stuck.

We pulled up at a rambling unpainted wooden house, weathered to a silver tone that glowed from among a stand of pine trees on an open meadow. A broad blue lake glistened behind it and scattered houses were in view, each the same rich silver color. An older woman was walking up the path barefoot, carrying a fifty-pound sack of charcoal lightly on her shoulder. We couldn't understand her words, but her warm smile and gestures made us feel sure we were at the right house.

Peter was kept busy translating Saastamoinen's stories as we sat two hours over what he called "a cup of coffee and a few cakes." His wife had quickly prepared a repast that definitely surpassed the bounds of "a few cakes." We marveled at the energy and hearty appearance of this woman who'd been the mother of Saastamoinen's *seventeen* children, who'd spent forty years skinning and preparing the hides of animals Saastamoinen brought back from his traps in the woods each winter. She had also looked after their twelve cows and vegetable garden at the same time. She turned aside our compliment on her fine fruit preserves and pickles by saying, "It's easy now. There are so few children about; only eight of my grandchildren and two of my children are in the house this summer." Saastamoinen took us to his tiny

soot-blackened blacksmith shop. The wooden building was far from any other dwellings and right next to the lake. He lit a fire in the brick hearth and soon had the hard coal glowing as he swayed on the huge hand bellows. He showed us some of the sharply honed sickles that made up most of his forging work, while he waited for a piece of round iron rod to heat to the proper temperature. Then he pulled the white glowing metal from the hearth with a huge set of pincers, forged and tapered it into a sweet-sounding triangle with a rhythmic pounding of his huge hammer on a much-used anvil.

Saastamoinen washed the soot from his face and arms in the lake, then regaled us with backwoods stories as we went back to his kitchen for a farewell drink.

"My attic is stuffed with liquor, must be hundreds of bottles there," he told us. "Everyone in Finland seems to think it's proper to pay a blacksmith with whiskey. Only problem is that I don't drink, not like my Canadian brother." And then he told us the gruesome story of his brother and the cat:

> When my brother and I were young, I had a cat. My brother wanted that cat and I agreed to sell it to him. He took the cat, but emigrated to Canada before he ever paid me for it. Well, I knew my brother would do well in Canada, he was such a shrewd character. So I wasn't surprised when he came back to visit us here, forty years later, dressed in fancy clothes and bragging about his wealth. "You never paid me for that cat," I reminded him. My brother didn't say a word. He went back to Canada and two months later a box arrived with my brother's return address on it. I opened the box and there was a dead cat!

Saastamoinen roared with laughter over that memory. But music was his real love, and before we drove off he played his accordion for us once again. "None of this music has been written down," Sastamoinen said in response to one of Larry's questions. "Real folk music is handed down from mouth to mouth, growing, living, and changing. As soon as you write it down, it dies." His wife tapped her foot; Saastamoinen swayed and sang in his rough voice. We could well picture this kitchen during one of Finland's long, dark winter nights when it would be filled with the smell of delicious cakes and the sound of Saastamoinen's many friends as their music grew and swelled until it drove away the loneliness of a snow-filled wild northland.

When we left, Peter directed us toward the east and when Larry said, "I thought you lived south of here," Peter answered, "I do, but I'm taking you sailing."

An hour later we drove up a long winding driveway to a rambling summer cottage set on yet another of Finland's tree-lined lakes. A warm multilingual lady gave Peter the kind of greeting reserved for very welcome unexpected guests. Within a few minutes she'd extended her greeting to us. "I've got another guest you'll really enjoy. But go off sailing now and light the sauna before you do," Moya said.

Peter started the pine logs burning in the pine sauna while Larry and I rigged the Lightning-class dinghy that bobbed to a light breeze on a mooring less than two hundred feet from the summer house. We skimmed across the lake, enjoying hiking out to steady the frisky dinghy. Then, two hours later, when the sun was lower than the treetops we returned to shore and went into the steamy hot sauna. After ten minutes of sweating, we ran to the water's edge and dove into the cool, refreshing lake, then back into the sauna to sweat again. After three stints in the sauna, I scrubbed all over and washed my hair in the crystal-clear lake. My skin felt glowingly healthy as we sat on the wooden veranda with our hostess, who turned out to be a journalist. Her other guest, a young Japanese who'd come to Finland to study Russian icon painting, joined us as we snacked on cheese and cold cuts. Our dessert was a huge bowl full of tiny wild strawberries from the woods around this peaceful retreat, smothered in fresh whole cream from the cow next door.

My mind seemed to take a step backward as all of us sat there discussing the art of icon painting. Here we were, two average people,

Larry diving out of the sauna into one of Finland's thirty thousand lakes.

thousands of miles from home, hundreds of miles from the sea, among people who'd been strangers only a day before, learning about a subject we'd never heard of until a few hours ago. Yet we felt warm, welcome, and as rich as any man on earth, and I knew *Seraffyn* had opened this world to us.

We had two pleasant surprises waiting for us when we returned to *Seraffyn* in Marianhamina the next day. The first was a big brown envelope containing our mail. Brian Cooke had watched it arrive at his house in bits and pieces during our stay in Poole and suggested, "Since you are always moving, you must miss a lot of letters. How do you know where to have people write to you? How do you know if you receive all the letters people send you before you leave a place? Our yacht club always seems to have letters lying around for visitors who have already moved on. Why not use my address at the bank permanently and have all your mail sent there? Then, once a month, or when you let me know your next forwarding address, I'll send you one registered airmail package containing all your post." We'd really seen the logic in this and when that first package arrived in Marianhamina with thirty letters, all rubberbanded together, we were sold. We've used that system for five years now, and our mail, usually a headache for cruising people, has been exceptionally dependable.

The second treat was a visit to the Erickson Museum, which was in a large house on the shore next to the square-rigged *Pommern*. Fortunately, we chose a quiet day, and the museum's curator Captain Kahre (Cory), who'd sailed around the Horn over twenty times, seven times as master of a full-rigged ship, was willing to give us a personally guided tour. The lost days of sailing cargo ships came alive to us under his guidance as we stood in the wheelhouse of the late *Herzogen-Cecile*, one of the last of Erickson's square-riggers. *Herzogen-Cecile* had sunk at the mouth of the Salcombe River in southern England. Erickson, a wealthy shipowner who had survived and prospered during the switch from sail to steam, and was then already building his museum, salvaged the deckhouse of *Herzogen-Cecile* and reassembled it inside the museum building. The few remaining sails of the *Pommern* filled one room of the museum. When we looked at the mound of decaying cotton and hemp, Larry asked, "Could the *Pommern* be sailed today?" Captain Kahre proudly informed us that her hull and spars were completely ready to set to sea. "The only concession we made to make her part of this museum was to install a fire sprinkler system. But unfortunately, most of her sails have been used through the years to make hatch covers and tarpaulines for Erickson's steamships."

We added our name to the museum guest book, then left to pace once again the three-hundred-foot-long decks of *Pommern*. It took little imagination to hear the bare feet of sailors running along her decks and hear their shouts in her maze of rigging. We ran our hands over the huge drums of the revolutionary Jarvis brace winches that stood abaft the *Pommern*'s mainmast. We could well imagine Erickson's disappointment when every modern invention he added to his sailing ships, every labor-saving device he used to pare his sailing crews from fifty men down to twenty-four on the five-thousand-ton ships, still failed to make the romantic sailing ship as practical as steam.

Two views from the yard of a square-rigger. *Seraffyn* looks like a toy until Larry put the 105-mm lens on the camera for a closer view.

~~~~~~

CHAPTER 14

Never on a Friday

A light breeze ruffled the sheet that covered us in our favorite
bunk, the wide cushion-filled cockpit. I got up and started the
coffee and tea, then took our logbook into the rumpled cockpit bed to
write in the poem my sister Bonnie had sent in her last letter.

> What matters?
> Very little.
> Only the flicker of light
>   within the darkness,
> The feeling of warmth
>   within the cold,
> The knowledge of love
>   within the void.

Larry and I read back through our logbook, which is more like an
informal dairy in which we paste favorite photos, postcards, and
memorabilia, than the formal logs some sailors keep. People, places,
and tiny daily adventures seemed to leap from its pages. Then Larry
brought both of us into the present by saying, "Is it really July 27? We'd
better move on today or we'll never see any more of Finland before
our docking date in Russia."

"We can't sail today," I told him. "It's Friday! But we'd better go
tomorrow because I'd like to be closer to Tallinn in case our visas do
come through." We'd been in close telephone contact with the Soviet
consul. Each time we spoke to him he'd sounded more hopeful. We
laughed at the idea of our personal visas causing so much trouble when
Seraffyn was already in free and clear.

"Now if we could have the two of you arrive on a registered Soviet carrier such as a bus or ship, then have your ship towed into Soviet waters, we could get you visas," the consul told us. "But I have our Moscow office working on the problem. Call me in three or four days."

His encouragement made my desire to see the home of my father's parents even greater. Larry had seen Denmark and England, the lands his ancestors came from. Now I hoped it would be my turn. Besides, we were dying to see the Hermitage and be the first post-Revolution foreign yacht to sail up the Neva.

As Larry folded the bedclothes and put the quarter berth cushions below in their places, the breeze filled in even more. The sun glowed warmly on our decks. "Lin, we've got to break this silly Friday superstition once and for all. Let's go sailing!

"But remember Lymington!" I started.

"Absolute carelessness," Larry answered.

I shrugged my shoulders, got out the chart, and stored away some dishes. Then I went on deck to hoist the mainsail while Larry cleared the spare line from the mooring buoy.

I stood at the helm while Larry hoisted the lapper, then cleared our mooring line from the buoy. *Seraffyn* slowly gathered way as I sheeted the mainsail in and Larry pulled the jib sheet. "Go to windward of the blue sloop," Larry suggested. I steered closer to the wind, but *Seraffyn* just didn't have enough speed through the water to clear the bow of the boat that had been moored a hundred feet away from us. "Fall off quick," Larry called, reaching to let the mainsheet run. I pulled the helm. *Seraffyn*'s bowsprit started to swing, and then it all happened, as if in horrible, unstoppable slow-motion. Our bowsprit went right between the shrouds of the twenty-five-foot sloop. Our bobstay hit its tow rail. *Seraffyn* stopped, slowly turned into the wind, trapped by wire and turnbuckles that grated against each other. Then hours (but really only seconds) later, slid slowly free with a ripping sound and drifted downwind, clear of the yacht club moorings.

Both of us were stunned. We got *Seraffyn* under control and then Larry said, "Take a pencil and paper over to that sloop and write a note to its owner while I reach back and forth here in clear water."

I rowed toward the sloop, concerned over the damage *Seraffyn*'s five and a half tons must have caused, and was vastly relieved to find only a twelve-inch surface scratch on the sloop's topside and a half-inch-deep nick in her toe rail. But large chips of varnish and spruce glared up at me from her white deck, so obviously *Seraffyn* had not come off so lightly. I was tied alongside, writing a note to the owner with our address, when the owner appeared. He thanked me profusely, saying, "She's just a sailing school boat so don't worry. She's been hit four or five times before this year. But not many of the culpits admit it."

His kind words didn't relieve the embarrassment Larry and I both felt as we ran out of Marianhamina. We were terribly depressed as we talked over all the possible ways we could have avoided the accident. "The real problem was that we were rushing and didn't take the time to discuss what we were going to do before we cast off the mooring line," Larry said after inspecting our bruised bowsprit. "If we'd thought for a minute or two, we'd have just cast off and drifted downwind free of the moorings, then set our sails. But it's all talk now. I don't think we should sail on Fridays. Let's find the first anchorage we can and stop."

So only five miles later we found a cove and anchored. We were both still depressed. The skies were clouding over and turning gray.

Sailing through the Finnish Archipelago.

Larry scraped the flakes of loose varnish off the bowsprit, put on a protective coat of varnish, then went and hid in the forepeak, his nose buried in a book. I sat moping on the side deck, watching a fisherman in a small varnished runabout pull up his net at the head of the cove. He started his motor and came directly toward us. "Larry, company coming," I called. The fisherman came carefully alongside, putting tiny clean fenders over to protect his shining varnished topsides. His wrinkled, weatherbeaten face was screwed into a look of careful concentration as he thought out each word of English and said, "I have caught too many fish. You must take some for your meal or I will have to throw them away." The fisherman wouldn't stay to chat. He just handed us four flounder-like fish and putted off as we were saying our thanks.

That broke our gray mood, and after a few last comments such as "Well, the only man who never made a mistake, never did anything," and "As long as we learn from our mistakes," and . . . we set to work

Chart in hand, we weave through the islands of Finland.

147

planning a dinner to do justice to those lovely sweet-tasting fish.

Sailing through the Turko Archipelago on Finland's southwestern corner was different from any sailing we'd ever done before. Unlike Sweden's well-populated islands, these had only a few scattered villages on them. Trees crowded right to the water. All of the hundreds of islands we passed looked the same, and without the excellent arrangement of beacons, lights, and stakes with brush-like heads of twigs that marked isolated dangers, we'd have had a difficult time with our navigation.

A brisk northwest wind sent us roaring through the islands. It was cool enough to warrant a jacket. The sea was absolutely flat because of the islands so close to windward. Larry was engrossed in a good book on the forward bunk. So I had a lovely private morning of guiding *Seraffyn* as she seemed to prance and surge, like the living, breathing personality she had grown to be.

When we burst through a narrow channel into a patch of relatively open water, I set Helmer to steer momentarily and went below to pour a cup of tea for myself. I climbed back on deck, glanced at the chart, then looked around. I was lost! Nothing looked the same. Just before I became frantic, I looked at our compass then at the direction of the black line we were following across the chart. A wind shift had caused Helmer to steer *Seraffyn* thirty degrees off. The profusion of islands fell into order as soon as I unclutched Helmer and steered back on course.

Helsinki had been our goal when we planned our Baltic cruise during the cold English evenings. But as often happens, the realities of cruising intervened. Our tour inland, the wonderful sailing in the Turko Archipelago, delays while we restocked *Seraffyn* in the excellent and very inexpensive markets of the friendly city of Turko-Abo—all ate up the quickly flying days of the short northern summer. As the dates set on *Seraffyn*'s Russian entry permit grew closer, we found ourselves clinging even closer to villages or towns with telephones. Each two days we'd call in for a report. Each time we were told, "Your visas have not been refused; but then, they have not been approved either." Finally, two days before we'd have had to arrive in Tallinn, our first proposed Russian port, a hundred twenty miles southeast of us, the distraught young consul for the Soviet Union informed us, "The immigration department in Moscow refuses to say yes or no." We realized it was their way of telling us, "Go away. Don't bother us."

Larry and I reacted just like two children. We went home, sat in the cockpit, and pouted. "We didn't really want to visit their lousy country anyway," one of us said. But we were both deeply disappointed. If only the Soviet consul in London had not been caught spying, the visa he'd arranged would have permitted us to be the first sailing yacht to visit the Soviet Union! In a way, we'd planned on that visit to Russia as the highlight of our summer. I guess it is a case of forbidden fruit seeming sweeter. Our spirits were pretty low.

But the next morning a note was lying in our cockpit when we returned from the huge flower-filled open market in Turko's main square. It provided pleasant thoughts that turned us from griping about Soviet restrictions. When we'd arrived in Turko and tied to the park-like shore of the river that goes right through the heart of the city, we'd mailed a note to Ake and Camille Lindquist saying, "Larry and I are friends of Leif Møller of Copenhagen. Leif said we'd enjoy meeting you. If you are free, please join us for a drink on board *Seraffyn* any evening this week." We'd found that this way of responding to intro-

Seraffyn is dwarfed by the unfinished hull of a ship at the Turko-abo shipyards that line both sides of the river.

ductions people gave us worked well. We didn't feel we were putting strangers who might be too busy to entertain unknown friends on the spot as badly as if we'd just walked up and knocked on their door, or even telephoned. If they couldn't join us, or didn't want to, they were free to ignore our note. But all of our notes seemed to get immediate responses, and this time had been no exception.

"Just came back to the city and found your note. Too busy to join you today; sail out to our summer house and spend the weekend. Enclosed chart shows the spot."

We set our alarm for 0400 when we went to sleep that night. We needed a few windless hours to row *Seraffyn* out the three-mile-long river. For the past week the daytime winds had funneled upriver, and in places it was less than a hundred fifty feet wide. To make matters more difficult, just one mile downstream the river was narrowed by hulls of freighters under construction in the local shipyards. We didn't relish short-tacking all the way down river. Our early rising paid off. Larry rowed *Seraffyn* downriver in an absolute calm while I prepared him a big breakfast which we ate as we took our first southbound voyage of the summer. We'd been at 60° 30′ north, only three hundred miles south of the Arctic Circle and probably as far north as *Seraffyn* would ever sail.

The Lindquists were already at their summer home, a Dr. Zhivago-ish rambling wooden building with large rooms, each dominated by huge porcelain, ceiling-high, wood-burning heaters. The house and its heaters were over a hundred years old and something of a rarity in the islands because, as Ake explained, "The reason everything in the islands looks so new is that we build of wood, then need huge fires to keep warm. So our homes and buildings often burn down. This one is standing because my parents rarely used it more than a few weeks each summer, and we do the same."

We spent two lovely days getting to know the Lindquists. Ake, the head of Lloyd's ship surveyors for Finland, was a keen racing and cruising sailor. He'd taken his Swan 43 sloop to England the previous summer and represented Finland in the Admiral's Cup races. When Larry mentioned our failure to get Russian visas, Ake, who had been to Russia many times surveying ships, told us, "Sailing boats and cruising sailors don't exactly fit in with Soviet ideology. The officials there are really concerned about letting people get any true idea of the freedoms of the outside world. Our yacht club decided to organize an overnight race out of Helsinki and contacted the Russian authorities, asking permission to race around a light-house that is only thirty miles south of Finland but within Russian territorial waters. It took months and piles of correspondence to get their permission. When we finally held the race, we found six Russian patrol boats sitting just off the lighthouse." Ake laughed and said, "Maybe the ships were guarding against Finnish yachtsmen defecting to Russia."

The third day there we had the first rainy weather we'd seen in our three months in the Baltic. We stayed on board, reading and writing letters, after the Lindquists commuted back to town in their runabout. The squalls let up in the evening and I was just debating what to cook for dinner when a small motorboat approached.

The dark-eyed owner, a man of about thirty, came alongside and, after introducing himself and asking where we had sailed from, said, "My sauna is hot. If you don't come and use it, the heat will go to waste." So we grabbed our towels and joined him. Three hours later he brought us back toward *Seraffyn*'s glowing anchor light, replete with the tasty smorgasbord his wife had served after the sauna.

"There it is, the first sign of winter," he told us.

"Where?" I asked.

He pointed at the stars that showed dully overhead. "When it's dark enough to see the stars again, we know that it is time to start getting our skis ready. Yes, it is an exciting time because we can start thinking of the fun of cross-country skiing."

He had a nightcap before leaving *Seraffyn*. "You should get moving, you know. You must be out of the Baltic before September 15 or you must take your boat from the water before the autumn storms come."

His words came to haunt us after we sailed away from the Lindquists' summer home. We kept planing to sail south, but we also kept meeting warm Finnish people.

We'd be sailing along, bound generally south, when another sail-boat would come into view. So we'd harden up our sheets and they'd ease theirs, and soon we'd be cruising alongside each other, chatting back and forth. We met Maija and Gabor Molnar this way. They were cruising on a Dragon class with their young son. "We are sailing to a party. Come along." So we tacked alongside them, going twenty miles off our planned route to join their friends at a lovely island retreat. And another few days would slip away.

By August 16 we looked at a calendar and realized that if we wanted to see any of Poland before the September 15 date everyone kept warning us about, we'd better get moving. We sailed to Noto, one of the southernmost islands of the Turko Archipelago and filled up with sweet fresh water at the village pump. For the previous three or four weeks Larry had been complaining of itchy skin and stomach pains, and I'd definitely noticed a case of short-temperedness. By nightfall the evening we'd anchored at Noto his stomach pains were beginning to bring sweat to his forehead. He spent a terribly restless night and in the morning I rowed into the tiny village and asked if the storekeeper could call a doctor for me. The island villages all have telephones, and soon I was speaking to the woman who was the district doctor for some two hundred fifty square miles of island people. "Sounds like kidney stones, extremely painful. Give him heavy sedatives, keep him still, but don't worry as there is no danger." She contacted the local guard and then called back, "We can't send the boat for him. It's off picking up a woman who is having labor pains. Can you bring him in on your own boat?"

I carefully copied down the directions to her island clinic on Nagu, then rowed out to *Seraffyn*. Larry was in bed, tossing and turning, unable to sleep or get comfortable, uninterested in reading. I gave him the dose of codeine tablets the doctor had prescribed after I read the list of medicines we carried on board. Then after I tried to make Larry as comfortable as possible, I looked at the chart. Nagu was over forty-five miles away. The channel was mostly unlit, so it meant two days of sailing since it was afternoon by this time. In spite of the doctor's assurance, I was worried every time I looked at Larry's pale, pain-filled face. He offered to help, but when he tried to stand I knew it was one bit of sailing I'd have to handle myself.

I blessed our compact bronze Plath anchor winch as I got a hundred fifty feet of five-sixteenths-inch chain and a twenty-five-pound anchor up. I also blessed Larry's foresight in arranging the anchor so that I could hook it onto the bobstay without having to lift it on deck. Then, as I hoisted the working jib, sheeted in the mainsail, and reached past the first island on our route, I remembered our fight back in Dartmouth. Because of that argument I had finally started handling *Seraffyn* myself. Larry had encouraged me, saying, "If ever something happens to me, you'll be better prepared to take care of all of us." He'd watched to see what problems I encountered as I used *Seraffyn*'s sailing equipment and then tried to simplify anything that gave me trouble. (Before I make Larry sound like an absolute paragon of virtue, I must admit his patience sometimes wore thin and at times he sounded just like any other husband trying to teach his wife to drive.) But now I sailed *Seraffyn* with my confidence growing every minute. When I had reached over twenty-five miles to the anchorage I'd selected for the night, I rounded *Seraffyn* into the wind, let the main and jib sheets fly, released the jib halyard, and doused the jib with its downhaul, then unclutched the anchor winch and let the anchor and chain run out. I'd been conservative and anchored over a quarter mile from shore so I'd

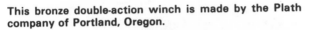

This bronze double-action winch is made by the Plath company of Portland, Oregon.

Using the Baltic's fresh water to do the laundry.

An evening bonfire and sausage roast on Snackholm Island, just south of Noto.

have a lot of room to maneuver the next morning, but we spent a safe night.

Larry was not better the second day and I was vastly relieved when we finally sailed into the tiny bay on the island of Nagu. I anchored and went ashore to find the doctor. She had me bring Larry ashore, and after a brief examination, sent him off to a hospital on the mainland by taxi and car ferry.

I went back to *Seraffyn* and stowed her sails properly, thinking of the times Larry had said, "What good is it spending hundreds of dollars on lifejackets, emergency radios, rafts, and so on, if I don't use the best piece of safety equipment there is, a well-trained crew?"

Larry did not have kidney stones. Although the Finnish doctors cured his stomach pains, it was not until we were leaving Poland that a doctor found the real cause of his recurring problem: "Vitamin B-12 deficiency. I used to see hundreds of cases during the war when flour was unavailable," the Polish doctor told us. It turned out that the high cost of meat in Scandinavia which had encouraged us to have a shipboard diet consisting mostly of canned food, combined with the fact both of us were trying to lose weight and so had avoided all bread, noodles, potatoes, and rice, had produced this deficiency. The results of a few vitamin tablets were nearly miraculous, and we became instant believers. Now, whenever we are at sea, away from the variety of fresh foods offered on shore, we take a vitamin supplement, as do many long-term cruisers.

Meanwhile the warm sunny days gave way to a northwesterly gale. Larry felt quite good, so we waited until we saw the barometer start to rise steadily and the wind to drop, then set our double-reefed mainsail and staysail and headed south, weaving our way through the southernmost of Finland's thirty thousand islands. The last lighthouse dropped below the horizon as we broad-reached swiftly along and we knew that we'd dream of returning to the "friendly archipelago" again some summer when we'd pray for another dose of the "best weather in recorded history."

CHAPTER 15

Poland and Politics

We ran across the Gulf of Finland, shaping a course that would take us well clear of the Soviet-dominated shore of Estonia. It was August 24, the northern summer was definitely fading away, and when I called Larry for his 2200 to 0100 watch, it was pitch dark with a heavy layer of scudding cloud hiding any stars.

I awoke half an hour after I climbed into the warm sleeping-bag-lined quarter berth and for a few minutes lay bracing myself against the toss and heave caused by the rising wind. Larry was pulling out navigation books, studying the chart, then going on deck only to return for another look at the chart.

I finally asked him what he was up to. "Since you're awake, how about coming on deck to see what you make of this?" Larry suggested. I struggled clear of the sheets, timing my climb out of the bunk with the roll *Seraffyn* made as another sea passed under her stern. Larry handed me my sailing jacket and came out into the cockpit. He'd taken down the mainsail while I slept and we were running under just the staysail. Helmer was steering well with two five-sixteenths-inch-diameter shock cords tied to the tiller to dampen a tendency to oversteer. The taffrail log was spinning at a rate I'd come to know meant we were moving at more than five knots.

"Look to port," Larry said. "We should be thirty-five miles from the Russian coast . . . there's not one navigation light shown on the chart for this area."

As soon as he said that, I saw what was bothering him. The loom of a huge light lit the undersides of the low clouds, just forward of our beam. It swept across the sky in a constant pattern that was unlike any navigation light we'd ever seen. Larry's search through the *Pilot* books, light lists, and charts had given no clue to this light, and with a strong northerly wind blowing, we doubted we'd been set far enough east to be in any danger. So we decided not to worry, but to keep an extra-sharp lookout.

I climbed back in the bunk and slept well until Larry called. As I pulled on my jeans and a sweatshirt, Larry told me, "Some kind of patrol ship came toward us from the east, circled about two hundred yards off, and put its searchlight on us. Then it headed due east again." He climbed on deck with me and pointed out the loom of the light we'd seen before. It was now aft of our beam. Then Larry pointed forward to where the loom of another light was just coming clear. "I'm steering a bit more to the west, just to be sure."

All that night we saw the loom of a line of very powerful lights. The next morning Larry was able to catch a glimpse of the sun with his sextant, and although the boat still surged and heeled along at over five knots, he got an accurate line of position. At noon the skies cleared and he took a noon sight. Our actual position was within two or three miles of our dead reckoning position, halfway between the Swedish island of Goteland and Russia. That evening we again saw the loom of huge lights on our port side but we didn't feel so concerned.

I had the 0100 to 0400 watch. The wind was still fresh, but had swung more to the east. *Seraffyn* roared along under just her staysail. I saw the lights of a ship approaching dead on our beam. I stood near the tiller, ready to change course if necessary. Then, exactly as Larry had described the night before, two hundred yards off the ship turned on searchlights, circled us at high speed, and headed away, due east.

The third night was the same. A patrol boat came and circled us at 0100. Lights loomed along the whole eastern horizon. By daylight our wind had decreased until we were able to set the mainsail, and by the time I served breakfast the seas were calm enough so that we could relax together in the cockpit while we reached along at five knots.

"The Russians must have had us on radar all the time. Those patrol boats never altered course when they came out and inspected us," Larry said. I ate the last peanut-butter-and-jam-covered biscuit, pondering about having to start each day without peanut butter now that we'd exhausted our supply. "I wonder if they thought we were trying to sneak into Estonia or Latvia?" Larry had no answer and we had little time to think further on the subject as we were fast approaching

Gdynia, Poland's largest Baltic port. I cleaned up inside *Seraffyn* as the high buildings of the city came into view. Larry checked our anchor and, at 1400 our third day out, we passed into the territorial waters of Poland. We'd taken two days and twenty-one hours to cover three hundred thirty miles, running most of the way under just a staysail.

We sailed past each of the six or seven basins formed by large stone breakwaters in front of Gdynia. Ferries, naval craft, and freighters filled their piers, but no one expressed the least interest in us. Then we saw the masts of several other sailing yachts and rounded the wall of the easternmost basin shown on our Admiralty chart. The submachine-gun-armed guard standing in front of a stone shed at the seaward end of the breakwater took a definite interest in us. He pointed his machine gun at our sails, then pointed the gun at the pier in front of his foot.

"I wonder if he knows that sailboats can't go directly into the wind," Larry joked uncertainly as we maneuvered *Seraffyn* toward the spot he was indicating. I hoisted our solid yellow quarantine flag to

Tied in the yacht basin at Gdynia, Poland, while a club boat practices docking under sail behind us.

show that we had no port clearance yet, then our small Polish courtesy flag. As soon as we had secured our mooring lines, the guard made a telephone call and then returned to stand on the dock beside us, his gun cradled in his arms.

We set to work putting *Seraffyn* into port order, feeling just a bit uneasy under the eye of the uniformed armed guard. Larry and I tried chatting nonchalantly as we performed the pleasant routine together, furling and tying the mainsail, stuffing the genoa into its bag, coiling the mainsheet, and tying off halyards. We'd just finished and started looking around at the wooden yachts that shared the basin with us when a line of officials came trooping down the docks.

Their warm smiles were in direct opposition to our guard's face. "Welcome to Poland," the harbormaster called as he removed his shoes before coming on board. He served as translator as the health, customs, and immigration officials presented us with about fifteen papers to be filled out. We showed them our visas and the letter from Theresa Remiszewski and the harbormaster rushed off *Seraffyn* and made a telephone call. He returned before we'd signed the last of the required forms. "Mrs. Remiszewski is not at home, but I'll contact her for you before tomorrow. I'll also call the head of our yachting association. He'll be glad to see you because you are the first Canadian yacht ever to visit Poland, and only the second yacht to come here this year. The other one was only from Sweden."

He apologetically explained that there were certain rules we had to conform to during our stay in Poland. Once we had *Seraffyn* secured to our satisfaction, we were not allowed to move her until we had cleared to leave. No guests were allowed on board until they gave their identity cards to the guard at his post. And finally, we had to leave the port before our visa expired, in twenty one days.

Since *Seraffyn* is so small and has such an open interior plan, we decided to tie our stern to a mooring buoy and have our bowsprit to the pier. Otherwise anyone—such as our omnipresent gun-totting guard—who looked down our companionway could see every move we made. We removed the dinghy and tied it alongside, scrubbed the decks down with seawater, then found an outside shower at the far end of the yacht basin. The cold water brought goose bumps out all over and I'll didn't willingly stay under its stinging spray one second after the last bit of soap was out of my hair. We wore sweaters as we ate dinner below decks that evening.

As soon as breakfast was cleared away the next morning it became obvious that the harbormaster had been busy. Petite, dark-haired, forty-three-year-old Theresa Remiszewski arrived, a bunch of flowers in one hand, a carefully wrapped packet of pastry in the other. Her sister Krystyna was with her, carrying another bunch of flowers and a bag of fruit. They had no trouble at all negotiating our bowsprit since both of them had thousands of miles of ocean sailing under their belts. Both held the rank of captain in the Polish sailing association, and worked in their spare time training other club members in offshore sailing and navigation. Each year they took a three-week-long Baltic cruise in charge of one of the club's forty-five-foot ketches. Theresa told us more about her attempt to win the 1972 single-handed transatlantic race. She'd done very well until the mast fitting holding her spreaders had started to split the hollow, unblocked wooden spar and she'd had to jury rig extra shrouds to take the strains. She'd climbed the mast alone at sea several times to do this and then completed the last eight hundred miles of the race under reduced canvas in the

Theresa Remiszewski on board *Comodor,* the yacht she sailed in the 1972 OSTAR.

forty-three-footer, still finishing in the top half of the fleet. Now she dreamed of being the first woman to circumnavigate the world single-handed and was trying to get government sponsorship for her project.

Before we had time to chat further, more people arrived, with more fruit, flowers, and pastries. We made everyone laugh by garlanding *Seraffyn*'s skylight and boom with our growing collection of bright autumn blossoms.

"How was your voyage from Finland?" one of our many guests asked. We told him about the strange lights we'd seen and the patrol boats that had inspected us. "Those were huge searchlights," the guest, a retired naval officer, explained. "The whole coast of Estonia, Latvia, and Lithuania is lined with them. There are smaller searchlights every hundred meters with machine gun towers in between. They aren't to keep you out; they are to keep Soviet people from escaping in small boats. No one is allowed to sail in those waters. The Soviets arrest any Polish fishing boat that even comes close to their territorial waters. Then our government has to intervene to get the fishermen free."

Another of our visitors went below to inspect *Seraffyn*'s interior and we noticed he was spending a long time lying on our forward bunk. Larry went in and found him reading a copy of Alexander Solzhenitsyn's *Cancer Ward*. "You can take that with you if you'd like. Lin and I have finished reading it," Larry told him. "I'd really like to have the book," our visitor said, looking at the slightly dog-eared paperback we'd bought in Finland. "It's totally banned here, but we've heard a lot about it."

"Take it then," Larry repeated.

Our guest looked very longingly at the book. "I can't take it with me. It would cause problems if someone caught me with it. But if you come to my house tonight for dinner, and if you wrap it up and put it in your wife's purse, then bring it with you. It would probably be all right. No one would stop a foreigner and insist on inspecting his wife's bag."

During our entire stay in Poland, hardly a day went by without reminders of the political restrictions of life in Poland. Hosts would check outside their apartment door before discussing anything about politics. Friends would suddenly go silent when we were walking down a street together and a passerby came close.

Meanwhile, our stream of guests continued throughout the day, more flowers turning our cabin top into a happy-looking garden.

Theresa was also fond of folk dancing and asked to know the name of the Polish dancers we'd met in Kaustinen. By that evening we had invitations to fill the next three days completely.

Theresa and her friends Julian and Margo Czerwinski came to take us for dinner our third evening. Julian was a naval captain who had been in charge of Poland's 135-foot, three-masted training schooner. Now he worked translating sailing books from English to Polish. We knew by the conspiratorial whispers that the three of them had a surprise for us. As the five of us were walking through the silent gray, partially reconstructed streets of Gdynia, past grass-covered ruins of pre-World War II buildings, Theresa finally bubbled over with the news. "We sent a telegram to your dancer friends in the mountains. They replied immediately and told us that you must come to stay with them. Marion, the leader of the Kaustinen dancers, has arranged for you to live in his brother's house for a week because both his brother and sister-in-law speak English."

Larry and I must have looked reluctant because Julian spoke up, "It is a wonderful chance for you. The mountains around Zakopane are the most beautiful in Europe. The Socialist World Folk Dance Festival will be on, and some of East Europe's best dancers will be there. Transportation will be no problem. I need a holiday and can drive you there, and act as translator, too! Theresa and Krystyna will watch *Seraffyn.*" We stopped Julian and assured him, "We think it sounds great, but are you sure we won't be inconveniencing a lot of people?"

"Poles love visitors," both Julian and Theresa insisted. So that was that.

Twelve hours later we were rambling across the coastal plains of Poland toward Lodz. The trunk of Julian's little car disgorged a magnificent lunch basket full of treats prepared by his wife Margo, who couldn't take time off from her job as an English teacher to join us. We ate the lunch under a tree by the roadside. All around us other traveling Polish families were doing the same. "Restaurants are few and far between, and then, only for very rich people," Julian told us.

Near Lodz we crossed the Vistula River and entered the small village that had been my maternal grandparents' home until just after the First World War. It stood on the flat endless-looking plain that had served as Europe's battlefield during countless wars. Julian drove slowly through the tiny farm community, its artisans mostly gone now, the streets full of chickens and geese. Then we stopped to try and get a few cold cuts to fill our basket again. The village women in their long black skirts and black shirtwaists whispered and stared as we wandered through the almost empty stores. I tried to imagine that one or another of them might have known my ancestors, or might even be a distant cousin. There were no sausages or cheese available. As we drove off, I thought, "Life sure would have been different if my grandparents hadn't emigrated."

We were fifty miles short of Krakow when Julian slowed down and questioned a bicycle-riding farmer by the roadside. "We should look for a hotel soon," Larry suggested. "There are no hotels within forty miles of here, but that's no problem," Julian told us as he turned off into the front garden of a flourishing farm. He went to the door and spoke to the husky farm wife, then came back for us. "These people have invited us to stay for the night. How many eggs do you want for dinner?"

We were given spotless linen-covered beds in a scrubbed but bare room just beside the warm kitchen with its huge wood-burning stove. The farmhouse was a rambling affair, sparsely furnished except for the main living/dining room which was filled by a lace-covered mahogany dining table. The three of us were served a dinner of six scrambled eggs each, with garden vegetables and hot honey-covered fresh bread. Then the whole farm family drifted in, along with several neighbors, and Julian was kept busy translating as our hosts asked us endless questions about "the world outside." Were the things they heard when they listened to the Voice of America really true? Could Americans really change jobs and homes anytime they wanted to? Did we have to carry identity cards at all times?

As we prepared to leave the next morning, we asked to pay for our meals and board. The farmer and his wife refused, saying, "It's not every day we have transatlantic sailors visit us." I was really glad we'd bought a supply of nylon stretch pantyhose at the suggestion of an English friend who had previously visited Communist countries. When I offered the farm wife and her eighteen-year-old daughter two pairs, the glow in their eyes showed us that these fifty-cent supermarket specials were better than money.

The mountain village of Zakopane, a favorite winter ski resort frequented by bargain-hunting Western Europeans, is beautiful. Tall stone peaks tower over the pine log houses and dark pines line the edges of grass- and sheep-covered meadows. Varnished carriages pulled by handsome light-boned horses in glowing bell-encrusted harnesses moved easily through the streets. They served as taxis, and Julian told us, "These carriages aren't for show, they are really practical. In the winter the wheels come off and are replaced with runners to make them into sleds. It's the most convenient and reliable way to get over the snowy lanes and ice-covered hills to the homes and ski lodges outside town."

Marion and his family did seem to love visitors. They made all three of us right at home, giving us a key to the house and suggestions for tours and ways to fill each day. We spent most evenings watching the carefully scheduled performances of state-sponsored dancers from Hungary, Russian, Georgia, Rumania, and eight other Iron Curtain countries, plus Austria. The costumes and dancers were professionally superb, but the festival lacked the informal spontaneity of Kaustinen. The performance I'll never forget was given by our hosts, the irrepressible Polish mountain people, or Podhale. They had a fiercely independent spirit and a delightful sense of humor that glowed through their performance. The international audience roared with laughter while our hosts danced, sang, and fiddled through a reenactment of a mountain-style wedding. The men tried to open a fifty-gallon wooden keg of beer. At first we thought it was part of the performance when they seemed to have trouble pulling the bung out of the top. But after they'd struggled on stage minute after minute, the fiddlers playing the same tune for the fifth time, the audience began to call suggestions. Finally one dancer took matters in his own hands. He gave a mighty wack with the heel of his decorated woodsman's ax, the bung disappeared into the barrel in a spray of foaming beer, and the dancers thrust their beer mugs under the flowing spout. Their jumps and whirls grew ever more daring and acrobatic as the agitated beer keg continued to foam.

During the warm autumn days we wandered through the mountains meeting friends and relatives of our hosts. Julian translated, and through him we learned the stories of men who had served as couriers and guides through the Tatra Mountains' snow- and ice-covered passes during two world wars. We became used to being offered a glass of creamy, foaming cow's milk alongside a glass of homemade brandy, no matter what time of day we arrived to visit.

Julian had to leave after five days, but we stayed on to enjoy scenes and a way of life we'd probably never see again. On the last night of

Marion and his son in their violin-making shop.

Our hosts, dancers from the Podhale folk-dancing group. These clothes are not only used for dancing, they are standard Sunday best.

Visiting the relatives of our
Tatra mountain hosts.

the festival our Polish hosts gave a party for the Russian and Austrian dance groups at a local restaurant. No one wore costumes except for the Poles, who, we learned, didn't consider their embroidery-covered natural-white-wool pants and cloaks costumes, but the normal clothes to use for evening dress.

We were seated with the Russian dancers at dinner, with Zofia, the beautiful blonde English-speaking cousin of our Polish hosts, by our side to translate. Next to her sat the Polish-to-Russian translator. Our chain of communication seemed to break down when Zofia asked us to show the Georgian dancers a photo of our little cruising boat. Their looks were both wistful and incredulous, and their questions showed that their carefully regulated way of life gave them no basis for understanding our fairytale-like wealth of freedom.

Before the dinner was half finished the Austrian musicians offered to liven up the party with some music. The wonderful strains of a Strauss waltz rang from three violins and a bass viol. The dark-eyed young Russian folk dancer seated across from me asked his translator to ask mine if I'd be willing to dance. I joined him on the empty dance floor. I had worn a pair of silk slacks and a fancy scarf top that was backless. As my handsome partner took my right hand in his and put his left arm around me, his hand touched my bare back—and shot away as if it had been burned. He blushed and put his hand lower until it reached the cloth of my trousers. That caused an even quicker reaction. Finally he put his hand firmly on my upper back where it was covered with my long hair. He nodded to the players and we glided off into a waltz. What a dancer! I was sad but slightly breathless when the music stopped after we'd danced to five or six different waltz tunes. My partner bowed to me, then asked our two translators to help him. He made me blush and glow all over when I heard his words translated. "That was wonderful! I'm fortunate to be the only man from my village who has ever danced with a beautiful American woman." Then the Poles took over on the bandstand and everyone joined in, filling the evening with song, dance, and friendly banter.

After ten days we took the train north across Poland, our bags full of handmade gifts from our mountain friends. We'd been given a packed dinner and ate it in the deserted first-class coach. By nightfall we were freezing as the rickety train rumbled over the plains. Larry found a conductor and in sign language tried to get the heater turned on. The conductor found an English-speaking student from the third-class carriage who explained, "Our law says that summer does not end until September 15. So the conductor is not allowed to turn on the heaters until September 15." It was September 14, so we pulled all our spare clothes from our bag and burrowed into them, but still we shivered and slept little that night.

Krystyna Remiszewski was manager of a large ship's chandlery in the port of Gdynia and she helped us fill *Seraffyn* with wonderful food and stores. The Polish government needs western currency and gave us a huge bonus on each dollar we spent. So all of the goods from Eastern Europe cost us far less than similar products in the West. Fine Bulgarian Reisling-type wines were thirty-five cents a bottle. Russian pink, dry champagne (a weakness of mine) cost eighty-five cents a magnum. But even better were things like the famous smoked sausages, hams, and sides of bacon from central Poland. We hung two sides of bacon in our chain locker, and by wiping them down with vinegar and water, they kept for three months and added a rich aroma to the focsle. Canned tuna and mackerel from the Soviet Union proved to be excellent, but one special treat was a case of expensive but much desired American Skippy peanut butter Krystyna located in a far corner of her warehouse. It had been ordered by some Dutch ship but never called for.

Once again *Seraffyn* settled to her lines as she filled with stores. Our Polish sailing friends urged us to try to extend our visas and stay on, at the same time saying, "You really should take your boat out of the water or leave the Baltic now as it is time for the equinotial gales." We had a hard time convincing ourselves that winter was on its way—an Indian summer gave us warm sunny days, although the nights were definitely becoming colder and longer.

We sunbathed on *Seraffyn* in the afternoon while we watched the superb boat handling displayed by the sailing club members. They maneuvered their forty-five-foot ketches in the confines of the yachting harbor completely under sail, dropping anchor and then backing them stern-to to the piers by shoving their booms to windward. The club sailors worked as a trained team on the state-owned boats. We met the owner of one of the few private yachts in Poland. The thirty-year-old boat builder told us that the cost of materials for a boat like *Seraffyn,* even after substituting items easily available in Poland, would be equal to a naval architect's complete salary for eight to ten years. He only owned a boat because he'd built it himself and had been given a large

Lin shopping in the public market of Gdynia.

pension when he lost both his legs below the knees in an industrial accident. This shocked us because we'd watched him at work, finishing the deck of a Carter-designed thirty-three-footer and seen him clamber out *Seraffyn's* bowsprit, never once realizing his handicap existed.

Farewells are always hard and in Poland there was one further complication. Seven armed officials arrived an hour before the departure time written in our port clearance papers. Two stood guard on the dock alongside us while five came on board and looked in each locker, Larry's toolbox, the bilges. They even looked inside our oven. "Are you looking for liquor or arms or what?" Larry asked. The most ribbon-encrusted official replied, "No, we are checking for stowaways." He signed the final release paper after his crew finished their inspection. "You must leave now," he told us.

"But our friends aren't here yet. We want to say good-bye!" Larry protested.

A hurried conference ensued. "You may wait, but no one is allowed to put a foot on your boat and you must stay on board. These two guards will stay until you sail out."

Theresa, Julian, and Margo arrived, leading about ten of our Polish friends down the dock just as the five officials were leaving. We tried to exchange hugs and kisses across *Seraffyn's* lifelines as they handed us more beautiful flowers and a lovely bag of fresh fuit. But all of us were acutely aware of the watchful guards standing at attention, their automatic rifles by their sides, less than five feet away from our farewell party.

"Please write to us as soon as you are safe for the winter," Theresa called as she helped cast off our mooring lines. We set the mainsail and lapper to catch the morning offshore breeze, and we took two extra tacks inside the breakwaters so we could exchange shouted last good-byes. The two guards rested their rifles alongside the guardpost and joined in the waves and farewell wishes as we eased our sheets and reached out of the harbor. "Dovidzania" we called out, repeating the lovely farewell word our warm Polish friends had taught us.

For a day and a half we ran wing and wing, along first the Polish, then the East German shore, the wind growing steadily fresher. "Visiting Poland made me realize how fortunate we are," Larry commented as we once again discussed the restrictions and economic problems we'd seen. "We Westerners take our freedoms for granted, especially the freedom of passports and traveling freely."

CHAPTER 16

The equinoctial gales our sailing friends from Sweden, Finland, and Poland had warned us about proved to be no myth. By the eighteenth of September 1973, the morning after we tied up in Bornholm's Ronne harbor, an easterly storm was blowing. *Seraffyn* lay comfortably in the corner of the fish haven, completely surrounded by almost a hundred Danish fishing trawlers. The wind moaned through the forest of rigging surrounding us and rain hurled down in sheets. For five days the wind blew at gale force with gusts to seventy knots.

At first we welcomed the enforced stay in port. I had mending to do. Larry was busy writing and reading. The local library had a large collection of English-language magazines. But we grew restless after our mail packet arrived at the local post office and we finished answering every letter in it.

"We're only about a hundred sixty miles from Thruro," I told Larry one evening after we'd returned from a walk decked out in full wet-weather gear plus three sweaters each. "Three good days' sailing and we'll be where we want to spent the winter."

Larry looked over my shoulder to study the chart of the natural harbor in front of Walstead's shipyard. "Looks good and safe, Lin. I'm sure we'll be able to take *Seraffyn* out of the water to revarnish her insides." We turned off the tiny butane heater we'd connected to one burner of our stove, then crawled into our Dacron-filled double sleeping bag. We quietly discussed the refit *Seraffyn* needed now that she was almost five years old. One or the other of us kept thinking of new items to add to our growing work list until we fell asleep, cuddled warmly together.

Each day the fishermen who owned the boats around us would come down from their homes in town to check their mooring lines, start their engines, and exchange news with their friends. One or the other would translate the latest weather forecast for us. On the sixth day the sky was clear and the wind did seem lighter when we opened our hatch in the early morning. By 1000 the wind was definitely lighter. The owner of the small steel yacht tied near us called, "Come listen to the forecast." He translated as a German announcer said, "Wind easterly, Force 6 to 7, decreasing to 4 or 5."

All around us the trawlers started to come to life. Their crews arrived from town shouting merrily across the water. A hundred fishing boats maneuvered out of the inner harbor, one after another. By noon there was only one trawler, the steel yacht, and ourselves left in the south end of the previously crowded harbor. "I'm not sure I want to go," I said, tapping the barometer that stood good and high at almost 1015 millibars. It didn't move. The flag on the harbormaster's office had stopped whipping and just waved gaily in the slightly gusty Force 5 east wind. Larry seemed reluctant, too. "It's dead downwind from here. Since it's about eighty-five miles to the light at Klintholm, we could leave as late as 1400 and still be sure of arriving during daylight. Let's wait another three or four hours. If the wind continues to drop, we'll set off."

I cooked up a pot of stew while I made lunch, figuring that it would be wise to have dinner ready in case the leftover seas outside were rough. At 1230 the people on the steel yacht prepared to sail. The four young Germans on board the thirty-foot *Tummler* had to get home to their jobs in Kiel. But still we were reluctant to cast off our mooring lines, although neither of us could put a finger on what was bothering us. At 1300 the last trawlermen cast off their lines and headed into the steadily calming sea. At 1400 neither of us could think of any logical excuses to stay in the harbor. We maneuvered *Seraffyn* around until she was pointing bow to the wind, then hoisted the double-reefed mainsail and staysail, cast off our doubled-up mooring lines, and reached into the center of the basin. As we tacked for the narrow entrance, the harbormaster came out of his office and called, "Good sailing." And it was good sailing as we ran wing and wing out of Ronne Harbor. The sea was calm, protected by the mass of Bornholm Island. Our small sails pulled us at top speed. We decided to eat an early dinner and really enjoyed the stew. Dark seemed to come extra early that evening as the skies clouded over and the wind began to increase. Before I went below to climb into the bunk, I helped Larry drop the mainsail, furl it, and secure the boom in the gallows. We'd already put one drop board into the companionway even though there was no spray on deck. We'd made it a rule that as soon as there was a reef in the mainsail, a drop board belonged in place. Since the first of the drop boards has its top higher than the level of our deck, water that gets into the cockpit during heavy weather can't easily find its way below decks.

Larry put our handy canvas companionway cover in place over the rest of the opening because the ever-increasing wind was cold. I was undressed down to a long-sleeve t-shirt, underpants, and socks when Larry pulled the canvas aside and said, "Hey, Bug, how about sleeping in my bunk tonight. It's on the windward side so if a bit of spray does come on board it won't get the sleeping bag wet." I was surprised at his suggestion because I prefer sleeping against the hull on the leeward side of *Seraffyn* when there is any motion. But I switched the bag across and set the lee cloth in place. One oil lamp glowed softly above the galley, swinging gaily in its gimbals as we roared off the backs of the growing seas. I squirmed around until I could lift the canvas companionway cover. I saw Larry standing in back of the boom gallows, his elbows over the stout piece of teak on which the mainboom now rested as we ran under just the staysail. Our oil-burning stern light bounced beside him, its light gleaming off his high black seaboots. He looked comfortable and warm enough in his sweater-bulged windbreaker and jeans. Our ship's bell rang four times and I secured the lashing on the lee cloth, turned over, and went easily to sleep.

How can anyone describe the horrid sensation I felt when I was thrown halfway out of the bunk? Only the lee cloth kept me from going further. *Seraffyn* made a huge whunking sound as she was hurled off the top of a breaking sea. The horrid crashing sound of flying cans, tools, books, floorboards, and dishes drowned out the rushing sound of the huge stream of water that pushed past the canvas companionway cover. We seemed to be upside down, then I was tossed just as violently back into the quarter berth. I struggled clear of the sleeping bag, sheet, and lee cloth in the solid darkness. I could only scream—"Larry, Larry!"—then my feet hit the water that sloshed fore and aft as *Seraffyn* resumed her running motion. I was standing calf-deep in water grabbing for a flashlight when Larry yelled, "I'm here. Start pumping!"

I found the bilge pump handle, inserted it in the pump, and started stroking. Floating floorboards hit my ankles, making watery-sounding thunks as they collided with the settee fronts. I had the water down three or four inches when Larry yelled, "Don't worry when the boat's motion changes." He poked his soaking-wet head past the canvas cover, "I'm going to head into the wind and heave to. Everything's all right now, Bug."

I flashed the light around the horribly littered cabin, pumping all the while. All the books from our navigation shelf were in the sink. The lenses from two oil lamps lay in shattered pieces on the drain board. Most of the tools from the locker in the starboard settee were now on top of the port quarter berth. Had I been sleeping there I'd have been hit by chisels, woodplanes, screwdrivers, wrenches—over a hundred pounds of flying sharp metal. Something kept tapping my leg. When the beam of my light picked up my toothbrush floating merrily on top of the remaining fifty or sixty gallons of unwelcome ocean that had invaded my previously tidy home, I finally broke down and started crying.

Larry hoisted the double-reefed mainsail. *Seraffyn's* motion changed as she heeled to a gust of wind on her beam, then rounded into the wind, slowed down, and finally stopped, heeling about fifteen degrees. She began to assume the comfortable, safe-feeling motion that I knew meant we were hove to.

Larry climbed below just then. "Got to get an oil lamp burning fast. We're surrounded by fishing boats," he was saying as he took my flashlight and looked around. Then he noticed my tear-streaked face. He tugged off his dripping windbreaker, put his soggy-sweatered arms around me, and started rocking me, whispering, "It's all right now, baby, we're okay."

I realized that Larry was shivering in his wet clothes. My stockinged feet were still covered with sloshing water. "Get out of those wet clothes," I commanded, trying to catch hold of myself. I grabbed for a paper towel to wipe my tears only to get a handful of soggy paper from the towel roller. Larry took charge. "Find me some oil lamp lenses. Every one in our navigation lamps shattered when they filled with water." Our linen locker on the starboard side had stayed completely dry, so I handed Larry a fresh towel along with his new lenses. He first got a cabin light going. Then he finished pumping the bilges. "I'm sure glad we moved the bilge pump to a position inside the cabin," he commented as our Whale Gusher 10 made sucking and gurgling sounds.

The kind golden light of two oil lamps made our mess look less frightening. Larry went back on deck, retrieved and lit our running lights, then finally stripped. When I rummaged in our clothes locker I found that over half of Larry's clothes were dry but all of mine were soaked because they were on the lower shelf. I stripped too, then both of us dressed in Larry's dry warm sweaters and jeans, laughing just a bit at the luck that made me store Larry's clothes on the upper shelves of our locker. "Can you imagine me trying to get into one of your sweaters?" Larry teased. Then we started storing things somewhat back in place. A cup of hot chocolate laced with brandy tasted wonderful, and I finally convinced Larry to climb into the miraculously dry sleeping bag when he started to shiver again. "You'll have to keep a good watch on deck," Larry warned me. "There are still lots of fishing boats around, so be ready to ease the mainsheet and bear off to move clear if anything gets too close."

His shivering soon stopped and finally he told me the deckside version of our mishap. "After you went to sleep the wind increased a lot more. The seas were growing, probably because we were clear of Bornholm's lee. *Seraffyn* was going too fast even with just the staysail. I considered heaving to, but there were all of those fish trawlers heading back toward the protection of the island. I figured it would be best to run past the last of them, then heave to. So I dropped the staysail and reset Helmer to put the wind dead aft. *Seraffyn* kept running at about three knots under bare poles. Helmer held her perfectly on course. I was standing on the afterdeck, behind the boom gallows, holding on, watching that keen little steering vane do its work. There was just a low-flying spray hitting my seaboats. I didn't even once consider putting on wet gear. Then I looked astern and said to myself, 'That one is going to get me wet.' Well, the wave broke right over our stern. Next thing I knew, I was completely under, plastered against the boom gallows by a huge weight of water. Boy, did I hold on tight! I'll bet you can see fingerprints in the teak. Then my head came clear. All I could see was white foam all around, no boat all. I can just remember thinking of you trapped below before I saw one tip of one spreader break clear of the foam. Then I knew she was going to come up. The mast leapt clear and seconds later *Seraffyn* seemed to shake herself dry. The windvane took over and we were running downwind again as if nothing had happened. The amazing thing is, the vane itself was bent at least thirty degrees to port yet it could still steer the boat. God, it all happened so fast! I should have hove to and stayed on deck with our big flashlight. When I think about it now, those fishing boats would have seen us; they must have been watching, too." (See Appendix C for a further discussion of storm tactics.)

Larry finally fell asleep. *Seraffyn* rode to the steadily howling storm, laying about fifty degrees off the wind. The wind and sea seemed to increase during the next three hours. Once a sea smashed against our bow sending a heavy clatter of spray against the cabin front, but no green water came on deck. A heavy rain started, and by dawn the wind abated enough so that we felt safe in laying off toward the Swedish harbor of Ysted, fourteen miles away on a reaching course. In the gray, rain-streaked dawn we could finally assess the damage we'd sustained. Our pride and joy, a thirty-year-old copper and brass oil-lamp-lit binnacle with a four-year-old four-inch Ritchie compass, had disappeared from its wooden bracket. The one-inch-diameter bronze pipe lifeline stanchion that we lashed the blade of our fourteen-foot oar to was bent at almost forty-five degrees. The dinghy, lashed firmly to its chocks on the cabin top, had been loosened up, and closer inspection showed that one of the bronze brackets holding the chocks to the cabin top had been bent like a pretzel and its two-inch, number 14 screws pulled loose from the oak framing of the cabin top. The inside of the cabin top was cracked from the force the dinghy had exerted. Inside, the damage was minimal: a lot of dented varnish work from flying tools, several broken bottles, loads of wet clothes, and five broken oil-lamp lenses. We were glad we'd had no engine because oil or fuel from the bilges would have made matters worse. Since the only electric equipment on board was the portable radio, which had been on the windward side and stayed completely dry, we were able to get all ship's systems working in short order despite the huge amount of water that had come on board. Every bit of the damage, both inside and on deck, occurred on the port side of the boat, the side that fell into the trough of the wave.

We used our hand bearing compass to steer by. Ysted came into view by 1000, although visibility was made poor by driving rain. We reached into its almost deserted yacht basin and sighed with relief as we tied our lines securely. I pulled all our wet clothes out onto the rain-soaked decks. Larry stuffed them into sailbags and we carted them into town. The lady at the laundromat was amazed at our soggy mass of clothes, so we explained what had happened. When we returned to the small harbor, we found that she had called the local newspaper— a reporter was waiting for us. "You know, a four-hundred-ton coaster sank only seventeen miles from here yesterday evening," he told us. Then he drove us to the main harbor to see the unhappy crew of a two-hundred-ton coaster slowly moving a shattered cargo of roofing tiles to correct the seventeen-degree list their ship had assumed after being hit by a rogue wave the night before. They'd lost most of their deck cargo, and only made port with the assistance of a huge car ferry that had responded to their May Day call. The ferry had stayed carefully to windward of the coaster, giving them a lee for the eighteen-mile voyage into Ysted Harbor.

We began wondering about the thirty-foot German yacht that had left Ronne an hour before us. And to this day we don't know what happened to *Tummler* and her crew of four. "You people should know better than to sail during the equinotial gales," the reporter commented, echoing the warning we'd had from dozens of Baltic sailors. We'd ignored them all and paid the price.

~~~~~

CHAPTER 17

Looking for Work

At first we were embarrassed when a local sailing family came rushing down the wooden dock to where we were busily drying fifty pounds of assorted vegetables, all our wet-weather gear, cushions, and floorboards. The family had read of our mishap in the storm and showed us the newspaper's slightly overdramatized article with its photo of *Seraffyn*, Larry, and me tied in Ysted Harbor. But our embarrassment soon changed to pleasure when they invited us home to dinner. They were the first of several Ysted families to stop by and make sure we were healthy, secure, fed, comfortable, and well entertained. For seven more days the equinotial gales blew, sometimes accompanied by heavy rain, other times by bright sunshine. Our Swedish friends provided us with evenings at home, rides around the countryside, and an evening at the local skindiving club where we watched beautiful homemade movies of a member's expedition to dive in the Red Sea. One of the local sailors located a spare box compass in a friend's garage, and when the storm cleared we were ready to sail.

This time we listened to the weather lore Ysted's sailors offered us. All seemed to agree that for the next month or two there would be only one or two days per fortnight with strong winds, but fog might be a problem. The locals also told us that by combining the information broadcast on longwave radio by BBC in England for the North Sea and German Bight, with that on the German broadcast for the southern Baltic, we'd get a good idea of the weather. After listening to the German broadcast four or five times we began to recognize the words that meant "storm," "fog," "sunshine," and "light winds."

On Wednesday the third of October we awoke to the *brrr* of our tiny travel clock's alarm. The two weather forecasts never once mentioned any wind over Force 5. By 0700 the sun shone gaily on our dewy decks. It was nippy cold, only a few degrees above freezing, yet when we ran clear of Ysted Harbor an hour later and set full sail, I wrote in our logbook, "beautiful, beautiful sailing."

For the next week the weather remained the same. We had delightful sailing as we explored Denmark's southern islands (Great Belt). I learned to sail with gloves, three sweaters, and two pairs of pants, feeling like a kid decked out for the snow. Larry reveled in the nippy weather, consuming hot cups of coffee or chocolate as fast as I could produce them. Each day's sail ended with Larry's winter drink, a hot rum punch: one part dark rum, two heaping teaspoons of sugar, one teaspoon of lemon juice, one shake of cinnamon powder or cinnamon stick, and three parts boiling water; mix well then put a dab of fresh butter on top and serve.

We could see a heavy band of fog rolling slowly toward us as we entered the Agerso Sound late one afternoon, and we were glad when *Seraffyn* whispered slowly through the breakwaters in front of the tiny town of Karrebaeksmin. There was a bit of tide running against us as

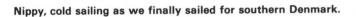

Nippy, cold sailing as we finally sailed for southern Denmark.

water flowed out of the huge estuary behind the town, so when we dropped our anchor approximately a hundred yards south of the big pier shown on our chart, *Seraffyn* drifted slowly back, taking up the slack in her chain. The wind had died completely and the water was as flat as gravy on a plate inside the protecting arm of the breakwaters. When *Seraffyn* hit something that sounded just like rock, we didn't worry but we were quite surprised. Larry got out the lead line and dropped it overboard. At our bow there was twenty feet of water, but our stern was aground on a rock. Larry climbed into *Rinky* and sounded all around us to find a patch of clear water. Then I winched in our chain and anchor while Larry set our oar in place. *Seraffyn* easily came free of the offending rock as Larry rowed her to his chosen spot and reanchored. Then a heavy wet fog closed in and we climbed below for dinner.

Early the next day we heard the sound of a sail being dropped close astern of us. Larry opened our hatch to see three sailors maneuvering a lovely-looking R boat under jib alone. As they tacked over in the seven-knot breeze, fog swirled and coiled around them. Larry let out a great shout of warning just before they hit our rock. The wooden

The R boat crew worked hard to free the boat from the rock we'd discovered the night before.

sloop came to a sudden stop, then stuck, its waterline exposed, its crew very surprised. They started their engine but that didn't budge them. We could see they had no dinghy, so Larry rowed over and offered to help. They handed him their big kedge anchor and Larry rowed it out with two hundred feet of line, then dropped it off the stern of *Rinky*. The crew tugged on the anchor line, rocked their thirty-eight-foot boat back and forth by leaning out first from the port shrouds and then the starboard ones, and finally the R boat shot free. There really wasn't room enough for them to join us at anchor in the area clear of rocks, so they sailed alongside the town pier and Larry went with them.

He rowed home half an hour later. "I just met a fellow from the local sailing club. Seems the pier over there used to be a hundred yards longer when our chart was drawn. It collapsed about three years ago and both boats anchored a hundred yards away from what is left, or right on top of the old foundations." In all of our cruising, this was the first time we'd found an inaccuracy on any chart that affected our sailing. But the local port authorities had written to the proper hydrographic office and reports of the pier's collapse had appeared in notices to mariners.

Larry came below and poured a cup of coffee from the still hot percolator. "Egon invited us to come to his house for dinner, and we have permission to tie up next to the pier," Larry said. "Who is Egon?" I asked. "The man from the sailing club," Larry answered, as he disappeared into the forepeak with a book he was reading.

By afternoon a strong wind was blowing directly through the opening in the breakwaters. Egon was waiting for us on the pier when we lifted anchor and sailed alongside with just our staysail. "Storm coming. You'd best sail under the bridge to the yacht club," he called. This made sense since the water alongside the pier was already starting to foam and boil against the tide as the wind increased. I stayed on board, making sure our fenders stayed in place between the rugged concrete and *Seraffyn*'s white-painted topside, while Larry and Egon made arrangements to have the bridge opened. The three of us sailed easily past the open bridge, and less than half a mile upstream secured to the clean wooden pier. We found ourselves surrounded by a variety of small yachts, which seemed strange this late in the year until Egon explained. "Because of the strong currents in this estuary, very little ice ever forms on the water. So most people leave their boats afloat waiting for those special sunny days that come even in the depths of our Danish winters." By midnight when Egon brought us home from a lovely dinner, a full gale was blowing. But we couldn't have felt safer.

We walked across the bridge toward the windswept village the next day. Only one other person was on the streets, an older man limping heavily along with a cane. His hat blew off as an extra-strong gust of wind swept through the wet streets. I ran after it, enjoying the exercise after the confines of *Seraffyn*. When I caught it and brought it back, Larry was talking to the man. A heavy drizzle started. Per Gustaffsen introduced himself and pointed to a whitewashed cottage right on the quayside. "Come in and warm up," he insisted. We followed him into his foyer, shed winter coats and boots, then walked in stocking feet across the highly polished wooden floors. "Watch that door sill," Per commented as we entered his cozy sitting room. His wife greeted us warmly and soon poured out hot tea and passed a plate of shortbread-like cookies as Per told us how he'd come to limp so badly:

I've been a pilot in this port almost forty years, sometimes bringing as many as five ships a week into the harbor in every kind of weather, and sometimes we get some pretty bad seas here, what with the tide and shallow waters and wind-driven currents. Last year in the middle of a huge winter storm I got a call to go out and meet a German freighter of about five thousand tons. It was early in the morning and the snow was coming down in heavy sheets blown by forty or fifty knots of wind. The streets were covered with ice. I met the pilot boat skipper at that cafe across the street and together we went to the pier. We had to climb down the ten-foot ice-encrusted iron ladder to get to the boat. The boat was covered in ice, icicles hanging from its rigging, a sheet of ice on its deck.

As soon as we cleared the breakwaters, we started hitting some of the worst seas I've ever seen in this sound. We were taking green water right over the bridge at times. My skipper located the German ship about three miles away and brought his boat masterfully alongside the wildly swinging rope ladder they'd let down for me, but the motion of those two vessels riding alongside each other in huge seas was horrid and I had to jump at just the right moment and rush up the ladder to avoid being crushed between the boat and ship. I somehow managed to do it and climbed up the slippery rope ladder, swinging first against the ship's side and then away from it. I finally made it to the deck and a seaman was there to grab my arm. He could barely stand on the ice-covered decks. I steered that ship into the harbor, using every skill I knew, and we got her tied up.

I had a hot drink with the captain, then climbed down the icy boarding ladder to the wharf and walked the half mile home, slipping and sliding, bowing my head to shield my eyes from the wind-driven snow. I reached our doorstep, opened the door, and stepped inside. I took off my coat, removed my seaboots, and headed toward the kitchen where I could smell the coffee my wife had brewing for me. I tripped over that dammed sill, fell, and broke my hip!

The irony of the whole saga seemed to hit Per once again and he laughed loudly as he pointed to the two-inch-high polished Danish oak sill at the entrance to the room we sat in.

It was the eleventh of October when we finally sailed into the channel leading to Thruro where Walstead's shipyard lay waiting for us. I was ready to settle in for the winter. Larry called it my nesting urge, but I was really looking forward to staying in the same place for a few months. I looked forward to doing my grocery shopping in the same stores each week and coming to know who had the nicest vegetables, or where to get the spices I wanted. I needed the friendly feeling of being recognized and greeted by the local merchants and maybe joining in a coffee klatch for a bit of female talk of recipes, sewing, and homemaking. These breaks in our cruising life were a refreshing change, and after three or four months my desire to move was always stronger than ever before. As soon as we'd anchored in front of the big sheds where *Puffin* had been built, Larry rowed ashore to find out about a winter job. I was busy looking around at the four or five shuttered cottages on the point about a quarter mile away from the sheds, daydreaming about starting a fire in one of their fireplaces and spending the long winter evenings toasting my toes and marshmellows in front of the flames.

Larry was away for almost two hours, and when he returned I could sense that all was not as we'd wished. "Didn't Walstead need any help?" I asked as he secured *Rinky* and climbed on deck. Larry began, "Walstead's wants any shipwright they can find. In fact, they've been advertising for help and not getting any replies. But Denmark has just become a full member of the European Economic Common Market this month and now anyone who isn't from one of the nine countries or their trading partners can't get a work permit. They've got an American guy there who is working for free just for the experience. They don't dare hire me—the authorities are watching too closely."

I was reluctant to let go of my dream. "But there must be some way of getting a work permit," I insisted.

"I doubt it," Larry answered. "The American fellow has been trying for six weeks. But I sure would like to work here. You should see the oven and jig they have for making laminated frames quickly."

We sailed six miles to the main town of Svendborg and tried to get a work permit. We were told that we could immediately start collecting welfare as unemployable residents, but there was no way we could work in Denmark because their quota of Canadian workers was full. "Now if you were Turkish there would be no problem," they told us.

We called Leif Møller in Copenhagen and he too tried to arrange the papers. He called everyone he knew including several politicians and the chief of police. When he had no luck, we gave up.

"Let's call England," Larry finally suggested. "I know I can work there. The Parkstone Yacht Club said if we gave them warning they could probably find room to store *Seraffyn* in their shed."

When Tom Hunt answered Parkstone Yacht Club's telephone he seemed delighted to hear that we planned to spend another winter in Poole. "Come right over and have lunch with me and we'll check the tide book and decide which day to pull you out," he said. I explained that we had over five hundred miles to sail and the Kiel Canal to transit before we could join him, but we would be there in time for lunch one day soon.

Leif Møller joined us to sail from Svendborg to Kiel. We once again had a wonderful frosty Danish winter special of a day as we first beat through the southernmost of Denmark's islands past Marstal, still the home port of many Baltic sailing trading ships. Then we eased our sheets and ran toward Kiel. Leif Møllar was a delightful guest as usual, lamenting the fact that some silly-sounding bureaucratic rules were keeping us from spending the winter where we could get together frequently. But then he decided he'd find some excuse to come to England during the winter and visit us. This weighty matter taken care of, he gave us a running commentary on all we passed. The night sail up to Kiel Fjord past a myriad of shipping absolutely thrilled Leif. "Do you think they know we're here?" he asked as we tacked to avoid yet another steamer when we saw both their port and starboard running lights at the same time. "I always assume they don't," was Larry's answer.

Beating through the islands.

We anchored in front of the Kiel Yacht Club at midnight. Leif left the next morning to take a ferry home to Copenhagen and we walked to the canal control offices. "How do we get our boat through the canal? She doesn't have an engine," I asked the man at the desk. "Easy," he replied, "hitchhike!"

And, following his advice, we did "hitchhike." We got our anchor up at daybreak and sailed over to the waiting area in front of the equalizing lock at the canal entrance. Thirty or forty ships of all sizes and shapes were anchored or steaming slowly in circles waiting their turn to enter the enormous lock. Larry slowed *Seraffyn* down by heading her into the wind. I climbed clumsily into *Rinky Dink*, encumbered by all my sweaters and wet-weather gear that barely kept me as warm as I wished in the bitting breeze. Weather reports on the radio told of a snowstorm less than eighty miles north of us, and the leaden sky overhead bore signs that it might move south.

I rowed among the freighters and coasters, yelling up at the crew of the smaller ones, "What speed do you make?" Everyone answered, "Nine knots," which was the top limit in the Kiel Canal. So I rowed on. Larry had warned me of possible dangers of towing a heavy-displacement boat like *Seraffyn* at over seven knots (theoretical hull speed plus one-quarter). It could impose strains that could jerk our bitts loose, besides causing *Seraffyn* to be difficult to steer. I was becoming dubious about finding us a tow that day. The lockmaster was beginning to call ships into the lock one at a time, his voice booming over a huge loudspeaker on the top of the lockmaster's tower. Then, just as I turned up to row out to where Larry was reaching back and forth with *Seraffyn*, I heard a beautiful sound—"tump . . . tump, tump . . . tump." I immediately knew I'd found our tow. I rowed past three steel coasters and there she was—a lovely old baby-blue Danish trawler, her icy-cold single-cylinder diesel blowing perfect smoke rings out the soot-blackened smokestack as it fought against starting for one minute more. I rowed up to the forty-five-foot wooden ship, yelled to a crewman on deck, and when he came over I asked, "Will you tow me through the canal?" He was the epitome of a Danish seaman, blond, blue-eyed, husky with a laugh to match. "Tow you? Hell, we'll lift you right on deck," he said when he looked over the rail at six-foot eight-inch-long fifty-pound *Rinky* and me. But when I simply turned and pointed out to where *Seraffyn* glided back and forth pretty as a white-winged bird, Larry waving from her tiller, the Dane laughed again. "I knew there had to be a catch. But never mind, we'll tow him, too!"

So I rowed to back to *Seraffyn*. Larry and I dropped her sails, pulled the dinghy on board, and got out fenders, mooring lines, and rigged a tow cable. Our Danish tow boat steamed alongside and then, side by side, took us slowly into the lock.

Over thirty small ships and ourselves filled the lock. The captains of each went to the lockmaster's office to pay their fees as water slowly filled the lock, lifting us all about ten feet to the level of the main river system that fed the canal. Our fee came to six dollars.

There are no pilots required for the canal on ships of less than five hundred tons, and as soon as we were clear of the lock our Danish trawler captain suggested we fall back on our long tow line so there would be less chance of damage from the washes of passing ships.

Seraffyn towed well at six and a half knots, but someone had to steer her all the time. Larry seemed to stand the cold better than I did, but only by downing cups of hot chocolate did he keep from turning blue as the headwind was increased by our forward motion. Halfway

Seraffyn under tow in the Kiel Canal.

through the fifty-mile-long canal our trawler slowed down. As *Seraffyn* glided alongside, the captain called, "This is Rendsburg. My favorite restaurant is here. Do you mind if we stop and tie up for the night?" Blue-lipped Larry thought the idea was great, and as soon as we were secured to the side of the trawler next to the huge timber wharf, I began thawing him out with hot rum punch and steaming thick beef stew.

The next day we reached the lock at Brunsbuttal and tied alongside our trawler as we waited for the lock to fill with ships that came straggling slowly in. The trawler men invited us on board and I brought along two big loaves of fresh bread I'd baked as Larry steered. They produced butter, honey, and strawberry preserves as we sat next to their roaring diesel heater in the sixty-year-old trawler's forward galley and sleeping quarters. Then they explained that they were taking her to the museum at Esberg, Denmark. "She was the first Danish trawler to have an engine," the engineer told us as he proudly gave us a tour of her engine room. The rough old single-cylinder engine had a seven-foot flywheel and moved the trawler at hull speed when it was going 100 revolutions per minute. "Lovely old engine. Nothing precision about it. We can machine up any old part that needs replacement ourselves," the engineer told us. He was sad to see his little ship retire after so many years of faithful service, but admitted that a museum was a good place for her to spend her retirement.

The lock filled with forty coasters and small ships, then emptied of ten feet of water. The gates swung open and the River Elbe lay before us. Our Danish trawler friends refused payment of any kind and wished us good luck as they motored out of the lock—tump, tump, tump.

We waited half an hour tied alongside the lock wall until a customs man arrived with two cases of duty-free scotch whiskey Larry had ordered in Kiel. Then we sailed out with the last of the tide and three hours later anchored in Cuxhaven, the North Sea entrance to the Elbe River.

The evening weather report from BBC in England told of gales and snow still to the north of us, but clearing was forecast within twenty-four hours. "This time we'll take no chances. We'll wait until there is not one gale within five hundred miles of us," Larry commented as he toasted his hands over our bravely glowing butane heater.

~~~~~

CHAPTER 18

A Different Kind of Weather

We only had to wait two days for a storm-free weather forecast. Even in Iceland the BBC reported light winds and no fog. We were really glad to be on our way because each day was perceptibly shorter, each night perceptibly colder. Besides, one stroll through the German city of Cuxhaven had given us a real fright. Food prices were the highest we'd ever seen (lamb chops were six dollars a pound, and tomatoes a dollar fifty a pound in 1973). We both like meat and fresh vegetables. With our tastes we'd have eaten up the last of our dwindling cruising funds in no time at all.

We were under way with the first of the ebbing tide bound for the notorious wintery North Sea with just enough breeze to give us steerage way. The sky was gray and streaky. A cold, damp haze cut visibility to about two miles. Shipping of all sizes, shapes, and ages chugged past us as we drifted by each marker buoy on the three-knot tide. The river traffic divided itself neatly, inbound shipping hugging the southern side of the well-marked channel, outbound traffic the north side. So we happily sailed right up the middle, taking advantage of the strongest tide, waving to the ships that passed two hundred yards on either side of us. For five hours this strategy worked perfectly. We traveled seventeen miles downriver until we were out in what looked like open water although our chart showed a maze of shoals and mud banks six hundred feet outside the channel. The shipping never thinned out, but as soon as dark fell our wind did. Then the tide began to turn against us. "Let's sail outside the channel and anchor till the tide turns fair," Larry suggested after looking at our chart. "We're right next to this buoy and there are two fathoms of water behind it for almost two hundred yards." I couldn't have agreed more. The thought of a night cuddled together in the warm bunk was much more appealing than one spent standing out in the cold and dark, steering from buoy to buoy, worrying in case a ship came too close, especially since we were barely moving. Larry looked around and said, "We'll fall off and run astern of that next ship." We eased the sheets and steered due south. The large coaster passed us, the masthead lights of the next ship were over a mile away, and the buoy that was our goal was less than two hundred yards ahead. We trickled slowly through the water, our speed dropping as the wind died even more. The green running light of the ship was joined by a red one. "They're going to hit us!" Larry gulped. I started flashing a D signal with our six-volt battery-powered quarter-mile lamp: –·· –·· –·· ("keep clear, I am maneuvering with difficulty"). The red and green lights grew steadily closer as Larry rushed to put our oar in place. The ship's masthead lights stayed right in line as Larry shoved against the oar. I kept flashing the light, swinging its beam across our sails. Larry was swearing up a storm as he worked, "Why don't they indicate they see us? They must have someone at the helm when there is such a crowd of shipping. Someone must be directing them through this channel." I could see the huge-looking ship clearly in the darkness, and when it seemed to be almost on top of us I dropped the tiller, rushed below, and grabbed the foghorn, then let out blast after blast. The ship never flashed a light or in any way acknowledged our presence. They never altered course; they never slowed down. And they only cleared our stern by what looked like fifty feet!

We were both unbelievably relieved to be out of the channel with our anchor down even though the boat rolled and bounced to the frequent wake of passing ships. I poured Larry a shot of whiskey and both of us vented our pent-up fear, calling the captain of that unknown ship all sorts of names. But as soon as we grew less tense Larry looked at our chart carefully, then said, "We were the foolish ones, Lin; we could have sailed all the way from Cuxhaven just outside the channel, clear of the shipping. There are two fathoms of water behind the buoys almost everywhere. We'd have had our own private two-hundred-yard-wide channel and we could have dropped anchor anywhere along the way. We're the ones who chose to sail without an engine. We shouldn't expect commercial shipping to stay out of our way. We've got to sail as if no one cares and no one can see us."

We set the anchor lite, hung it on the staysail stay and then slept soundly until 0300 when *Seraffyn* started to snub against her anchor chain. In our forward bunk we could hear the chain grumbling across the bottom when the wind changed direction. It served as a warning buzzer. Larry went on deck just as our alarm went off to tell us when the tide was changing. A fresh breeze blew from the east-southeast. Our course for the next hundred miles was due west. We lit our running lamps, hoisted our mainsail and lapper, and set off at five knots through the water with the fair tide under our keel increasing our speed over the bottom by three knots. There must have been some special star shining on us because our passage down the dreaded North Sea, through one of the busiest concentrations of shipping in the world, was delightful. Although it was cold and cloudy, the wind was always fair. In fact, it was always aft of the beam. When we had to alter course past the Hook of Holland and sail due south, the wind seemed happy to give us a break and within an hour it changed from east-southeast to northwest. The sea stayed almost flat. There was only a bit of morning fog, and the low clouds reflected navigation lights so we often spotted them and identified their sequences eight or ten miles sooner than we normally could have.

Three and a half days later we started to lose our wind when we were less than two miles from Folkstone Harbor in the narrowest part of the English Channel. "Let's reach in there and spend the night at anchor," Larry said. "The tide will be turning against us soon anyway. Maybe we could clear Customs in time to get real English lamb chops for dinner."

The tide was at its lowest spring ebb when we anchored a hundred yards away from the Customs house on the huge roll-on/roll-off ferry dock at Folkstone, England. We hoisted our flag and a Customs man came out of his office and yelled, "Come ashore with your dinghy and pick me up. Bring your passports." So we unlashed *Rinky* and slipped her over the side. When we rowed alongside the dock, the Customs man looked down at little *Rinky* where she bounced about at the bottom of a slime-covered forty-foot-long ladder. We could see the look of indecision on his face as he called, "Do you have much liquor on board?" Larry kept a straight face as he called back, "Only enough for our own consumption."

The Customs man looked vastly relieved and answered, "Come on up, then, no need to inspect your boat. We'll clear your papers at my office." We clambered up the ladder and went into his warm office. I glanced at the clock, "Oh, darn it, the shops will be closed in twenty-five minutes," I said. The Customs man was really sympathetic when we told him we'd had no lamb in over five months. "I'll keep your husband and passports as hostages. You run, left at the first corner, then up two streets. Tell the butcher Bill sent you," he said, opening the door for me. I ran and just caught the butcher and a green grocer and spent the two pounds I had left from the winter before. The ship's papers and our passports were cleared and stamped when I got back and the Customs officer wished us a good stay in England as we climbed back down the forty-foot ladder to the dinghy.

As we rowed back to *Seraffyn* I teased Larry, "Two cases of whiskey, one case of Russian champagne, three cases of Bulgarian wine—only enough for our own consumption!" Larry looked at me seriously, "It *is* only for our own consumption. We don't plan to sell any, and that's all the Customs people are worried about." And Larry was technically correct. We did consume it all, although we shared it with lots of friends when they came by for visits all during the long English winter.

We stayed in Folkstone only twelve hours because as soon as our alarm clock rang for the early-morning weather report we could see we had a fair wind for Poole. We ran before an ever-increasing south-east wind, each familiar landmark on England's south coast moving past us at five knots. It was the first time in five years of cruising that we'd ever sailed back through the same waters. All during the twenty-five hours it took us to run the 135 miles from Folkstone, past the Isle of Wight, right up to Poole Town Quay, one or the other of us would pipe up, "I wonder how Alf is doing. Let's call him as soon as we get in," or "Do you think Paul is still going to the same pub?" or "Won't it be fun to have another dinner at the Green Bottle?" or "Do you think Leslie still wants to go on the Round-Britain Race?" We couldn't wait to see people we now thought of as old friends, even though we'd only known them for three or four months the winter before.

We reached up Poole Harbor's now-familiar maze of channels on November 1, 1973, a warm feeling of homecoming growing inside. Poole Town Quay was almost deserted when we maneuvered along-side just astern of the two tugboats *Wendy Ann* and *Wendy Ann II*. Their captains took our lines and called, "Welcome home!" We packed our kits, clean clothes, and towels, and walked toward the bus stop past

Piplers, the local yacht chandlery. "Welcome back," Mr. Pipler called. We grabbed the first No. 2 bus that passed and rode to the Parkstone Yacht Club. "We're here to take you up on that lunch offer," Larry said as soon as we'd had a long hot shower. Tom Hunt looked up in surprise. "How did you get here so soon? Good to see you, welcome home!" And so it went.

Our winter plans seemed to make themselves. Within four days of our arrival *Seraffyn* was hauled out of the water, chocked securely among two hundred other club boats, her mast hoisted out and stored in the mast shed. We acquired a Morris 1000, a tiny gray whizz of a car we came to call Samantha. Larry was offered all the boat repair and alteration work he could handle at Cobb's Quay Marina on a contract basis. I was offered the same situation at Paul Lees's sail loft as Larry had enjoyed the previous winter, a chance to build a new sail in exchange for three mornings a week of my labor. But best of all, Paul Lees helped us find and rent a five-hundred-year-old town house, right in the middle of the quietest part of the town, only two streets away from the shops, two miles from the yacht club, and three miles away from Cobb's Quay. What a treat it was to wander through the four-story stone house with its saggy wooden floors, painted fireplaces, Elizabethan windows, and four-square staircase. We only had to pay twenty-five dollars a week for this marvel of a house because the owner was an antique dealer who used the house to store and display his collection and he worried about it if the house stood empty. It was wonderful to eat off hundred-year-old Worcestershire china, sitting on Chippendale chairs, chatting with all the friends we'd met the year before and many new ones, while around us the ghosts of a home that was built when Columbus was only twelve years old played their little tricks and refused to tell their secrets.

Our winter days fell into a comfortable pattern. Larry worked at his boat repairs ten hours a day, five days a week. I worked at the sail loft three mornings a week and spent my afternoons refitting *Seraffyn,* going over every piece of gear on her, making new covers for everything at the sail loft and putting three coats of fresh paint inside and outside *Rinky Dink.* Both of us used our spare time to write, and at least two days a month went toward the project that was to be the highlight of our next summer—the two-man Round-Britain Race.

Larry had always been fascinated by this race. "It's the only race that really tests crusing equipment and proves what kind of boats two

Leslie Dyball, commodore of the Parkstone Yacht Club and skipper of *Chough*.

people can handle well, both at sea and entering and leaving harbors,"
he told me when Leslie reiterated his desire to go on the race. It was
over a course that covered twenty-two hundred miles, starting in
Plymouth, England, going west past Ireland, north past the Outer
Hebrides and around the Shetland Islands, then south down the North
Sea to the English Channel, and ending in Plymouth. There were four
compulsory stops: Cork in Ireland, Castle Bay in the Outer Hebrides,
Lerwick in the Shetland Islands, and Lowestoft on England's east
coast. Participants had to stay exactly forty-eight hours in each of these
places. Any type of mechanical self-steering gear was allowed. The
race was held every fourth year. Leslie Dyball had asked Larry to crew
for him using his thirty-foot Sparkman and Stevens–designed half-
tonner. *Chough*, a finkeel, skeg-mounted rudder, fiberglass sloop of
moderately light displacement, was almost the exact opposite of *Seraffyn*, and Larry was curious to see what she'd be like to handle with

only one person on watch at a time. He and Leslie held long evening conferences on the equipment and stores *Chough* would need for the race. Larry helped install a Hassler self-steering gear on her, and I began to be just a little bit jealous as sixty-six-year-old Leslie and thirty-four-year-old Larry grew as excited as sixteen-year-olds preparing for their very first regatta.

Meanwhile, we began to notice a strange fact. Our pleasure in the beautiful three-bedroom stone-floored house with its often-used grand piano seemed to diminish as our freedom fund increased. At first we loved having so much room to spread out, and often dined in front of the living room fire when the dining room table was covered with *Seraffyn*'s freshly varnished hatches, blocks, and bunk boards. But I began to tire of forever leaving the one thing I needed for my downstairs projects in one of the upstairs rooms. I began to resent having to vacuum and dust five rooms when we only used two most of the time. The delight of knowing exactly where to buy each thing I needed

Our five-hundred-year-old home came complete with grand piano. Most of the house beams were originally from old ships. You can just see *Seraffyn*'s forehatch and sextant box with a fresh coat of varnish under the piano. *Peter Stevens*

in the local shops soon turned to boredom when I never saw a vegetable that was new to me and never found a sausage I hadn't tried before. The novelty of being able to go to a movie any time we wanted, or listen to live folk music at the local club, or hear a symphony orchestra soon lost their glamor when we always had to drive through the same streets to reach them. It took four and a half months of work before our cruising fund reached the minimum figure we'd set—three thousand dollars. The minute it was fifty dollars over, Larry finished up his last contract and quit working, and we knew it was time to migrate. Together we finished giving *Seraffyn* one complete fresh coat of varnish inside, from bilges to deck head including the underside of the teak decks, behind the waters tanks, inside the lockers, and under the table. We waited only until our bunk cushions arrived back from the sailmaker's glowing new in their blue imitation-leather covers. Then we moved out of the old house and back into *Seraffyn* even though she stood high and dry in the Parkstone Yacht Club shed with ten days to wait for a tide high enough to float her free.

I felt like I was coming home again. Even though we had to walk three hundred yards to use the club's toilets, we still found we loved our turtle shell of a home and longed to be under way.

All sorts of friends stopped by as we finished our refit. Leif Møller appeared unexpectedly from Denmark and stayed three delightful days. We gave farewell parties on board land-locked *Seraffyn*, our guests climbing a nine-foot ladder to join us. Then the yard crew arrived and jacked *Seraffyn* onto the wheeled launching car. She looked magnificent as she immerged from the shed, her white paint glowing brightly, her whale strip a proud royal blue, *Rinky Dink* pristine on the trolley under *Seraffyn*'s bilge. Peter and Valerie Stevens, two new Poole winter friends who had introduced us to long walks in the green rolling hills of Dorset, came by to help us restep our freshly varnished mast. On the morning of the launching rain threatened, and the Stevenses, Leslie Dyball, and Larry worked like devils to put on the last coat of antifouling paint as the tide rose up the launching ramp. Then, less than twenty minutes before the highest tide of the month, one of the few days when we could launch *Seraffyn*, the yard manager walked by and, like the voice of doom, announced, "Aren't ya going to grease her seams? She'll leak like a sieve after a dry spell like we've had the past three weeks." Larry looked at *Seraffyn*'s bright-red bottom where the seams between each plank were just visible. We couldn't see day-

During our winter refit Larry spliced
up new halyards.

Then he added a coat of enamel to
our topsides.

light through any of them. "She didn't leak a drop when I first launched her," Larry said with confidence. "She shouldn't leak now. Put her in the water."

I stayed below decks storing the last of our provisions as *Seraffyn* was wheeled slowly into the water. I couldn't believe my eyes as salt water shot through tight-looking seams, right across the boat. A jet of spray drummed on the bottom of the oven until I threw a dish towel over the seam. The jet quickly soaked through the towel. I pulled open a floorboard; the bilge was filling by inches every minute. I grabbed the pump handle and began pumping as fast as I could. Larry called from the dock, "Lin, come cast off the cradle lines."

I poked my head clear and yelled, "Help, we're sinking!" then rushed back to the pump. Larry jumped on deck, looked inside, and said, "Can you keep ahead of the water?" I looked up from my praying position in front of the pump. "Yes, just barely," I answered. Then Larry said, "I'll be back in three or four hours. I have to finish our new reefing lapper and deliver Samantha to Paul; then we'll be free of our car and ready to sail whenever we want. Don't worry, she'll take up quickly."

The yard men towed *Seraffyn* free of the cradle, down the half-mile-long tidal channel, and out to where a club mooring was waiting, half a mile from the clubhouse. The water was still flying three feet in the air from the seams that had been close to the electric heater we'd used while we worked inside during the cold winter days. I was really shaken to think that my safe little home could actually leak, but this was the first time in five years she had been out of the water for more than two weeks. She did take up quickly. I recorded in our logbook the strokes it took to keep the water below floorboard level:

> 1115 — 50 strokes every 3 minutes
> 1300 — 45 strokes every 4 minutes
> 1700 — 32 strokes every 10 minutes
> 1900 — 42 strokes every 26 minutes

The only problem was that Larry didn't come back in three or four hours. By the time he finally rowed home at 2100 and threw our new lapper on deck, I was close to exhaustion. I'd spent the last two hours laying on the settee, hanging my hand into the bilge so that when I fell asleep the cold salt water rising in the bilge hit my fingers. Then

I woke up with a start and began pumping madly. I was furious with Larry for leaving me alone so long on our sinking ship. But he conned his way back into my affections by saying, "I knew you could cope with almost anything, Lin, and I told the yard crew to keep an eye on you. If there had really been an emergency I could have depended on you to sail the boat on the beach or get some help. Now, you go to bed. Forget making dinner. I'll take over pumping and tomorrow I'll show you the jib you worked for. Paul says you were a great help in the loft."

So Larry did take over. He made me two of his gourmet-style peanut butter and jam sandwiches, then set the alarm for each forty-five minutes and slept in the main cabin near the pump. By the next evening we only needed to pump forty strokes every four hours. On the third day *Seraffyn* was leaking so little that we went off for a day sail on board *Chough*, which had been launched on the same tide as *Seraffyn*. We returned six hours later to find only a few gallons of water in the bilges. By the fourth day our bilges were absolutely dry.

We said our last farewells, but this time our friends in Poole just teased, "You'll be back." And somehow we knew they were right. Even though we were headed for the Mediterranean as soon as the Round-Britain Race was over, we would come back to Poole some day.

We sailed once again to Brownsea Island and spent a week wandering through the Solent while westerly winds blew. Finally, on June 3, 1974, we got a good weather report with southerly winds and we headed west toward Dartmouth to find a place where I could enjoy cruising alone while Larry came back to join Leslie for the estimated five or six weeks the Round-Britain Race would take.

CHAPTER 19

A Busman's Holiday

The wind freshened as we beat south to clear Portland Bill. When water started splashing up *Seraffyn*'s sharply tilting lee deck we decided to stop admiring the shape of our pure-white brand-new lapper and try to reef it. With the lapper we'd had before we'd had to take the sail down, unhank it from the headstay, bag it, get out the working jib, unbag that, hank it on, and hoist it, then store away the lapper. Now, shortening sail was simply a matter of dropping the lapper in the jib net, tying in the reef points, retying the sheets in the reefing cringle, then hoisting the sail again.

We had to retie the reef points in our new lapper three times that first day to get the foot of the sail setting perfectly, but once we figured out the tricks, we became believers. "We'll sell our working jib to the first person who can use it," Larry said, admiring his handiwork on the tautly pulling, reefed lapper. We've since become completely converted to reefing headsails. We now have two reefs in our staysail, one in our lapper, and one in our genoa. These three reefing headsails give us a complete range of sail combinations. The alternative is an interior full of bulky, expensive sails that are nowhere near as handy.

Dartmouth was absolutely beautiful in its spring finery, flowers edging the roadsides, tourists in their summer frocks strolling along the quay. The river was full of holidaying yachtsmen, including two long-distance cruisers. Nick Skeates and a friend were Azores-bound on *Wylo*, Nick's twenty-nine-foot, forty-year-old cutter (see Appendix B for details of *Wylo*), and Dan Bowen on his sleak, T. Harrison Butler–designed wooden thirty-footer *Romadi* was bound for the Caribbean.

A Busman's Holiday

All of us sailed up the River Dart about five miles to Dittisham to visit a famous pub Dan knew about. I'd heard there were oysters on the mud banks in the middle of the river. It was still low tide when we anchored and Larry and I rowed over and found absolutely no oysters, but returned happy and muddy as can be with a bucket of cockles. I set the cockles to clean themselves in a pail filled with fresh salt water. Then we joined the cruising crowd at the two-hundred-year-old stone "Ferryman's" Pub on Dittisham's tree-covered shore. An old-timer played folksongs on his concertina as local fishermen and summer tourists filled the pub until there was barely room to move. We were among the last to leave, and all of us rowed back to *Romadi* where Dan boiled up a pot of tea, then brought out his guitar to continue the evening's entertainment. After we'd exhausted the usual supply of cruising sailors' standard discussions—self-steering gears, anchors, hard dinghies versus inflatables, running rigs, floor timbers, and leaking decks—we talked of voyages past and future, anchorages we'd like to visit again, storms we'd like to have avoided, and wine we dreamed of tasting.

Larry ties a reef into the lapper as the jib downhaul holds it into the jib net.

We sailed back to Dartmouth's main anchorage and spent several evenings visiting on board various yachts that were gathering for the "Old Gaffers Race." One evening as we shared some of our fresh clams on a new friend's yacht, I decided to use his marine toilet. I thought I'd turned off all the proper valves when I'd pumped the bowl clean. A half hour later our host's face took on a look of shock as he saw a stream of water running out from under the loo door. He ran into the loo, and I heard him cursing under his breath and pumping furiously. Then I heard him turning a valve. He came into the main cabin and tried to reassure me. "My fault, Lin. I should have made sure you turned off the right valves. It's happened before." The overflowing loo and soggy carpet definitely put a damper on the evening and we left shortly thereafter. "What did I do wrong?" I whispered to Larry as soon as we rowed clear. "It wasn't really your fault," Larry told me. "His head installation was poor. The hoses should have looped high above the waterline and had antisyphon valves at the top of the loops. The way he has it now, everytime anyone uses that head he has to open the valves, then pump the loo, and finally close all the valves. It's a pretty dangerous situation. If the same thing had happened when we were all on our way ashore for the evening, his boat could have filled with water and sunk. I've heard of that happening before." I looked at our blue plastic bucket and its lid with more respect after that. It had its inconveniences, but it would never sink our boat!

Henry North, with his inimitable sense of humor, joined us the day of the Dartmouth Annual Old-Gaffers Race and we sailed the course, enjoying the sight of thirty gaff-rigged sailboats, twenty-two to eighty feet long, some built before the turn of the century, topsails pulling, crews working to spread clouds of canvas to gain every inch they could on the ever-dying wind. *Dyarchy*, the husky, well-known forty-five-foot Laurent Giles cruising cutter, was queen of the day, glowing magnificently in a fresh coat of black enamel and varnish. But our fishermen friends from Falmouth walked off with the first two prizes in their open oyster dredgers, and when we joined them for beer in the Royal Dart Yacht Club after the trophies were given out, several of them said, "Bring *Seraffyn* to Falmouth. We'll keep an eye on her and make sure Lin has a good time."

Their invitation was irresistible, and on the next day we set off on an impromptu race westward, twenty-six-foot, seventy-year-old *Evelyn* taking the lead, *Seraffyn* in the center, and twenty-two-foot *Magdelena*

Elizabeth and Mary, an old Plymouth hooker, had a few worms in her deadwood so her owner hauled her on the tide and . . .

Larry helped fit a worm shoe and get her ready for the Old-Gaffer's Race.

Magdelena in the foreground, *Evelyn* closest to the shore. Two fine examples of seventy-year-old Falmouth oyster dredgers.

right on our heels. Each boat set its spinnaker and ran toward the River Yealm. A heavy fog threatened and we took bearings just before it settled over us. *Evelyn* was ahead and out of sight. The breeze grew lighter and we dropped our spinnaker and drifted along under mainsail and genoa. We plotted our position on our detail chart and steered a careful compass course. Then we heard the putt-putt of a small outboard motor and looked astern to see *Magdelena* emerge slowly from the fog. Arfie had inflated his rubber dinghy, lashed it alongside the engineless *Magdelena,* and put the outboard motor on the inflatable. The little three-horsepower Seagull moved five-ton *Magdelena* at over three knots, and as he caught us Arfie called, "I know you guys are yachtsmen. I figured you'd have a compass and chart on board. Mind if I follow you in?" We laughed and offered to boil up a pot of tea. But Arfie's girlfriend Sue emerged from under *Magdelena*'s tiny enclosed forepeak with an already-brewed pot of tea she'd cooked up on a primus stove. Arfie turned off the outboard and the four of us chatted comfortably as we sailed through the fog side by side, until we reached the black rocks at the entrance to the river. We tacked across the bar, caught the first of the incoming tide, and beat upriver, sounding with our lead lines as we went. Once anchored, we settled in to wait for the fog to clear.

It took us another ten days to reach Falmouth even though it was only forty-five miles away. We dawdled along, visiting each of the

Larry sailed *Rinky Dink* on the river Yealm while I got dinner ready.

beautiful anchorages and rivers we'd seen almost two years before. It was special fun feeling like old hands as we remembered the names of each headline and recognized the bar men in the pub we'd visited before. When we sailed into Falmouth there were only three days left before Larry had to take the bus back to Poole to join Leslie. Commander and Mrs. Coxwell had been told that we were coming and immediately offered us the use of a spare mooring in front of their home which they used as a sailing school. It was about two hundred yards upriver past the Royal Cornwall Yacht Club. "I just set that mooring," the jolly, twinkle-eyed commander told us, "so Lin will feel safe leaving *Seraffyn* there no matter what blows up. I'll have my nephew put a longer pennant on the pickup float so Lin can reach it more easily when she comes back from a day sail."

Larry finished attaching a boathook to the end of *Rinky*'s seven-foot-long boom. "That will make it easier for you to pick up that pennant under sail. You won't have to lie on deck to reach water level when you come back from a sail," he told me as he stored the now dual-purpose boom back in place.

When I rowed Larry across the river to the center of Falmouth on June 28, *Rinky* was full to the brim. Larry was borrowing *Seraffyn*'s 450-square-foot nylon drifter and 1,050-square-foot spinnaker to add to *Chough*'s wardrobe. He also had our new Negus taffrail log and a little whiskey from ship's stores. "Now don't be afraid to take *Seraffyn* out for a sail," he said as he climbed on the express bus. "Worst you can do is scratch her paint. She's your boat, too!"

I'm terrible at good-byes and kissed Larry self-consciously under the steady stares of the fifty holidaying British lady members of the garden club that filled the bus. "Try and win that race," I said as I turned to leave. "I'll take care of *Seraffyn*—you have fun!"

I rowed back toward the far side of the river wondering if I'd want to go sailing now that Larry wasn't there. As odd as it sounds, I didn't know whether I really liked sailing or if I went because going places and being with Larry was what I enjoyed.

No one in Falmouth gave me time to be lonely. Within hours of his departure several people had sent messages inviting me for meals, and the day after Larry left Mrs. Coxwell asked me to help collect money for raffle tickets at the fishermen's festival at Flushing, the village across the river from Falmouth. I watched the hilarious fishermen's parade, roared with laughter as several men tried to walk out a greased pole set over the water, and held my sides while the same men had a pillow fight on the grease-smeared varnished spar. I was conned into joining the ladies rowing race, and put up a very poor showing against the husky local fishermen's wives when I tried to row a four-hundred-pound dory with ten-foot oars set on tholepins. I was used to fifty-pound *Rinky* with her closed bronze oarlocks. The lady who won must have weighed a hundred sixty pounds. She made that sixteen-foot dory fly over the water, its long oars groaning on each stroke. I learned afterward that she often joined her husband to pull nets on his mackerel trawlers. With that kind of competition, I felt I had some excuse for coming in last.

The next day I sat on deck sipping a cup of morning tea, feeling free as a bird in the warm sunshine. Dean and Carolyn rowed up in their little rubber dinghy. We'd first met them in Dartmouth and they were bound for Texas in their twenty-two-foot fiberglass sloop. After I invited them on board and poured them some tea, I heard myself saying, "How about joining me for a sail upriver to see Restrounget Creek? Tide's fair." Minutes later we'd secured the rubber dinghy to the mooring, reached off the mooring, and jibed around, *Seraffyn*'s sails filled for the run downriver. I loved it. Being in charge of our lively

A rollicking crowd cheered on the fishermen as they batted at each other with soaking wet pillows.

little ship, I felt confident that I could make the right decisions and bring her up to the mooring at just the right speed so that my guests could easily pick up the mooring pennant. I was out sailing around Falmouth estuary with *Seraffyn* and some friend or other two or three hours every day. When Pat Daniels, a lady friend from Poole, came to join me for her one-week summer vacation, I thought nothing of saying, "Let's sail to Plymouth and help Leslie and Larry get ready for the race." The two of us had a bit of a struggle getting *Rinky* on board, but we managed, and just as we were ready to drop the heavy mooring chain, the Coxwells' six-foot four-inch nephew David James called out, "Where are you two girls going?" "To Plymouth," we shouted back, and David was soon on board, too. The three of us had a rollicking sail on a fresh northerly breeze. All doubts I had about my love of sailing were dispelled. Larry or no Larry, as a sport, sailing is great! It requires practice and careful planning, but offers a tremendous feeling of freedom and accomplishment.

We picked up one of the double moorings in outer Millbay Docks, and secured *Seraffyn* bow and stern. Then all of us walked to the inner dock where sixty-one boats were being measured and prepared for the race.

Thirty-foot *Chough* looked tiny surrounded by boats like eighty-foot *Burton Cutter*, skippered by Leslie Williams and crewed by Peter Blake; seventy-foot *British Oxygen*, the catamaran sailed by Robin Knox-Johnston and Jerry Boxall; and *Manerava*, the huge aluminum trimaran being sailed by the two Colas brothers from France.

It was just great being part of the preparations for a race like this! Pat and I did bags of laundry, spent hours shopping for stores to last Larry and Leslie twenty-five days, and turned *Seraffyn* into a steaming galley ship as we cooked up and prepacked enough food to last Larry and Leslie for five days. Brian Cooke on his lightweight fifty-foot trimaran *Triple Arrow* had to be extremely conscious of every pound he put on board his boat, and he gave Leslie a bit of ragging when we carried two cases of wine and a fly-fishing rod and reel on board *Chough*. But Leslie turned to Brian and said, "Just because we're racing doesn't mean we have to suffer, and I plan to do some salmon fishing in the Shetlands."

By the time we followed *Chough* to the starting area, on Saturday the sixth of July 1974, I was exhausted from dinner parties, race preparations, and one last private evening with Larry on *Seraffyn*. But Larry

Larry was busy helping Leslie prepare *Chough* for the race, but even so he had time to enjoy the prerace festivities.
Chip Mason

Chough of Parkstone and her two-man crew sail out to the starting line.

and Leslie looked great as they posed for the cameras of the eight sailing friends who were with me on *Seraffyn*. There was a nice light breeze for the start and all sixty-one of the competitors safely cleared Plymouth's breakwaters, the multihulls showing occasional bursts of speed as puffs of wind blew through the hills of Plymouth.

As soon as we sailed back to Millbay Docks, all of my guests, including Pat, left and there I was, all alone, forty miles from Falmouth where I had a date in three days. I'd never considered single-handed sailing, but here was my chance to try it. I'd met five-foot three-inch Claire Francis who was skippering thirty-two-foot *Cherry Blossom* in this race with Eve Bonham as crew. Claire had single-handed across the Atlantic. So had five-foot two-inch Theresa Remiszewski. If they could do it, so could four-foot ten-inch me. I sat on deck enjoying the quiet of the deserted docks, contemplating the adventure ahead of me, when a twenty-six-foot blue and white fiberglass sloop came into the dock under power. The two men on board backed between the mooring buoys that lay less than thirty feet to port of *Seraffyn*. As they secured their lines to the rings on the buoys, I called over, "Please take up real tight on your mooring lines. It's high tide now and when the tide's out these moorings have just a bit too much scope and we'll bump." The men seemed to give me the usual "who wants to take notice of a girl" look, and after chatting about the weather for a few minutes they went below decks.

I was sound asleep in our forward bank, dreaming someone was knocking. Then I woke up. Something was knocking against *Seraffyn*'s hull. I looked out the hatch. It was 0500 and just beginning to grow light. That fiberglass sloop was banging against *Seraffyn*'s port quarter, the only part of our topsides not protected by fenders. I was furious. I became an instant Women's Libber, roared on deck, grabbed two of the wire shrouds of the offending sloop, pulled them apart as hard as I could, then let them loose. *Twang!* The fiberglass sloop vibrated, making a sound like a plastic guitar breaking a string. Two heads flew out through two hatches and turned quickly. The look of confusion on their faces turned to one of definite interest. They didn't say a word, only grinned, and I could sense that something was not as it should be. I followed their gaze, looked down at myself, and realized that I was completely nude. I jumped into the cockpit and rushed below, yelling, "Get your bloody boat off my bloody boat."

I heard a few whispered comments and chuckles as the men tightened their mooring lines and their boat pulled clear. I took a book and retreated into the forward bunk, trying to calm down and regain my shattered composure while I waited for the 0630 weather forecast.

The weather forecast gave me no reason to stay in port, so I got dressed and started to remove the sail covers before my confidence ebbed away. One of the men on the next boat asked me what I was up to, and then offered, "I'll row over and help you sail clear of the mooring. Then I can row back here."

"Thanks, but I can do it myself," I replied. Then I almost wished I hadn't been such a smart aleck when I looked at the boats moored less than twenty feet on each side of *Seraffyn* and considered the careful short-tacking I'd need to sail out of the dock area. I poured another cup of tea and slowed down to think out each move I'd have to make. Then I climbed into the dinghy and removed the mooring lines that held *Seraffyn* and replaced them with long lines that I first cleated on deck, then ran through the rings on the moorings and back to *Seraffyn*, where I cleated the end. That way when I was ready to be free, I could simply cast off one end, the line would run through the mooring buoy ring, and I could gather it in once I was under way. There was a fresh southeasterly breeze blowing at an angle across the docks. I set the mainsail and sheeted it to a close-reaching position, then tied the tiller just a bit to windward. *Seraffyn* started pulling against her stern mooring. I hoisted the staysail and sheeted in. Since I had no reason not to go, I cast off the stern line. *Seraffyn* slid a few feet to leeward of the buoys and then immediately began to gather headway. I rushed forward to cast off the bow line. Its free end threatened to snag around the tip of our CQR anchor, but I gave it a quick jerk and the line slipped free. I pulled the two lines on deck as *Seraffyn* glided past the mooring buoys into open water. One easy short tack and I reached past my would-be assistant, waving nonchalantly although my heart was just falling back into its proper place. Then I eased sheets to run out of Plymouth Sound. I felt as tall as the sky and was almost convinced that single-handed sailing was the greatest sport on earth when, eight hours and thirty-five miles later, my warm sunny beam reach turned into a cold blustery beat with a backing wind. Then I began to think differently. The tide was against me as I beat the last six miles and I came to appreciate the assistance and security a sailing partner offered. By the time I picked up my mooring in front of the Coxwells' home I began to understand the problems and dangers of sailing alone, especially without an engine. But I was as proud as punch and eager to share my adventures with Larry.

The Falmouth fishermen and members of the Royal Cornwall Yacht Club kept me busy and happy as I eagerly followed Leslie and Larry's progress in both newspaper and radio reports. They quickly took the handicap lead in the race, and by the time they reached Lerwick in the Shetlands, were nine hours ahead of the nearest competition. The weather reported by most of the competitors proved that this was not the type of race I'd have enjoyed. The yachts had had to beat three-quarters of the course in Force 7, 8, and 9 winds. One after another, competitors began to drop out of the race. The multihulled entrants seemed to suffer the most; *Peter Peter*, a forty-eight-foot catamaran lost its mast, retrieved it, restepped it, and sailed another thousand miles in the race, only to lose its mast again; *John Willy*, a forty-six-foot trimaran, split up and was abandoned; *Triple Arrow*, the fifty-foot trimaran sailed by our good friends Brian Cooke and Eric Jensen, flipped over in a sudden gust of wind off Lerwick and had to be towed into harbor and righted by a crane—all in all there were twenty-one retirements in a fleet of sixty-one, almost all caused by heavy weather damage. And when Larry joined me again one month later in Falmouth, he was the glowing joint winner of the fleet handicap prize. I was anxious to hear the sea stories he'd have to tell.

"Leslie sure was one hell of a partner," was the first thing Larry told me. "The second night out of Lerwick he made three complete headsail changes all by himself in one three-hour watch; number-two genoa, working jib, finally ending up with the storm jib beating into a really rough headsea with winds gusting Force 9! Later I made him a special breakfast, scrambled eggs and corned beef hash, to celebrate his sixty-seventh birthday. Hope I've got that kind of determination when I'm fifty."

I asked Larry about the complaints I'd heard about the handicap system being faulty. "Of course it was inaccurate," he replied.

It's impossible to handicap multihulls with monohulls—there should have been two categories. But I feel we had a real victory. *Chough* was forty-sixth from the top of the fleet according to overall size, and we were the thirteenth boat to cross the finish line. The huge multihulls didn't show the speed people expected from them. *British Oxygen* was seventy feet long with a sixty-foot waterline and took ten days and four hours to sail the course. We took fifteen days

A map of *Chough's* course in the 1972 Round-Britain Race.

and twenty-two hours with only a twenty-one-foot waterline. They had three times the waterline length yet only turned in a thirty-four-percent faster time. That was probably because there was a lot of windward work in the race and multihulls are faster off the wind.

One thing I did notice was how tired people seemed to be when they finished each leg. Leslie and I were quite tired when we finished the first leg at Cork. Leslie had done a wonderful job using his local knowledge to catch each lift of the current and tides. He knew the area from Plymouth to Cork like the back of his hand, knowledge gained on seven Fastnet races. He took us right into the bays to beat the foul tides and got us the lead. But I knew that we couldn't keep it up if we didn't get more rest. So when we were in Cork, I suggested, "From now on, the man off watch should climb right in the bunk, even during the day. The man on watch should handle everything, with the windvane doing the steering: sail changes, navigation, chores. If we get more rest, we'll do great." Well, it sure worked. When we reached Lerwick, Leslie was so rested he stepped right off the boat, fly-fishing rod in his hand, and asked directions to the nearest salmon creek. The young guys on some of the other boats couldn't believe their eyes. This race proved it to me—thirty-five feet is the biggest boat two people can keep racing efficiently. *Quailo,* the fifty-four-foot boat that was successful in the Admiral's Cup, had a thirty-nine-foot-long waterline but only moved twenty-two percent faster than *Chough.* Her crews complained of being too tired to want to change big, heavy headsails halfway through the race.

I wanted to know what Larry had thought of sailing an IOR-type boat over such a long distance.

I prefer *Seraffyn* anytime, Lin. She's so much easier to steer and her motion is much more comfortable. Besides, *Chough* could never have carried the gear and stores *Seraffyn* does and done as well. Downwind with a spinnaker *Chough* was mannerly, but the minute we got near a reach with the chute, she was horrid. And on a beat in heavy conditions she pounded like hell; in fact, she shattered the sliding glass doors in the loo and threw the glasses and bottles right out of the specially designed liquor locker. But we were really pushing her hard. Leslie refused to show his boat one bit of mercy. You wouldn't believe how she could go to windward. We often had her moving at six knots and above, close-hauled! She didn't respond to self-steering as well as *Seraffyn*, but I'll say one thing—after the unbelievable pounding we gave her, I sure have more respect for a well-built fiberglass boat. The hull never gave us one worry.

For the next few days Larry and I shared sailing adventures. I learned how the thirty- to thirty-five-foot boats seemed to be the ones that could be driven hardest by their crews, and that the people on them always seemed to be the ones having parties at the rest points while the men off the fifty-footers slept. Larry shared the fun moments of the race, the bottle of champagne at the finish line, the songs and beer at tiny Castle Bay pub, and the kindness of people in each port. He told me about their trials and tribulations, such as when *Chough* sailed into a maze of gill nets off northwest Ireland and they had to waste three hours finding a way out of the mess. And the time they beat into Lerwick Harbor on a Force 9 headwind, then rested forty-eight hours while the winds blew fair, and had to leave again just as the winds backed and turned into a Force 9 headwind again. When I asked Larry if he'd go on the race again, he said, "I was thinking of asking you: if we're in England in 1978, what do you think of taking *Seraffyn* in the next Round-Britain Race? I'd buy you a good warm pair of sailing gloves. You may not be as tough as Leslie, but we'll have had ten years of two-man sailing practice by then."

Fortunately I never had to give him a definite answer since we were sailing the Pacific in *Seraffyn* when the next Round-Britain Race came around.

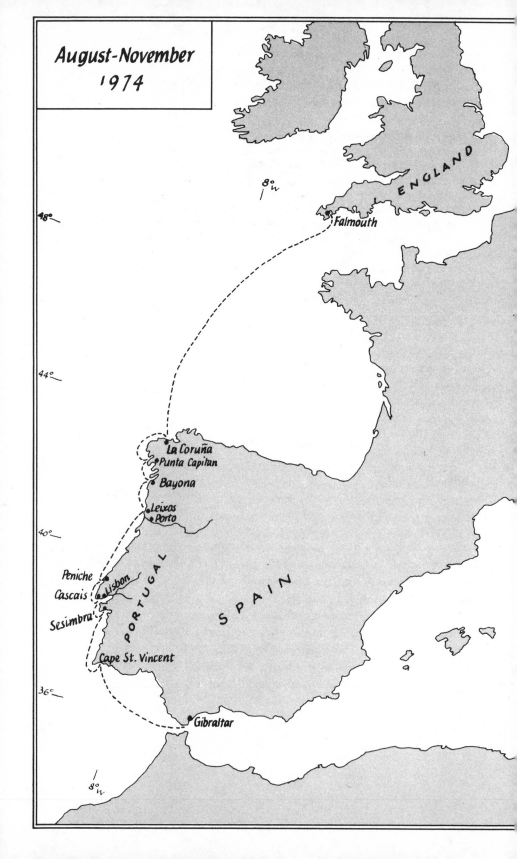

August-November
1974

ENGLAND

8°u

48°

Falmouth

44°

La Coruña
Punta Capitan
Bayona

Leixos
Porto

40°

PORTUGAL

Peniche
Lisbon
Cascais

SPAIN

Sesimbra

Cape St. Vincent

36°

Gibraltar

8°u

CHAPTER 20

Heading for the Sun

O nce again we'd reached that difficult point—we had to make a
decision. The English days were warm and sunny those first
weeks of August, but we remembered the fickle weather September
usually brings to European waters. Both of us longed to visit Scotland
with its lochs and islands, and Larry's brief stop at Castle Bay in the
Outer Hebrides had made him more interested than ever before in
getting to know the Scottish sailors better. Mayne, the Irish barman
from the Royal Cornwall Yacht Club, added his voice to those who said
we'd be sorry if we missed Ireland's wild west coast. But Dan Bowen
had poisoned our minds with stories of Spanish wines, brandy, and
champagne, served alongside buckets of mussels and oysters on the
sun-warmed waters of Spain. We didn't have to toss a coin to make our
decision; I just reminded Larry of the freezing days he'd spent working in the boatyard in Poole, coming home blue and shivering from
the rain and winter wind. "I've heard there's a real shortage of yacht
repairers in Gibraltar," Larry said. A quick telephone call to the Gibraltar Information Service Office and we knew that getting a work
permit would be no problem. So our plans were made, and we set to
work getting our international vaccination cards brought up to date,
buying stores, scrubbing and antifouling *Seraffyn*'s bottom, and gathering last memories of Falmouth to take along with us.

My parents arrived from California on a three-week tour of England and drove their rented car down from London to join us for three
days. One of the main drawbacks of a boat as small as *Seraffyn* is that
she doesn't have room to provide a separate private stateroom for
guests. So, few people can join us for longer than two or three days

without feeling cramped. It was fun to show my mother the exciting antique shops in Falmouth and to take her for tea and cakes in the two-hundred-year-old Greenbank Hotel. The two of us sat by the hotel window watching Larry and dad short-tack *Seraffyn* up the river after a long day sail. We tried to cram two years of memories and family gossip into two hours.

After telling me of yet another divorce among friends in California, my mother looked at our tiny home coming to rest at the mooring across the river and said, "How do the two of you live together twenty-four hours a day in such a small home? Don't you miss your privacy? Don't you get bored with each other?" I tied to explain that the two of us were drawn closely together by the shared work required to take care of *Seraffyn* and voyage in safety and comfort. With our common interests, we never seem to run out of things to talk about—places we'd like to go, people we'd like to meet, things we'd like to do, changes we'd like to make to our floating home, things we'd like to write about. We didn't have the outside pressures caused by jobs, mortgages, and a hectic social life that steal time from the average shoreside couple. Because we couldn't easily hide from each other, we had to face our personal problems and work them out way before they grew too big to handle. We had the time to really communicate, uninterrupted by telephones or life-insurance salesmen. Despite our limited living accommodations, we'd learned to find the moments of privacy everyone needs. Larry would say, "Excuse me for a few hours, I'm going to read a book." Then he'd climb into the forepeak or lounge back against a sailbag and I'd work happily away in the main cabin or row ashore for a walk. Every year or two we'd arrange to spend three weeks or a month separate from each other. This sometimes happened naturally such as it had during the Round-Britain Race. At other times we chose a convenient meeting spot so that one or the other of us could take a trip inland to visit friends or go sightseeing while the other enjoyed having *Seraffyn* all to himself. We'd use the time learning not to take each other for granted, and I know I always came back appreciating our partnership more than ever. About once a year when we've stayed in the same harbor waiting for weather to clear, mail to arrive, or a check to be cleared, one or the other of us becomes short-tempered or generally obnoxious. But we've come to recognize this as a disease we call "port fever," and since boats are made for going places it is simply cured—we set sail and move somewhere new. Now, four years later, after we've lived on board for over nine years, we are busy scheming and planning a new boat we might build some day. As we do that, I realize that our shared projects and mutual goals are the reason we rarely get bored with each other.

After three sunny days my parents departed amid a flood of tears and good-luck wishes and we went back to our preparations. The August weather deteriorated. Rain came to mar the holiday makers fun. Strong southerly winds gave us an excuse to have more time with the Falmouth oystermen, spending delightful days racing on their rugged gaff-rigged cutters. Finally, on the morning of August 22, 1974, the depression and bad weather moved east and we rushed to buy our final stores so we could set sail that day. It was Thursday and if we hadn't gone then, we'd have been trapped by the lessons we'd learned about sailing on Friday.

At 1330 we reached clear of Falmouth and for the next three days we had headwinds varying in strength from less than two knots to more than twenty as we beat across the Bay of Biscay. We passed the time pleasantly, sharing our memories of two winters and part of a summer in England. We were going to miss the people we'd met there. "I'd become used to being able to communicate well with people. So many of the Englishmen were on our wavelength with their love of boats and sailing," Larry said as he went on deck to check for ships.

We made just over sixty miles a day along our rumbline, always close-hauled, Helmer in charge, catching each lift or heading of the fickle wind. We'd tack every time we got a definite heading, plot our position, then settle in while *Seraffyn* chewed away at the miles, heeled about twenty degrees with her deck not quite touching the water. On our fourth day out of Falmouth the wind drew to the southwest and we could finally lay our course direct for Corunna on Spain's northwest corner. Five days out the wind veered until we could ease our sheets. *Seraffyn* carried her full mainsail, staysail, and lapper, beam-reaching at five knots. Spain lay about seventy miles ahead of us and I sunbathed on deck considering a matter of relativity. Moving at her top comfortable speed of six knots, *Seraffyn* could cover a maximum of 144 nautical miles in a twenty-four-hour day, or about 165 land miles. Our average speed for over sixteen thousand miles of cruising had been 3.56 knots or eighty-five nautical miles a day (ninety-five land miles) including tacking in and out of harbors and waiting out calms. That really wasn't much until you stopped to consider that we were moving our home and all we owned, using the natural power of the wind.

At 1500 that fifth day we spotted the gray outline of Spain's hills on the horizon. The wind had freshened until we were carrying only a double-reefed main and staysail, reaching on an ever-growing easterly wind. Large waves started to march out of the Bay of Biscay. By 1800 I had a rough time holding myself in the tossing galley while I heated up a can of baked beans with another can of hot dogs poured into the same deep pot. I buttered up some bread that luckily I had baked the day before, and handed it to Larry who'd come below after setting the oil running lamps in place.

I didn't even consider eating—my stomach threatened to rebel just from the aroma of the hot baked beans. "Isn't it a bit rough?" I asked Larry, wedging myself into a corner of the settee. Larry wiped his bowl clean with a fourth slice of bread and answered, "If it gets much worse I'll heave to, but we're only thirty miles out of Corunna. In less than twenty miles we should pick up some protection from the land." *Seraffyn* lurched over one sea and a roaring sound of water shooting away from her bow resounded through our wildly moving home. "I'll go on deck and hand-steer. You climb into the bunk and get some rest so you'll be fresh to help us navigate into port. I'll call you as soon as I pick up any navigation lights."

The motion seemed to get even worse as I lay against the hull in the leeward bunk. I tried to sleep, but with little success. The cabin lamp we'd left burning ran out of oil and in the complete darkness each sound was magnified. Books on the shelf thudded, wine glasses clinked, a pot in the oven screached as it shifted, a can in the locker beneath me thumped against the wooden bunk front. I heard the hiss of passing waves, the slapping crash as our channel and chain plates hit the waves. Spray splattered against the windward cabin side; wind shrieked through our rigging. I was becoming really nervous and concerned when Larry called, "Lin, open the companionway!" I scrambled out of the bunk. "What's wrong?" I yelled over the roar of wind that filled the night.

"Everything is under control," Larry reassured me. "It's magnificent out here, but I've just picked up a light and I need you on deck to take a bearing and time the light sequence. Put on something warm under your wet-weather gear."

I lit another cabin lamp and found an extra sweater in my locker under the forward bunk. With light glowing through the cabin and my mind occupied by studying the information on our approach chart, I lost my apprehensions. I climbed over the drop board in the companionway, pushing the heavy canvas cover aside.

The sight that met my eyes *was* magnificent. Huge waves ranged toward us in even rows, their crests glowing green with turbulent phosphorescence, white spray streaking their faces. Larry steered, one hand on the tiller, the other clutching the bulwark, with the end of the mainsheet tied around his waist. *Seraffyn* roared across the face of the waves, sometimes burying her whole bowsprit in the foam that lifted from her bow. The white swinging anchor light we used as a stern lantern threw light that gleamed off our soaking decks.

"Tie the end of the jib sheet around yourself and go up next to the shrouds. The light I spotted is just on the windward side of our bow," Larry told me, giving a big grin as *Seraffyn* gathered speed from an extra-heavy gust. I passed the end of the jib sheet that was tied to my waist around two shrouds and secured it so my hands could be free. I had to shield my eyes from the spray as Larry headed *Seraffyn* up into a particularly big sea. Then I caught the flash he'd seen. Flashlight in one hand, arm around a shroud, stopwatch in the other hand, I finally figured out the beginning and end of the light sequence and timed it. It definitely was the huge light of Corunna and we were right on course. I unlashed myself from the shrouds, sat down on deck, and scooted back to the cockpit, the jib sheet dragging on the deck behind me. Larry reached over and secured my jib sheet safety line around a cleat, gave me a quick hug, and went back to steering.

Together we enjoyed the majesty of the stormy night as *Seraffyn* charged across the waves like a racehorse, averaging close to seven knots. Within another hour we could feel the huge seas swinging more toward our stern as they curled around the northern corner of Spain. Soon they began to lose their power. Within four hours of the height of our "quicky" storm the wind lost its force as it became blanketed by the hills, and within another hour we were almost becalmed.

It was 2300 when Larry said, "How about standing a watch for me?" I readily agreed, since by then we had an accurate fix on our position from two different navigational lights. *Seraffyn* moved slowly through the water on the offshore breeze. Helmer steered and I spent my time enjoyably washing dinner dishes, putting away the various small items that had been dislodged in the gale, and drying wet-weather gear as our stormy Biscay Bay farewell blow became just another memory.

In six years of cruising this had been one of only three or four times when we'd used anything like a safety harness. But *Seraffyn* had strong twenty-four-inch-high lifelines, eight-inch-high bulwarks, and a massive boom gallows frame to hang onto. And from the first day I sailed with Larry he had told me, "One hand for the ship, one hand for yourself." We'd often discussed safety harnesses and always carried two in a convenient place in *Seraffyn*. But, as a good friend once said, "You can't buy safety. You have to earn it by learning good sea habits." Safety harnesses are a great assistance if you happen to be wearing them at the right time. But in practice few people wear them every minute of the time they are at sea. Good hanging-on habits, strong and convenient handholds, and the awareness that death is only one misstep away are just as important and will stop you from falling overboard when there is an emergency that gives you no time at all to find and put on your harness. The time in the Baltic when we were suddenly broached, Larry didn't have a safety harness on—it was good hanging-on habits that saved him.

It was midmorning before we finally sailed into Corunna. We'd both had over five hours of sleep. *Seraffyn* was scrubbed and tidy inside and out. Fifteen minutes after we let go our anchor we were in the dinghy bound for shore to see if we still remembered the Spanish we'd learned when we'd cruised through Mexico and Central America two and a half years before.

CHAPTER 21

The Five Rias

The Club Naval at Corunna is one of the most magnificent yacht clubs we've ever been in. Marble floors, mirrored staircases, mahogany-paneled rooms. The showers were complete with an attendant to hand you a club towel at a cost of twenty-five cents. After a shower we went onto the veranda and looked over the oil-covered basin where the club members kept their boats. Three other cruising boats were tied there, and the two men off a thirty-foot Swedish yacht soon joined us. One was definitely under the weather. "What's the problem?" Larry asked. "He's suffering from the Spanish-Swedish disease," his partner answered. "Stomach trouble?" I asked. "No, it's just that a whole bottle of good brandy here costs less than a glass would at home in Sweden. He's been like that every morning for over a week now."

We all laughed except for the afflicted sailor and the hours passed quickly as we shared the club's specialty, tortillas. This was completely different from the tortillas of Mexico. Those had been pancake-like pieces of unleavened bread. A Spanish tortilla turned out to be an egg omelette filled with fried onions, potato chunks, garlic, and spices, and served chilled with salt and pepper. It became a favorite of ours.

Corunna is a big city with a busy harbor. Shopping was delightful but the harbor traffic and strong winds made our anchorage uncomfortable and we definitely didn't wish to move into the oily club basin to wait for the winds to die down, even though it was well protected. So four days after we arrived, we set sail to explore the coves and bays of the much indented coastline.

For six days God worked hard creating the earth. On the seventh he was tired and lay back to rest. He rested his hand down on the northwest corner of Spain and made five great dents. When God saw what he had done he felt sorry, so he blessed the area and made it bountiful.

So goes a legend about the coast of Galicia, and as we cruised this green hilly coast with its five great estuaries, locally called "The Rias," we came to believe the legend was true. Never have we eaten such a variety of delicious seafood, and nowhere have we found lighter, more palatable inexpensive wines. Only three small industrial cities marred the coast; most of the time we could only see small tidy fishing villages and farms.

After two hours of sailing in protected waters with a fresh north-westerly wind blowing, we came to the village of Nada. A huge gleaming power yacht was anchored in the bay just off the town's fishing boat harbor. As we circled the yacht, its name stood out proudly, carved and gold-leafed, *Arturo*. An old, tall, heavy-featured man waved and called "buenos dias" to us as we tacked in closer to shore to anchor. A police boat came rowing out: "Sorry, but you must move," the young officer said in hesitant English. When we asked why, he told us to come with him to the *commandante*'s office.

"You must move at least five miles away from here immediately," the *commandante* told us as soon as we walked into his office. "Why?" we wanted to know. We told him about the strong winds in Corunna and said how peaceful and welcoming his small port looked to us. The *commandante* only repeated, "You must move immediately."

We set sail again, grumbling more than just a little bit, and beat five miles out to the center of yet another deep fjord, when we ran into El Ferrol. We noticed an American yacht tied alongside and an English yacht next to a pier in a comfortably enclosed fishing boat basin. As we tacked by them, a sandy-haired man yelled, "Toss me a line." We set fenders and sailed carefully alongside the forty-foot *Summer Salt*, secured, and soon were chatting with Spencer and Dale Langford and their three children.

"Did you happen to see Franco?" Spencer asked. "He's supposed to be cruising around here in his power yacht. It's huge and named *Arturo*." We remembered the lone man who'd waved and smiled at us from *Arturo*'s flower-decorated afterdeck. We didn't envy him at all as we joined in the friendly atmosphere that spreads over any group of cruising boats that happen to share the same harbor.

Pedro Lema, a local sailor who was also harbormaster and pilot for the huge shipbuilding yard at the north end of town, came by to have a chat. He invited the whole cruising crowd home to meet his wife Marisa and have a real Spanish dinner. Then he took Larry and me for a tour of the shipyard. The three of us climbed into the drydocks and up the steep boarding ladder of a 186,000-ton Swedish oil carrier that was undergoing repairs and alterations. Its captain gave us an interesting tour of the huge ship. We used its elevator to go up eleven stories from the engine room to the ship's bridge where the captain and first mate had created a small vegetable garden in planters around the electronics of the computer-like room. "I've just picked up a strange report," the radioman told the captain as we stood examining the million dollars' worth of navigation equipment around us. "A hurricane is reported heading this way. It's only six hundred miles west of us with winds to eighty-five knots." The ship's barometer was dropping steadily. The sky outside was filled with cirrostratus clouds thickening by the minute. The wind on the bridge anemometer read forty knots. We rushed back to *Seraffyn* to prepare extra mooring lines and Pedro went to check his harbor boats. Fishing boats filled the harbor. There had never been a hurricane reported this close to Europe before. By the next morning the weather had cleared but the Bristol Channel, seven hundred miles north in England, reported winds of up to one hundred miles per hour. I was glad we'd come south before September.

After a week in El Ferrol we decided to move south. Locals all told us that we had to be south of Cabo San Vicente, Portugal's southern tip, before October 25 to avoid winter and we still wanted to explore the other four "rias." "Sail to the Ria Arosa, then turn east and go past three islands, head north, and on the very last point before the end of the estuary you'll see a yellow stone grainery and a very tall line of eucalyptus trees. Anchor there. Marisa's family owns a seafood farm there. We'll take a holiday and meet you," Pedro suggested. Although he and Marisa spent an hour more telling us all of the fun things we'd do together if we sailed to Punta Capitan, we'd been convinced from the first, and so were the Langfords.

We had unremarkable sailing south past Cabo Finnisterre. The navigation lights were reliable, currents ran as we expected, and winds were light but fair. Four days of pleasant, sunny sailing later, we rounded up and anchored next to *Summer Salt*. Pedro, Marisa, and two of her brothers rowed out with two one-gallon galvanized buckets full of clams, oysters, limes, and fresh grapes. We ate them all. The party moved from *Seraffyn* to *Summer Salt* to the farmhouse, and from there to the local bar where the light-yellow local wine was served in flat white bowls instead of glasses. Marisa's eighty-year-old aunt shared stories of the family's two hundred years on this same farm. The second afternoon we all drove to the town ten miles away and bought ten large locally caught fish to barbecue that night. I just couldn't make it ashore for the party—I had an upset stomach and headache that made all my previous illnesses seem small in comparison. "I must have eaten a bad oyster at lunchtime," I moaned to Larry. He had less sympathy than usual when he replied, "Bad oyster, that's a joke. Anyone who eats five dozen oysters for one lunch deserves to be sick." So I stayed in bed feeling sorry for myself as the laughter and songs on the shore two hundred yards away from our quiet anchorage rang through the night.

It must have been 0400 when I heard shouted good-byes from the beach, then the sound of oars striking water. I was just beginning to be sure I'd survive when Larry climbed clumsily on board. His movements were a sure sign of "one too many."

"Lin, you should have seen it. The most mesmerizing thing I've ever experienced, it was almost pagan. We drank lots of homemade wine, the fish was delicious. Marisa and her family entertained us with haunting Spanish songs. We reached over our heads to grab the bunches of grapes that were ripening in the arbors. When the fires burned down real low, Marisa brought a large silver bowl from the house and filled it with some brandy-like liquor. Her brother hummed softly in the dark, strumming his guitar. Then Marisa lit the brandy and took a ladle and poured the burning liquid through the air, the flames throwing dancing shadows across her face. She caught the brandy in the wine cups and handed one to each of us, still flaming. We drank the hot liquor and its fumes went right to my head. When my cup was dry the fires had died. We stood in the darkness, only the sound of crickets and the guitar calling softly through the night."

We had a rude awakening only four hours later. *Seraffyn*'s bow dipped and bobbed violently to the waves of a near gale. She snubbed against her anchor chain and spray found its way through our open forehatch onto our bunk. I went on deck to see the rock retaining wall that fronted Punta Capitan less than a hundred yards from our stern. An unusual northeast wind blew. The nearest shore to the north lay over two miles away, and a nasty sea was starting to build.

Spencer and his family were up and preparing to move, showing signs of wear and tear from the night before. Larry really didn't want to get out of the bunk; his eyes were red indicators of what his head must have felt like. But *Seraffyn* moved a few yards closer to the rocks as she straightened out her chain. So we reefed the mainsail, set the staysail, and beat two miles to calm water and reanchored. That took just over an hour and we were both ready to climb right back into the bunk when Pedro and his irrepressible cousins appeared in a car on the road opposite our new anchorage. "Come ashore," they yelled. "We'll take you to visit a friend who has a wine shop." But not one of us had the energy to accept. "Come back in three hours, we need some more sleep," we yelled.

The fishing fleet in the village across from Punta Capitan.

The days passed quickly, and we only decided to sail on when Pedro and Marisa left to return to El Ferrol. We reluctantly waved good-bye to Punta Capitan and sailed swiftly south toward Bayona on a fresh northerly breeze.

The friendly village of Bayona nestles under a beautiful parapeted castle at the entrance to the Ria Vigo. It is one of the most popular stops on the nautical route to sunshine. Almost every European yachtsman bound for the Caribbean via the Canary Islands stops here to rest after escaping from the Bay of Biscay. The Bayona Yacht Club makes voyagers welcome, and even goes to the trouble of having an English-speaking manager. The club was enlarged and their docks modernized for the 1972 transatlantic race, but most of the dock space was filled with local yachts when we arrived, so we happily anchored out among the cruising yachts.

Wanderer III, the thirty-foot sloop which had carried Eric and Susan Hiscock for over one hundred ten thousand miles, lay looking fresh and clean in green and white, just astern of us. It was now owned by a young German couple bound for the United States. Six-foot-plus Svend Kaee had his twenty-one-foot *Optimist* nearby, with its oversize Danish flag. He rowed over to visit us in the smallest rubber dinghy we've ever seen. Svend had to lie down to row, and his feet hung over the stern. He was bound for the sun after a chilling visit to Iceland the previous year. (See Appendix B.) Two couples from Belgium, Paul and Pierrette Benoidt and Marc and Françoise Besirre, were bound for Barbados on their two French-built fiberglass sloops. They invited us for a barbecue on one of the deserted islands ten miles north of Bayona. We joined them and ate mussels pulled from the rocks at low tide and then steamed in a mixture of tomatoes, onions, and garlic.

One young English couple had arrived in Bayona just a few days before we did on a thirty-year-old, thirty-five-foot ex-racing sloop. They had fallen in love with her the first time they saw her up a river on England's south coast. She'd been built by a famous Scottish yard, designed by an artist, and her sheer was a delight to behold. So they paid the low price the owner was asking and bought her without a survey. Then the two of them, both new to sailing but full of dreams, put most of their life's savings into buying cruising equipment and stores. They set off with only a little money left, bound for the Caribbean where they heard they could earn more by doing charter work. Halfway down the Bay of Biscay their inboard rudder started to loosen up. When they reached Bayona they put the boat on the concrete ramp next to the club and waited for the tide to go down so they could check the rudder. A bit of surge kept the boat from settling close to the wall. So they put a bulk of timber between the concrete wall and the mast of the sloop with heavy padding to protect the varnish. When the boat settled and leaned its weight against the mast, the mast split open just below the deck partners. It had been made up of laminations and was rotten where someone had tacked a piece of copper over the split glue joint. A close inspection of the inboard rudder and its shaft running up through the stern timber showed that extensive repairs were necessary to both the rudder and the shaft alleyway. The rudder needed at least six feet of clearance below the keel to drop out of the hull and that couldn't be done on the concrete ramp. So the boat was shifted to the beach as soon as the mast was hoisted out. Then by setting several anchors she was held upright as the tide went out. The couple

Mussels are cultivated throughout the five rias on huge rafts built of girders. Ropes hang into the water and mussels cling to these ropes and develop until they are harvested when about two inches in length. This family had five rafts fifteen feet by forty feet long in the bay at Bayona.

dug a deep hole under the rudder and removed it. As the days passed
their dream ship began to turn into a nightmare. As they tried to find
some way of replacing their mast with very limited funds, Larry
offered to help build a new one, but the price of decent timber was
beyond their budget. When we left two weeks later, the handsome but
crippled old sloop was still on the beach, rudderless and mastless. We
never heard what finally happened to her and our hearts ached for the
couple who could have saved thousands of dollars and weeks of worry
by spending only a hundred dollars to hire a surveyor in the first place.

Another sad story was tied to the club docks. The forty-five-foot-
long, almost-new aluminum French sloop had been on its way north
from Portugal. Its crew of four were tired after motoring north into
headseas and headwinds for two days. They arrived at the entrance to
the Ria Vigo at night and spotted one of the range lights that mark the
clear passage north of a group of submerged rocks. They decided they
were well clear of Wolf Rocks even though no second range light came
into line with the first as the chart indicated it should. "Must be out
of order" was the navigator's comment. They headed into the ria and
seconds later a wave lifted them beam-on onto the rocks. A second
wave washed right over them. A third wave sent them clear, and it was
then that they realized that one man had been washed overboard.
Their flares quickly brought help from Bayona, only two miles away,
but despite a careful search the man was not found until his body
washed up on the beach three days later. The aluminum hull had a
dent almost a foot and a half deep and five feet long in its side, and the
boat had suffered some internal damage. The comment someone made
at the club was particularly poignant, "Yes, that proves it, you can put
an aluminum or steel boat on the rocks and it will float off again. But
the whole idea of this sport is to keep off the rocks!"

We were sitting on deck early one morning, watching fishing boats
leave the harbor with their trail of seagulls, when a tall Spaniard came
powering out in the club launch. "Remember me?" he called in perfect
English as he came alongside. Both of us shook our heads no. Then he
pointed to the far side of the mooring area. There it stood, the white
and blue fiberglass sloop that had swung against *Seraffyn*'s side when
I was alone in Millbay Docks at Plymouth. I must have blushed from
head to toe at that memory because Adriano gave a teasing smile and
said, "I have some movie pictures I took of you that your husband
might especially like to see!" We ate dinner at Adriano's house later

that evening and his wife helped us with our faulty Mexican-accented Spanish. Since the evening was cool she'd draped the dinner table with a long quilted cover and set a small heater under the table. It glowed against our legs and felt great.

No home movie ever interested me quite as much. I glowed with delight as Adriano showed *Seraffyn* and me maneuvering out of the close confines of Millbay Dock looking completely at ease. "I wish I'd had my camera ready a few hours before I took these," Adriano said. "I'd have had even more interesting photos to share with you then." He ran the four-minute film through at least three more times just for our entertainment.

The days were growing cooler. I had jeans on more often than a bikini, and along with most of the last southern-bound cruising boats we set off for Portugal on October 1, giving Wolf Rocks an extra-wide berth.

CHAPTER 22

Looking for
the Portuguese Trade Winds

Only twenty miles from the entrance of Bayona lay the notoriously uninviting coast of Portugal. Even though there are several rivers running out of the hills and through the coastal plains of this western-most corner of Europe, almost all are fronted by sandbars. In the three hundred miles from Bayona south to Cabo San Vicente, there are now only four all-weather harbors available to ships that draw over three feet. Three of these harbors are man-made, two of them constructed in the last twenty years. Over ninety percent of the fishing done off this coast is in boats that can be landed on the beach or surfed over river bars. Yet this is the country which produced and sponsored some of the world's most adventuresome navigators, men like Vasco da Gama, Magellan, and Amerigo Vespucci. From this inhospitable coast sailors have ventured into the cold, ice-laden waters of the Grand Banks to bring home catches of cod in their handsome sailing schooners.

This coast is also known for its northwesterly wind, which usually blows so steadily that it is called the Portuguese trade winds. But that wind was nowhere in evidence when we left Spain. In fact, even though the Atlantic stretched in an unbroken reach for over three thousand miles to the west, the sea we trickled slowly over was almost as flat as a plate.

We reached Leixos (Lay-show-ez) at 0130. Even in the dark we could tell it was an industrial harbor. The flares of a huge fire, burning off waste gases at a refinery, dwarfed the twenty-mile range navigation light at the north end of the harbor. The sound of generators hummed across the still water combined with the roar of trucks and screech of heavy cranes. We sailed slowly past the red and green lights on the end of the breakwater. Our harbor chart was in the cockpit, inside a clear plastic chart case we'd been given in England. I used a flashlight to study the details as Larry short-tacked up the channel. At first we thought a fishing boat was busy at work in the harbor entrance, but as we came closer to what turned out to be a light-covered barge, we decided it was some kind of drilling platform. Someone on the platform flashed lights at us and yelled. We couldn't make out his words over the noise of generators. A large bell rang. A horn blasted. Suddenly a huge "be-humph" resounded through both air and water. *Seraffyn*'s cockpit sole jumped under our feet and less than two hundred yards astern a geyser of water, mud, and rock shot fifty feet into the air. Even though we finally found a berth at the far end of the harbor, almost a mile away from the blasting operations being carried out to deepen the rock bottom of the harbor entrance, we never quite felt comfortable as the shock of underwater blasting shook our home at unexpected intervals both day and night.

Leixos had a filthy harbor. Crude oil covered our waterline within hours after we tied to a fishing boat in the rock-wall-enclosed inner basin. It smelled like rotten fish at low tide and sour oil at high tide. Normally we would have moved on immediately, but the man on the fishing boat told us, "Come into Porto. Help us celebrate our happy flower revolution." His description of the beauties of the town where port wine was blended sold us on it. We rowed to the dinghy landing, secured *Rinky*, and found the wonderful old No. 1 tram. This tiny, electrically run wooden carriage had carried passengers along the waterfront from Leixos to the entrance of the River Duro, then along the riverbank to Porto, for over fifty years. It was a delightful ride, past the swirling mud banks at the river's entrance, alongside boatyards still repairing the wooden cod fishing schooners, past women washing their laundry on the river's edge. Frolicking children stopped to wave and yell to us as we rumbled quietly past. Twenty minutes later the old-fashioned cane-seated carriage came to stop at the foot of Porto. As soon as we stepped off into the hustle of the open market along the riverbank, an English-speaking man appeared and said, "Because of our revolution there are not many tourists right now. So you'll get a warm welcome if you visit one our wine cellars on the other side of the river." He directed us along our way and we spent the whole morning on a slow, enjoyable guided tour of the two-hundred-year-old wine cellar. We stood watching as men made new oaken barrels for the mellow red wine. We met the wrinkled old winetaster and shared glasses of wine with the charming, black-eyed young girl who'd given us our tour. After tasting over ten different types of port we couldn't really tell one from the other. Two relaxed and contented cruising sailors stepped out of the cool stone cellars and walked the one mile into the ancient city that climbed the hills on the north side of the river.

Everyone we met was wearing a carnation in his lapel or pinned to her blouse. All seemed to notice us and wave, then shout, "Viva Portugal!" When we came to the main plaza, a crowd was busy tearing revolution posters off marble monuments and building fronts. A young man had climbed a huge bronze statue of a general on a horse. He secured a red carnation on the general's bronze breast and worked to secure a Portuguese flag between the horse's ears as the happy crowd below laughed and shouted encouragement. We were the only foreigners in the crowd and people tried to tell us what was happening. But our Spanish, similar as it sounded to Portuguese, just didn't work. Finally, a young student came and translated. "We no longer have a dictator. Portugal is free! Now we can build a modern nation. These are all students and citizens giving a day of their time to clean the city." We watched as the crowd hosed down the plaza with fire hoses and worked to remove some of the thousands of posters and painted slogans that defaced the beautiful old stone buildings of Porto.

It is possible to sail up the River Duoro right into the heart of Porto. But after speaking to a pilot and seeing the complicated, tide-swept, shoal-encumbered shifting river entrance, we decided it was safer to stay in Leixos. Besides, we'd watched piles of refuse running down the river, dead rats included. Health authorities who'd stamped our ship's papers had warned us of reports of cholera in the city. Besides, we liked having an excuse to use the antique No. 1 tram.

We left the harbor of Leixos five days later laden with beautiful fresh vegetables and seafood from the huge public market. Prices had been extremely low (people told us it was because of the revolution). As we worked very slowly south being pulled by a one-knot current, close-reaching on a light southwesterly wind, we became convinced that the Portuguese trade winds were a myth. We spent a calm night anchored off the beach and the next day found the entrance to Aviero, a small town whose river entrance was shown in detail on our chart.

Piles of refuse float past women who are washing their clothes in the river Douro.

Below left: The young Portuguese student tried to secure his flag to the horse's ears as the crowd below cheered him on.

Below right: The beggar king celebrates Portugal's hard-earned freedom.

The bar at its entrance should have had seven feet of water at low tide, but even in the calm weather there were breakers right across the entrance. We could see no clear passage into the harbor even after reaching slowly across the entrance three times. So we continued slowly south, our big blue and white drifter pulling us along at two knots.

Our charts indicated a fishing harbor behind a point called Peniche. Although our British Admiralty *Pilot* book for the coast of Portugal did not mention this harbor, the American edition we happened to have on board gave a careful description of a new harbor with fifteen feet of water, a new breakwater, and room for up to two hundred fishing boats with good holding ground. "Let's head in there and wait for a change in the weather," Larry suggested. "I don't particularly like being out here in the shipping lanes with so little steerage way." We only had fifteen miles to go when a heavy fog settled over us. The wind died completely. We stood watches through the night, blasting our foghorn in answer to ships that passed eerily by. Occa-

We found the ends of the breakwater at Peniche after ten hours of heavy fog.

sionally the fog would clear enough so that we could take a bearing on the Peniche light and the one on the small island of Berlenga, five miles off the mainland. Then whoever was on watch would recompute our position and work to try to sail on any puff of wind that drifted by. The fog and sporadic winds persisted but we found the ends of Peniche's breakwater after taking sixty hours to cover one hundred ten miles. The fog lifted and a fresh northwesterly breeze filled in within minutes after we set our anchor amid a fleet of gaily painted fishing boats.

We rowed ashore to the small village and wandered across the peninsula, carefully investigating the wooden fishing boats under construction along the beach. We watched two men sawing frames from a huge piece of oak, using the same kind of cross saw we'd seen in museums. The building methods didn't seem to have changed in two hundred years. But the fifty- and sixty-foot-long fishing boats that resulted now sported huge Spanish-built diesel engines.

The quiet village seemed untouched by the revolution or the outside world. A stone windmill worked quietly grinding corn, its canvas sails moving ever faster as the October wind freshened. We ate dinner in the village's one restaurant that evening. There was no menu and the waitress spoke no English or Spanish. We still spoke no Portuguese. After several frustrating minutes of noncommunication, Larry had an idea. He pulled the last of our supply of Portuguese escudos from his pocket, the equivalent of three dollars, and set them in front of the waitress. She smiled, then drew first a fish on her pad, then something that resembled a pig. "Which one?" she indicated in sign language. We chose the fish. She disappeared into the kitchen and came back minutes later with a loaf of hot fresh bread, a carafe of vino verde (the local young white wine), and a chunk of fresh butter. We stalled our appetites with this and ten minutes later she emerged again, proudly carrying a platter with two huge, perfectly grilled fresh fish steaks seasoned with garlic and oregano, a mound of french-fried potatoes, and a fringe of juicy bright-red tomato slices. Dessert was a bowl of grapes and fresh fruit. As we left we wished we'd saved some escudos to give her as a tip. But our one word of Portuguese had to suffice. "Thank you" was all we could say.

I wanted to stay in Peniche longer. But when we woke up the next morning and heard a fresh northwesterly wind blowing through our rigging, I couldn't help but agree with Larry, who said, "Come on, let's

Two men use the same methods their fathers and grandfathers used to cut sawn frames from huge slabs of oak. The adze is being used to shape a keel. This is one boat-building tool that is still widely in use today. These fishing boats will work out of Peniche, using trawl nets.

set sail and use this wind." I stored things away below while Larry put a reef in the mainsail and led the staysail sheets. "Ready to flake the chain?" he called. "Okay," I answered as I climbed over the forward bunk to the chain locker. Larry cranked the chain in, our handy bronze Plath double-acting winch clicking happily. I scattered the chain as it dropped through the chain pipe so it wouldn't stay in a pile and overflow the edge of the chain locker or fall over itself and jam when *Seraffyn* heeled. When the five-fathom marker came into view, Larry called, "Come on deck, I'll hoist the main." I scrambled out into the cockpit, glad of my sweater and jeans in the Force 6 wind, and took hold of the tiller. Larry hoisted the main and I stood ready to pull in the mainsheet. Larry pulled in the last five fathoms of chain and called "Anchors up!" I sheeted in the mainsail. *Seraffyn* gathered way. Larry hooked the anchor onto the bobstay and hoisted the staysail as I jibed the boat. Then he came back and trimmed the staysail and I steered for the harbor entrance. As soon as we were clear, Larry suggested, "How about plotting a course to Lisbon. Is it possible to get another cup of coffee?"

So in the pattern that had almost become a ritual, I handed Larry the tiller and climbed below, plotted our proposed course, reheated the coffee and tea, and poured out cups three-quarters full. Then Larry sat at the helm, I perched on the companionway sill, and we chatted as Peniche dropped quickly away behind us.

What a glorious sail we had that day! The sun warmed our decks and we shed our sweaters as soon as we'd put *Seraffyn* on a dead downwind course, the staysail on the whisker pole, reefed mainsail vanged and prevented on the opposite side. When we cleared the lee of Peniche Point the ocean swell caught us. *Seraffyn* would rush down the face of the large long swells at what seemed like ten knots, then she'd slow down to climb the back of the next swell, seem to pause for a moment as she reached the crest, then surge down its face, throwing spray and foam twenty feet on either side. If we hand-steered, *Seraffyn* tried to surf off almost every wave. But if we let Helmer stay in charge she didn't, because he couldn't anticipate and give her rudder that little twitch right at the top of each wave that got her going.

Landmarks flashed by as we roared along, clocking seven knots over the bottom. But we knew that at least half a knot of that speed was due to current. By midafternoon we could see the cliffs of Cascais, marking the entrance to Lisbon, and couldn't have been happier as we shared a bottle of Portuguese wine and a plate of crackers with white farmer's cheese in the surprisingly steady cockpit.

Ahead of us a large power yacht came pounding directly into the seas, going north, spray flying right over the bridge driven by the twenty-five-knot wind. It passed close by us, rolling heavily, its motors growling and rumbling, and Larry raised his wine glass to the man at the helm and said, "I'll bet that man is looking at us and thinking, 'It's an ill wind that blows no one some good!' "

Although we thought little of that incident at the time, it had an ending almost three years later. We were at the 1977 World Half-Ton Regatta in Trieste, Italy. Larry was off *Seraffyn* crewing on the Canadian half-tonner, and I was hanging upside down varnishing under the bowsprit, when a tall, lanky West Indian came by. "I know where you were at 1530 on the twelfth of October 1974," he said to me. I had to think hard as I varnished, then I answered, "We must have been somewhere in Portugal about then."

"Yes," he answered, "You were running free, looking beautiful as can be about twenty miles out of Lisbon and I was having my guts rolled out in a sixty-five-foot motorboat, wishing I were you. I saw you salute with your glasses of wine and felt like turning and running, too." Jeff Bishop, a delivery skipper, had been taking the motorboat north to England.

We roared upriver to Lisbon, past the tower of Belem where Henry the Navigator had watched for his explorers to return. We tied in the visitors' basin just at dark. We'd sailed fifty-five miles in only nine hours including the time we'd spent maneuvering into the tight little basin. The decks had stayed dry the whole time. "What a fine little boat! Give her a bit of wind and she flies," we both agreed as we settled in to eat our dinner.

Lisbon turned out to be one of the loveliest capitals we've ever visited, rivaled only by Copenhagen. Its naval museum took a whole day of our time. Not only was the collection beautifully housed, it held some of the finest models we've seen. The carriage museum, just a quarter mile from the harbor, is definitely the most unusual we've visited. Housed in an indoor riding academy building constructed during the eighteenth century, its collection of close to fifty horse-drawn luxury carriages came from craftsmen of over four centuries. Three of the largest carriages, ornately carved and cushioned in velvet, had carried Portuguese royalty during a papal procession a hundred fifty years previously, and each had a cleverly concealed chamber pot inside for the relief of its elderly passengers.

The city was particularly quiet as there were few foreign tourists about and the local people were settling back, peacefully waiting for the promised elections. The second day after we arrived, we returned from a day of touring feeling slightly footsore. Some people were on the deck of an interesting-looking local yacht moored two boats away. "Who designed your boat?" Larry called over. José Da Veiga Ventura and Judy Kuenzle, his fiancée, introduced themselves and invited us over. Judy worked as a stewardess and José as airport manager for Pan American Airlines, and after we'd shared drinks and tours of both boats, they took us for a walk in the old city of lisbon by night. Then we went to their apartment and cooked up a dinner together. They shared their dreams for Portugal with us and the worries they had about the growing pains their country had yet to face. "Our students are all dreamers and believe the promises the Communists make. But

The happy cook at a tiny restaurant in Lisbon fans the flame under her brazier while three-inch-long fish sizzle on top.

our small farmers and fishermen are the backbone of the economy. They don't want communism, they just want the right to own their own land or their own boat and the peace to work them," José told us. He and Judy made our stay in Lisbon pass far too quickly. They took us into the country to meet farming friends and taste the wines that city people rarely enjoy. They showed us their favorite shops. But they too warned, "You should be moving on. Winter storms will be coming at the end of October." Their warning, combined with the fact that our cruising funds were really getting low, made up our minds to move on quickly. We'd known when we left England that we had only enough freedom chips to last five months more. The one thing we didn't want to have happen was to arrive in Gibraltar flat broke and be forced to take the very first job that came along, even if we didn't like it. So after only a week in Lisbon we invited Judy and José to join us for a day sail.

They seemed to love it as the wind freshened just outside the yacht basin and we flew downriver on a beam reach under a reefed main and staysail. José directed us to an anchorage he liked near the handsome village of Cascais, ten miles outside Lisbon. Soon after we anchored, Larry rowed all of us ashore in the dinghy for dinner.

The anchorage had been quite calm when we'd left the boat three hours earlier. But when we finished saying good-bye to our new friends at the train station and walked back through the quiet streets toward the waterfront, we couldn't believe the surge and swell we saw in the anchorage. Launching *Rinky* off the concrete ramp in front of the Cascais Sailing Club was a real challenge. Larry timed the incoming three-foot surge and shoved the dinghy off the ramp. On the next surge he jumped into the dinghy and rowed clear. He waited until there was a momentary lull and rowed stern to the ramp. "Jump!" he called. I just made it into the dinghy as a large swell ran along the seawall and up the ramp, crashing against the beach. I got my trousers wet to the knees.

Seraffyn rose and fell gently to the swell that ran under her from astern. The wind still came gusting off the beach. We'd never seen anything like it, but José had told us that this was quite normal. He'd described how the formation of the headland turned the northwesterly swell around until it ran into Cascais from the south, even when northerly winds blew fresh. "Sometimes the swell is as high as ten feet," José had told us when we stood watching the local fishermen bring their twenty-five-foot-long fish-laden dories up the beach on log rollers.

We slept quite comfortably all night, so I was doubly surprised when I opened the hatch in the morning and saw eight- or ten-foot-high rollers coming into the anchorage. When *Seraffyn* was in the trough of the waves, the forty-foot pilot boat on a mooring two hundred yards astern of us disappeared from view. The twenty-knot wind kept us perfectly aligned, stern into the smooth rolling swell, so we didn't roll. But as we watched the swell becoming roaring breakers on the beach three hundred feet in front of us, we decided to forget trying to row ashore for a last bunch of fresh fruit. "Let's get out of here quick" was what I said, and within minutes we were running wing and wing into that ten-foot swell.

Five miles later the sea pattern straightened out. We had another headlong dash south on the Portuguese trades as far as Seisembra, the newest harbor on this coast. It was tiny, with room for only about

Larry carries water to *Rinky Dink* on the ramp at Seisembra.

twenty fishing trawlers and maybe two yachts. Heavy gusts of wind blasted the harbor, dropping off the high cliffs and whistling through the rigging at fifty knots although the wind outside ran no more than twenty. So we spent less than forty-eight hours here before setting sail to run away from winter.

Cabo San Vicente came clear on the horizon on Tuesday the twenty-second of October. The wind was fresh and cold, laden with moisture. Clouds of fog rushed along with us, obscuring the headland, then lifting momentarily to show us the bold cliffs that marked our turning point. As we rounded the cape, heavy squalls rushed off the land, some so strong that we had to luff up when they hit or risk getting water in the cockpit over the lee deck. We anchored in the lee of the land for the night and the next morning awoke to find a warm, sunny day. "Remember what Pedro told us when we were in El Capitan?" I asked Larry as we worked to again be under way. "Yes," Larry answered, "Get past Cabo San Vincente by October 25 and you'll miss winter. He was right on."

We set every sail we could on a romping beam reach. The wind pulled aft and we set our huge blue and white spinnaker, laughing like two school kids as we scudded along at four and a half knots. "Just think—no real winter, no heater, no gloves, no three layers of sweaters." We shouldn't have laughed so loud.

A gust of wind from dead ahead collapsed our spinnaker. Helmer sent the tiller hard over to correct for the wind shift, and seconds later we were headed back the way we'd come. Down with the spinnaker, up with the lapper. We disconnected Helmer, tightened in the sheets, and reset the steering vane to head toward the straits of Gibraltar hard on the wind. Squalls began to grow in the north. By midnight we were down to storm sails and I'd pulled out our winter sailing clothes. By morning we were hove to as Force 8 squalls swept over us, kicking up a nasty sea. Rain slashed against the decks and we stayed below most of the day while *Seraffyn* lay comfortably hove to. We only glanced out once in a while to check for ships. Larry beat me again at cribbage, the cards held in place on our tilted table by a bunched-up towel. "That'll teach us to laugh at winter," he said as he warmed his hands on a cup of hot chocolate.

If I believed in weather gods I'd have said one was listening in just at that moment because soon the wind lightened and drew back to the northwest. We set sail and by nightfall were on a close reach, moving

All plain sail set in the Mediterreanean sunshine. *Ton Steen*

beautifully. The stars were out, the seas grew steadily calmer, the decks dried, and the air warmed. The current caught us.

Larry was reluctant to go below and climb in to the bunk. He sat with his arm around me in the cockpit. Helmer steered and the taffrail log hummed as it counted the miles we covered. We could see our oil lamps burning through the open companionway, turning *Seraffyn*'s main cabin into a golden glow of varnished mahogany and teak. The chime on our ship's clock rang clearly over the hiss and mumble of our churning wake, eight bells. "I'm kind of looking forward to doing some work," Larry commented. "It's a good change, isn't it? Three months of work, nine months of cruising. I wonder what kind of jobs we'll find in Gibraltar."

I thought of the six-and-a-half years we'd been cruising on *Seraffyn* and the ten years Larry and I had been together. We'd always seemed to find some way to replenish our cruising funds. Larry could do wood repairs or splice rigging. Quite often owners of large yachts wanted their boats moved across an ocean and didn't have enough spare time so paid us to deliver their yachts for them. As long as we kept our expenses low and some money in our cruising emergency fund, we always seemed to find interesting work when we needed it. "I guess having to work as we go makes our whole life more interesting. If we never had to think of earning money it would all seem too easy," I said to Larry. "I wonder where we'll moor the boat. There seem to be lots of places to go for a daysail. Hope the markets have some interesting foods." Larry took over the daydreaming, "Wonder if there'll be any cruiser races we can take *Seraffyn* in. Hope there's a good library and some English movies."

He finally went below to sleep. The lights of Trafalgar passed quickly by during the misty night prompting Larry to comment, "Nelson's ghosts must be nearby," as we changed places at 0200. It was my watch when the first gray of dawn showed on the horizon. Since there were no ships around, I began tidying up inside the boat and made a cup of tea as *Seraffyn* ran smartly along. The sky turned to a rosy glow. I climbed on deck, tea in hand, and almost gasped in awe. The sun rose slowly, a majestic red globe, perfectly framed on one side by Europe, on the other by Africa. "Larry, come on deck," I called. He sleepily climbed into the cockpit. We watched in quiet warm companionship as the sun seemed to beckon *Seraffyn* toward the new adventures waiting for us in the Mediterranean.

Glossary

boom gallows: A metal and wood structure on the afterdeck that supports the main boom when it is not in use.

carlin: A fore-and-aft structural member of the deck framing.

channel: A wooden strut over which the chainplates pass so that the shrouds do not crush against the bulwarks.

drop boards: Stout wooden boards that are dropped into a slot to close off the companionway.

Force 8 to 9: Wind speeds of thirty-four to forty-seven knots.

head: See loo.

heaving to, hove to: A way of stopping the boat's forward motion so that she lies at an angle of about fifty degrees off the wind and creates a wide wake or slick water on her windward side; this action can be taken to wait for a change in the tide, to rest, or to be safe during a storm.

Helmer: The name of *Seraffyn*'s wind-activated self-steering gear.

lapper: A small genoa that just reaches aft of the mast when sheeted tight in.

lazy jacks: A set of lines secured on both sides of the boom which serve not only as double topping lifts but keep the mainsail from falling all over the cockpit and helmsman when it is dropped; usually found on gaff-rigged vessels.

loo: A marine toilet, often called a head, an object of much discussion and many bad jokes on board cruising yachts.

quay: An English name for any dock to which a ship or boat may tie.

Rinky, alias *Rinky Dink* (*Wrinkles* when she needs a paint job): The six-foot eight-inch pram-style Montgomery dinghy we use as a tender to *Seraffyn;* the dinghy was originally christened *Rubicon* but that seemed a bit grandiose.

scope: The ratio of the length of anchor chain let out to the depth of water the boat is anchoring in; a scope of five to one is our minimum for strong winds in anchorages with good holding ground (chain doesn't do you any good in the chain locker).

telltails: Twelve-inch lengths of nylon yarn that are attached to the shrouds and backstay to serve as wind direction indicators; total cost for a ten-year supply—fifty cents; cost for one electronic wind direction indicator—one hundred and fifty dollars.

wing and wing: To run with the mainsail on one side of the boat, the jib on a pole to the other side; our favorite course, dead downwind.

APPENDICES

~~~~~

The Idea Is Freedom

"How can the two of you live on a twenty-four-foot boat for eight years?"

"Isn't *Seraffyn* a bit small for safe extended cruising?"

"Don't you miss the comforts you could have on a thirty-five-footer?"

The only other question we've heard as often as these is "How can you afford to cruise around like you do? Where do you get the money?"

Two basic questions—size and money. The answers are simple. We chose between the physical luxuries of a big boat and the freedom of a small one.

But we're not the only people who choose to cruise in a small boat. Gordon and Annabelle Yates are now enjoying their fourth year on board twenty-eight-foot *Amøbel*. Nick Skeates is approaching Australia after three years of cruising from England on twenty-nine-foot *Wylo*. The Hiscocks sailed for ten years and one hundred ten thousand miles on thirty-foot *Wanderer III*. When we think of the cruising friends we've met in the past eight years, one fact becomes obvious. Most people who cruise away from home waters year in and year out, living on money they earn before they leave or as they cruise, have small yachts. By small we mean thirty-two feet or under. Even those with private incomes who cruise year in and year out usually choose boats around thirty-five feet on deck.

Cruising Represents Freedom—Small Boats Ensure Freedom

If we had waited until we could afford a forty-five foot yacht and all its luxuries, we might never have gone cruising. Yachts of any size are expensive. The bigger they are, the more they cost. A quick walk around any boat show will prove the difference between a twenty-eight-footer and a forty-five-footer. Then comes outfitting. We have taken a cost survey, asking people who are currently cruising away from home for a minimum of twelve months to fill out our questionnaire. So far, thirty-eight cruiser from eight different countries have obliged. Some of these people have been cruising as long as ten years on their present boat. Every one of them listed outfitting as costing an additional twenty-five percent above and beyond the purchase or construction price of their boat, be it new or secondhand. So, if you pay sixty-thousand dollars for your boat, you'll spend an additional fifteen-thousand dollars getting it ready for offshore work. If you buy a thirty-footer for thirty-thousand dollars, outfitting will be seventy-five-hundred. Since we have no private income, we equate money with time off. The difference between the outfitted forty-five footer and the outfitted thirty-footer means starting to cruise years sooner, or having money for extra years of cruising. We are willing to give up a lot of physical luxuries for all those years of freedom.

Someone is bound to counter that statement by saying, "I'm handy with tools. I can buy a forty-five-foot hull and finish and outfit it myself for twenty-five-thousand dollars." If the expenses of cruising ended right after purchasing and outfitting your boat, we'd say, "Great, have at it." But they don't. The survey answers proved that cruising expenses are directly related to size. The fifteen families who cruised for over two years on boats thirty-three feet and under (five of these listed private incomes) had monthly expenditures of a hundred-fifty to three-hundred-fifty dollars with an average of two-hundred-fifty dollars. The twenty-two people on boats from thirty-four to forty-nine feet (fourteen of these listed private incomes) had monthly expenses ranging from two-hundred-fifty to a thousand dollars a month with an average of four-hundred-fifteen dollars. Displacement seemed to have little effect on monthly expenses; they always related to length on deck.

*See update, page 313.

Everything costs more for the larger boat. Mooring fees are charged by the foot. Cruising permits (an unhappily expanding custom) cost according to size. Hauling, gear, and equipment costs depend on boat size. And finally, human nature being what it is, tradesmen and suppliers identify with the man on a small boat. But they see a forty-five-footer and assume the owner must be rich, so *they* charge accordingly.

Can You Handle It?

Any reasonably healthy couple, no matter what their ages, can handle a forty-five-foot yacht in average conditions with the aid of an engine. As long as there are enough winches and a bit of forethought, people can sail seventy-footers alone. The Observer Single-handed Transatlantic Race proves this. But cruising year in and year out is not like taking one dash across the Atlantic, with only one harbor to enter. When a couple are cruising for pleasure they will each have to handle the boat single-handed at times, if only during night watches. They'll have to take care of the boat and themselves in storm conditions and while entering strange harbors time and time again. Since engines are not infallible, long-term-cruising people are occasionally going to be forced to short-tack into some strange harbor under sail alone. On a thirty-footer it's a pleasant challenge; on a forty-five-footer it's plain hard work.

Although we've often heard that sail area is the limiting factor as to the size of boat two people can handle, cruising has proved to us that it's in harbor that a boat's size matters. If all hell breaks loose at sea, it's not too difficult to heave to and wait it out. But when a fifty-knot squall blows through your anchorage and dislodges your ground tackle, either you or your spouse may have to set another anchor or get the first one up—quick and alone. The thirty-five-pound anchor on a twenty-eight-footer is all I'd want to handle, the seventy-five-pounder on the forty-five-footer is far beyond my (Lin's) capability, especially when the motion and emergency factors are added to the equation. Even more frightening, but an event that unfortunately happens too often when you are cruising, is when that same squall catches you lying against a dock or seawall. The chop builds up in the harbor. Your fenders start popping out of place, leaving your handsome, vulnerable topsides exposed, four inches from a grinding pier.

While you are struggling to push your boat away from the wall so you can put in another fender, consider what size boat you really want to cruise in. Our criteria for the absolute maximum size we'd enjoy is one that either of us could shove off a pier against a thirty-five-knot beam wind while the other ran to secure another mooring line or set a beam anchor. We've worked around yachts for thirteen years together and cruised for over nine. We've delivered yachts ranging from thirty-five feet to fifty-four feet, and I'm convinced that our safe limit based on harbor criteria is thirty-two feet on deck.

Often people in forty-five-footers seem to have lost the joy of sailing. Yes, they still make passages mostly under sail, but they rarely seem to go "out for a day sail." Once again, this is caused by the problem of handling the big boat. It's too much work to lift a forty-five-footer's anchor and set its sails just for a cruise around the harbor. Then, to make it worse, designers and builders of many of today's production cruising boats have sold people on the idea of forty-five-footers by saying, "You can handle it—only seven hundred square feet of sail area, less than four hundred feet in the mainsail." The boat is vastly underrigged, so it moves like a monument in anything under ten knots of wind. Not much fun for sailing. We've found that sailboats that are a joy in light winds (three to eight knots) usually have eighty to eighty-five square feet of working sail area (jib and mainsail) for every ton of weight. It's sail area that drives a sailboat. Light-weather racing machines like *Windward Passage, Ondine,* and Holland half-tonners have as much as one hundred five square feet of working sail area per ton, and this doesn't include genoas, spinnakers, and so on. At the other end of the scale is the Tahiti ketch, known for its slow passages in anything less than fifteen knots of wind. It has fifty-five square feet of canvas for each ton of weight. To get good light-weather performance on a forty-five-footer you need big sails. These sails are more than two people can easily handle. That's why thirty- to thirty-five-foot boats finished well ahead of forty-five- to fifty-footers in the last two-man Round-Britain Race and swept the fleet handicap prizes.

Safety

No boat, no matter what its size, is safe without good seamanship. The ability to make the right decision, the ability to handle the boat in all conditions, the ability to maintain your equipment so it's ready at all times—these determine a boat's safety. When it comes to storm conditions, no boat is really comfortable no matter what its size, but the man on the thirty-footer might have one advantage. Because his gear will be smaller and easier to manhandle, be it storm trysail, sea anchor, warps, he might be ready to take preventative measures sooner. Because of his boat's smaller size and generally shallower draft, the man on the thirty-footer would probably find more places of refuge available to him than the man on the forty-five-footer. Yes, the small-boat sailor will have to think twice before choosing to round the Horn or take a winter passage. He may choose to lay in port and wait out a gale the man in a forty-five-footer may challenge. But prudence and good seamanship, not the boat's size, are where safety lies.

The Question Is Comfort

Yes, I'd sometimes like the physical luxuries of a forty-five-foot yacht—an enclosed shower, a powered anchor winch, hot water, refrigeration. But from delivering big yachts we've learned that each of these items not only requires constant maintenance but seems to break down just when you want it. When you are tied up in a marina for four months trying to get repairs done, waiting out winter gales, or working to earn money for your cruise, even a forty-five-footer is a poor excuse for an apartment. The fun of cruising is going places, meeting people, making new landfalls. When you are on the move, the smallest boat is a joy.

It all comes down to deciding what comfort is. To us, it means being free to go. The reason we can afford to go is because of *Seraffyn*'s small size. By working three months each year, we can have nine months of freedom. Because of her low maintenance costs, we have the "comfort" of extra money to explore inland in the countries we visit, money to take a shoreside apartment for three or four months if a winter turns cold, wet, and miserable. We have the "comfort" of being able to buy the very best equipment for *Seraffyn*. If we want an anchor, it will cost about eighty dollars for the finest twenty-five-pound CQR. The seventy-five-pounder needed for a forty-five-foot yacht is three hundred dollars (Malta prices, 1977). Since we can afford the best equipment and can be sure *Seraffyn* is well maintained from masthead to keel, we have the mental "comfort" of confidence.

We know we can push *Seraffyn* to her sailing limit if it becomes necessary. And we are "comforted" by the knowledge that either one of us can handle her in almost any situation.

There may come a time, no matter how much we are enjoying the cruising life, when we need to move into a community ashore. Twenty-four-foot *Seraffyn* has one final advantage—she's not such a big investment that we'll have to sell her. We can put her on a mooring while we rejoin society. And there she can be used as a weekender, waiting patiently until we again get the urge to wander.

Come on, join the wonderful community of long-distance cruising people. If you have a small boat now, look it over and consider ways to make it more comfortable, seaworthy, and fun to sail. If you are trying to find a boat, don't be trapped by the glitter of the forty-five-footers. Their glamor soon palls when you are broke or covered with sweat and grease from working in the engine room trying to keep those luxuries functional, while the folks on the twenty-eight-footer astern of you are free to wander ashore or set off for an afternoon sail.

We received a letter from two of the most experienced cruising people afloat, Eric and Susan Hiscock, cruising New Zealand's waters on *Wanderer IV* (January 13, 1977). Their comments sum it up well:

> To judge by the many people we have met during our recent world voyage, I would say that it is those in the smaller vessels, simply but efficiently equipped, who get the greatest pleasure and satisfaction. (We . . . met *Wanderer III;* she came sailing into Taiohae Bay while we were there, and was the only one of many that did *sail* in.) With the small-boat people, as with ourselves still, although we now have so vast a ship, I would say that they prove the point: "It is better to travel hopefully than to arrive." The owners of larger, more sophisticated craft tend to regard their yachts as most people do cars, i.e., as a means of getting themselves from one glamor spot or tourist attraction to another in the greatest possible comfort and the least possible inconvenience, and with safety as a high priority. . . . So you see, my thoughts on this matter are much like your own.

The whole idea is freedom. Go small, go simple, go now!

The Small Boats

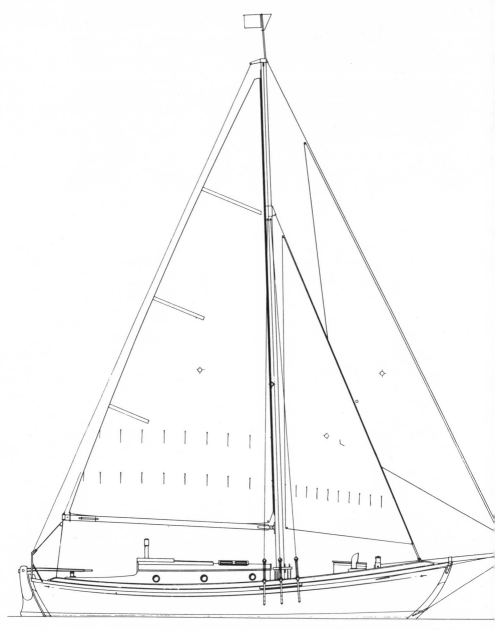

Kion Dee, sail plan. *François Graeser*

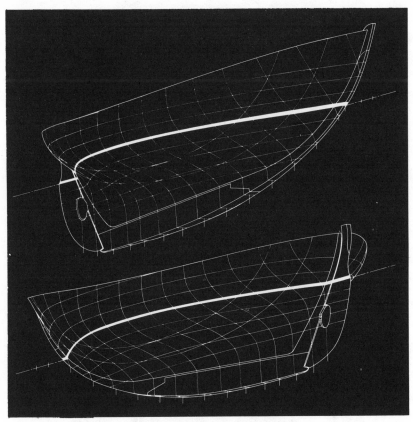

Kion Dee, **hull design.** *François Graeser*

KION DEE

Owned by: François and Rosemary Graeser

Designer: François Graeser N.A.
Ch. de Bellerive 19
1007 Lausanne, Switzerland

Built of wood by owner

Length: 26' on deck
Beam: 9' 1"
Draft: 4' 3"
Displacement: 8,000 lbs.
Ballast: 2,400 lbs.
Rig: cutter
Working sail area: 323 square feet

Maximum sail area: 440 square feet
Spars: wood
Whisker poles: alloy
Rudder: outboard
Self-steering: self-made, trim-tab type
on main rudder
Dinghy: inflatable

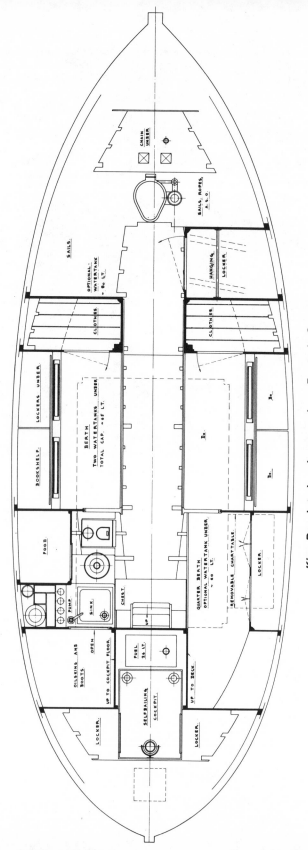

Kion Dee, interior plan, top view. *François Graeser*

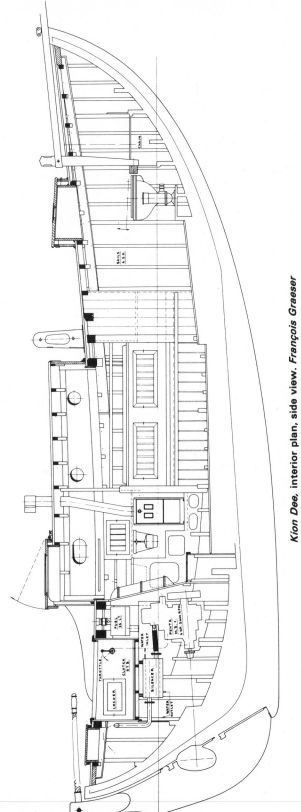

Kion Dee, interior plan, side view. *François Graeser*

François Graeser, black-bearded, six foot four inches tall, and slim, is a serious, prudent sailor with a vast technical knowledge and skill in yacht design and drafting. He is the physical opposite of his tiny, laughing, fondue-cooking wife Rosemary, and the two of them could often be seen sharing long walks ashore in Gibraltar and José Banus, Spain, where we came to know them well. François would stride along with Rosemary's legs doing two steps for each of his long ones.

Kion Dee, teak-hulled, classic-looking double-ended cutter, is our favorite cruising boat next to *Seraffyn*. She was built piece by piece by her designer who then trucked her down from Lake Zurich, Switzerland, to her natural element, salt water. The Graesers spent three years cruising Europe, covering over five thousand miles. By living, sailing, and cruising on *Kion Dee*, François tested his own design in a thorough, long-term way few cruising yacht designers can ever dream of.

Lin and I first looked over *Kion Dee* when we arrived in Gibralter. We liked her because she had small port lights; a low profile; strong sea-going deckhouse; bulwarks and teak decks for safety; lots of anchor chain; a hand-operated anchor winch; an easy-to-remove outboard rudder which facilitated a simple but effective trim-tab type windvane; a generous beam, which gave her a good motion at sea and added volume below to carry all the food, water, and spares that are vital to a cruising yacht; a long, triangular keel profile which allows her to tack with ease; good windward performance with her efficient rig; a simple hand-start single-cylinder Volvo diesel without any electrics; and oil lamps for navigation and cabin lamps. (Both *Kion Dee* and *Seraffyn* are without electrics and neither suffers from any electrolysis.)

Kion Dee's interior is very traditional for small yachts of about twenty-six feet, fine for two people who plan on a lot of ocean work and spartan cooking. The small galley with one burner and no oven is enough at sea, but for a couple living on board and cooking three meals a day, it is (in our opinion) too spartan. I also know that most couples who live on yachts these days demand a double bunk to use in port. This could be added to *Kion Dee*'s fo'c'sle.

Two of my previous keelboats were double-enders similar to *Kion Dee* and I don't have any strong feelings for or against double-enders or transom yachts for cruising. With a wide-sterned transom yacht I might want to heave-to a bit sooner than I would with a double-ender. But on the other hand, I do like the security of the wide decks aft with boom gallows, stanchions, and lifelines out in the quarters as is possible on a transom-sterned yacht. The boom gallows frame is a great place to hang onto in any kind of weather. The double-ender is harder to plank when it comes to fitting and bending the after ends of the topside planks. The transom-sterned yacht is slightly weaker in the quarters or fashion timber area. The double-ended hull form, with its similar waterline shapes fore and aft, is generally considered easier to steer and balance, although not so fast to windward as the transom-sterned yacht. I am not convinced that the double-ender is any more seaworthy than a transom-sterned yacht—both types have been pooped while running too long before heavy seas. It's simply a matter of personal preference, since both types have their good points and not-so-good points, just like two automobiles, one with rear-end drive the other with front-wheel drive.

The only drawback to a custom-designed, nonproduction yacht like *Kion Dee* is that you can't order one from Sears and Roebuck for next-week delivery. The only way to get a yacht built to your personal specifications is to build it yourself or to contract with a boatyard. The first method requires hard, meticulous work and is time-consuming. The second also takes time and is usually expensive. But the rewards are well worthwhile if you end up with a yacht like *Kion Dee*.

The *Kion Dee* under construction. *François Graeser*

The *Kion Dee* is double-planked of teak set in Resorcinal glue with double-sawn frames of acacia (locust). Her backbone is iroko, and, held by silicon-bronze fastenings, she should be good for fifty years or more. *François Graeser*

The good little ship at rest in Barcelona, Spain. *François Graeser*

The *Kion Dee* running at hull speed in the Golf de Lyons. Note the nice bulwarks and the beautiful teak decks, with plenty of space for easy sail handling. *François Graeser*

A clean wake and a well-cut, light genoa. *François Graeser*

François put on the dodger so he could have headroom in the chart table–galley area. Note the boathooks which double as handrails on the cabin top.

Kion Dee and the first mate, Rosemary.

Careened upriver to clean and paint the bottom. *François Graeser*

François is the physical opposite of his tiny, laughing, fondue-cooking wife Rosemary.

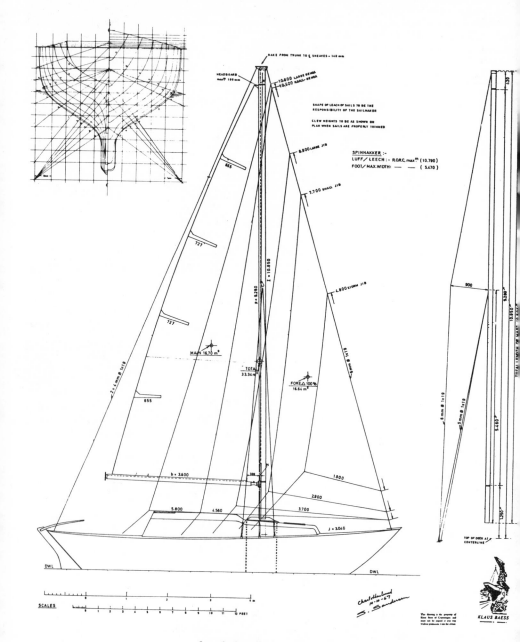

Amøbel, sail plan. Klaus Baess

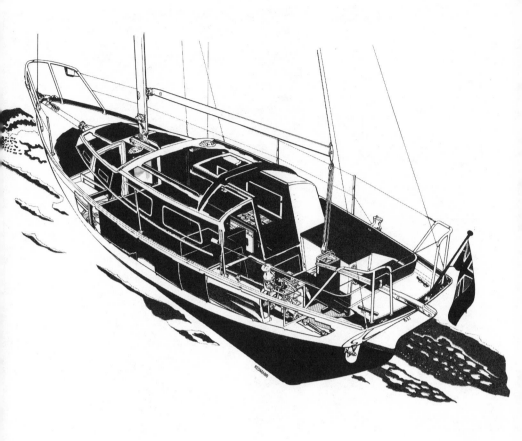

AMØBEL, Great Dane 28

Owned by: Annabelle and Gordon Yates

Designer: Aage Utson
c/o Baess Boats
21 Livjaegergade
DK 2100 Copenhagen
Denmark

Built of fiberglass by Klaus Baess, Copenhagen, Denmark

Length: 28' on deck
Beam: 8' 3"
Draft: 5' 0"
Displacement: 8,500 lbs.
Ballast: 4,000 lbs.
Rig: masthead sloop

Mainsail: 167 square feet
Jib: 166 square feet
Spars: alloy
Rudder: outboard
Self-steering: QM (cost: $300)
Dinghy: inflatable

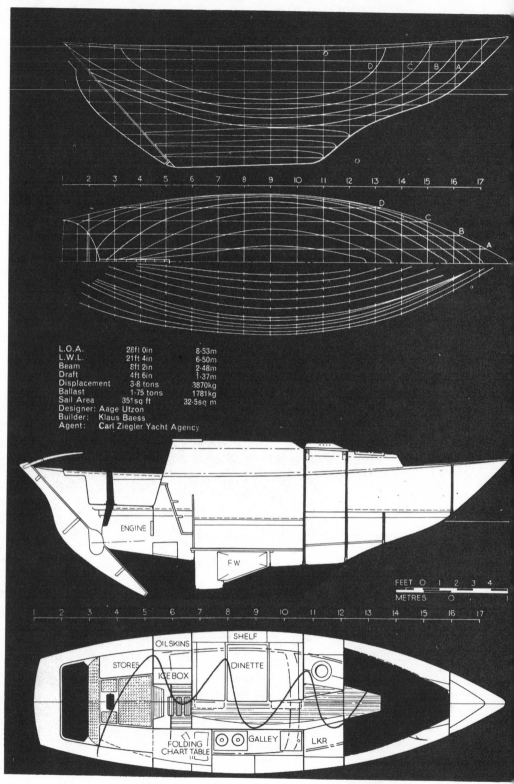

L.O.A.	28ft 0in	8·53m
L.W.L.	21ft 4in	6·50m
Beam	8ft 2in	2·48m
Draft	4ft 6in	1·37m
Displacement	3·8 tons	3870kg
Ballast	1·75 tons	1781kg
Sail Area	351sq ft	32·5sq m
Designer: Aage Utzon		
Builder: Klaus Baess		
Agent: Carl Ziegler Yacht Agency		

Amøbel, **hull design and interior plans.** *Yachting World*

Nine years ago we sailed into La Paz, Baja California, in Mexico. As soon as we'd anchored, Gordon and Annabelle Yates rowed over in a black Avon dinghy. "Welcome to La Paz," they chimed and then proceeded to answer all of our questions: where to buy beer by the case, which restaurant had the best combination plate *(cielo Azul)* where to buy Mexican brandy ($1.10 a bottle). The four of us formed a fast friendship, sampling the restaurants in the evenings and sharing quantities of beer during the day while we talked of anchors, windvanes, Vietnam, politics, cruising Baja. Annabelle and Lin talked about how to cook shellfish and Spanish mackerel, about galley arrangements, buckets, husbands, children, and mothers-in-law. There was hardly a subject the four of us didn't tackle in the eight months we cruised the Sea of Cortez.

Gordon, a civil engineer, had designed and built his own trim-tab type self-steering gear. In Acapulco he solved Helmer's main problem, showing me how to rig a differential in my linkage between the windvane and trim tab. Since Acapulco, Helmer has steered *Seraffyn* beautifully for over twenty-four thousand miles. Thanks, Gordy!

Annabelle and Gordon are an unusually determined couple. They raised five children and then, at the age of fifty, were both still mentally and physically flexible enough to adapt to the rigors of small-boat cruising. They had kicked the steady job habit and gone cruising a year before we did.

We asked Gordon to write about his three boats:

First, in Las Vegas, Nevada, I built a thirty-foot Piver trimaran which later tried to capsize us twice. In 1967, we sailed from Los Angeles to within six hundred miles of Hawaii where Captain Dittler on the U.S. naval vessel *Prairie* rescued us. [The Yateses hit a freak storm and had been hove-to for several days when Captain Dittler spotted them and offered assistance, lifting the trimaran on deck and taking them to San Diego, California.] We fixed up and sailed the Mexican coast as far as Acapulco, where I lost my nerve. I had to get a good boat.

We flew to Annapolis in 1970 and bought a twenty-two-foot Cirrus, *Amøbel II*. We sailed down to, across, and around Florida and the Bahamas. The Cirrus was too small. No way could she carry enough to cross an ocean. We sold her but we are still wistful. She was so close-winded and cozy.

We flew to Copenhagen in 1973 and bought a Great Dane 28. Larry had said, "Folkboats are okay," so we got the closest boat to it with room for an engine and a head. Annabelle would not go for a "bucket and chuck it." I was too old to wait out in front of ports wishing for wind. Larry was worried about my buying a stock boat, but "time's a-wastin' " so we got it and learned "What's hidden is either not there, loose, or iron." In *Amøbel* we sailed to England, Madeira, Tenerife, Barbados, Tortola, Panama, and north to San Francisco in 1975. Our total time logged at sea in ten years is eighty-five hundred hours.

Twenty-eight-foot *Amøbel* is a fiberglass, full-keel, outboard-rudder, masthead sloop. Loaded for an ocean crossing with a ton of stuff, including two fearful old sailors, she is one inch below her scribed waterline. She has four thousand pounds of sealed-in lead ballast, with a quick, five-second roll that snaps the buttons off my shirt. She has four diesel horsepower per ton, which is what is needed to go north up the West Coast from Panama. Her galley should be at the center of motion on the port side; where it's now located, *Amøbel* can throw soup out of the pot. I think her windows should be smaller, but she dances up and over the seas and has never scooped up green water. QM self-steering rules her (cost: $300).

Gordon Yates, skipper of *Amøbel*. Phil Lum

Amøbel's owners and crew,
Gordon and Annabelle Yates.
Phil Lum

Annabelle
and her galley.
Phil Lum

A Great Dane 28 fitted out for cruising.
Note the reef points—two in the mainsail
and one in the jib—the windvane, and the
CQR anchor ready to go over if needed.
Phil Lum

In a second letter Gordon writes about *Amøbel*'s handling, anchoring, and motion at sea:

> First the good things: anchoring and docking, she works under main only, dinghy-like. She steers herself to weather under working sails or main only. I kill time waiting for dawn or the tide under main; with helm tied to weather, she tends herself on a slow beat. In a gale she slowly works to windward under deep-reefed main and self-steering. Bob Burn of GD-28 *Blue Gypsy* heaves to by sheeting his boom to weather. QM steers her downwind with main (vanged and prevented) plus poled-out jib. In a stronger wind the heavy-weather jib sheeted amidships dampens rolling. Her full keel and outboard rudder shed kelp, fishnets, and anchor rodes.
>
> Bad things: at anchor she charges about like a bull. [Because of her motion] she broke one of my ribs in the English Channel, making me tend her with one arm till Madeira. In light wind she snaps the air out of her genoa, which bugs me.

Gordon's comment about *Amøbel*'s whippy motion is a familiar complaint of owners with highly ballasted (forty-six percent for *Amøbel*) high-freeboard, high-cabined, light- to medium-displacement yachts. The lightweight hull will initially heel quickly and easily until the tremendous amount of lead jerks the heeling movement to a stop, giving the "button-snapping motion" Gordon speaks of.

The cutaway forefoot and full bow sections would probably be the cause of her restlessness at anchor. When a gust of wind hits her bow she has no depth or sharpness of forefoot to grip the water and stop her from falling off and charging around. An all-chain anchor rode can often help prevent this problem because of its weight and drag on the bottom.

If you plan on living afloat and cruising full time, your interior layout should (1) be comfortable and convenient in port, and (2) comfortable and convenient at sea. The facts are that most people who call their yacht "home" spend only ten percent of the hours in any cruising year actually sailing or at sea. *Amøbel*'s layout is good for an eight-foot two-inch by twenty-eight-foot yacht. The forward area has been converted to a double for a separate shoreside bunk that is always ready for use, if only just to lay down on to read a book for a couple of hours. You don't have to make it up each time you want to use it. If one of you wants to go to bed early, it's ready and you won't disturb anyone in the main salon. Across from the loo, Gordon and Annabelle have installed a solid-fuel central heater which is great for cool winter nights in the San Francisco Bay area where they are now cruising.

Lin and I have delivered a number of new yachts with the dinette-type table and find it great in port. At sea you need something to hold plates and cups secure, but this is true with all fixed tables. If something on the dinette table in *Amøbel* does spill, it will usually go to port or starboard, not on the eater. With the more common fore and aft table and settees, you have a fifty-fifty chance of hot soup or coffee on your lap.

The quarter berth on the starboard side would be a good sea berth with one person on watch, one in the bunk.

The Great Dane 28 is a fiberglass production boat and you can get one quickly, outfit it, and be off cruising without too much cost, too much waiting, or too much personal labor. As Gordy says, "Time's a-wastin'."

GD 28 fitted out for racing or local cruising. *Klaus Baess*

NORDISKA FOLKBÅTEN

Construction and Arrangement Plans

A Norwegian Folkboat, side and top views. *SNAME Transactions*

A Folkboat, the F-117, out cruising. *SNAME Transactions*

FOLKBOAT

Original Nordic Folkboat designed by Jac N. Iverson of Stockholm and
Tore Sunden of Gothenberg

Built of wood, various builders

Length: 25' 1"
Beam: 7' 2 1/2"
Draft: 3' 11"
Displacement: 5,000 lbs.
Ballast: 2,000 lbs.

Rig: three-quarter sloop
Sail area: 235 square feet
Spars: wood
Rudder: outboard
Dinghy: inflatable

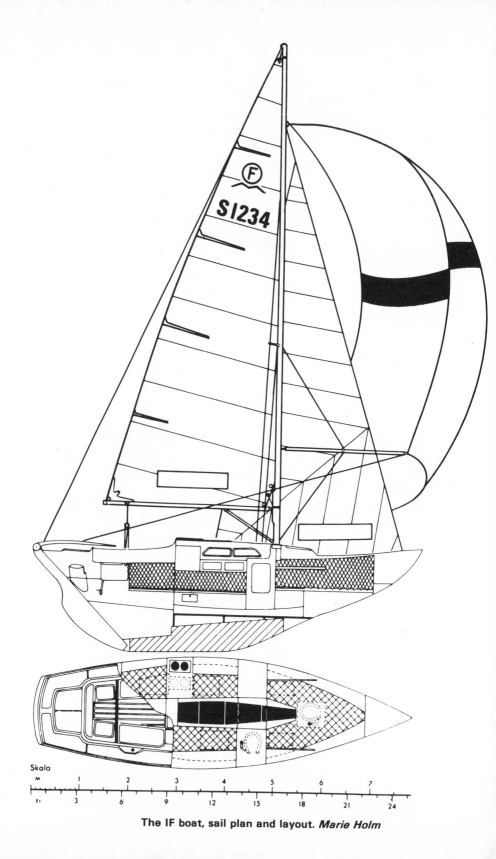

Skala

The IF boat, sail plan and layout. *Marie Holm*

IF BOAT

Designer: Jac Iverson

Built of fiberglass by: Marieholms Bruck AB
                          330 33 Hillerstrod
                          Sweden

Length: 26′ 0″	**Mainsail:** 160 square feet
Beam: 7′ 4″	**Jib:** 100 square feet
Draft: 4′ 0″	**Genoa:** 150 square feet
Displacement: 4,800 lbs.	**Spars:** alloy
Ballast: 2,425 lbs.	**Rudder:** outboard
Rig: seven-eights sloop	**Dinghy:** inflatable

"I say, if I were young, I would get a Folkboat, a sweep, drink my beer warm, and go." We quote Gordon Yates.

The Folkboat is also my stock answer for young would-be cruisers. The Folkboat is easy to handle, it's cheap, it's easy to fit with a wind-vane, and with a few modifications it can be outfitted to sail the Atlantic.

Folkboats were designed in 1948 to be inexpensive. In fact, Folkboat means "people's boat" and is yachting's answer to the Volkswagen. Many of the older wooden ones can be bought quite cheaply, depending on condition. The newer fiberglass versions are reasonably priced since the Folkboat is of moderate displacement and new sailboats can be priced like beefsteak, so much a pound.

I have always liked the Folkboat since I saw *Bambi,* in the West Vancouver Yacht Club in 1959, twenty years ago. She was an original lapstrake Folkboat with low freeboard, a sweet sheer, and modest overhangs. At times I'm wistful and wish she had been for sale because somehow I would have found the money and bought her. As it was, I took ten years to get organized, build *Seraffyn,* and save some money for the insurance fund and cruising fund. *Bambi* and I could have been away at least five years earlier. But the Folkboat is a minimal cruiser for two, or three in a severe pinch. Carrying enough food and water is always a problem in a small boat, and to cruise in a Folkboat extensively you can't afford the space and weight an inboard motor takes. A small outboard, or a sweep or sculling oar will stretch your Folkboat's interior and keep the load waterline in sight. The Folkboat, with its small three-quarter rig, loses light-weather performance rapidly if she is overloaded. Most of the older wooden versions were built without self-draining cockpits. A self-draining cockpit is a necessity for extended cruising.

Bill Isreal, saved his money while working in an electronics factory and bought a secondhand wooden Folkboat, then modified it for long-distance cruising. He sailed from California, down the coast of Mexico to Costa Rica, single-handed, taking over a year for his voyage. Bill removed his Folkboat's cockpit seats and flush-decked the area aft of the cabin. This gave him enormous storage space below plus the extra stiffening and strength of full-width deck beams and decking. He remarked that the deep cockpit was not necessary for protection from wind and rain as he stayed below during rough weather, letting his windvane do the steering, and only came on his large uncluttered afterdeck to reef or change sails, or steer into harbor.

He used a three-horsepower outboard motor on a small rubber dinghy for his tender. With this tied alongside his Folkboat, he could maneuver in harbor or move along in a calm at about three knots.

Bill paid about twenty-five hundred dollars for his older lapstrake Folkboat, then spent about fifteen hundred more for his sextant, radio receiver, extra anchors, and afterdeck modifications. For four thousand dollars he had a nice mini-cruiser. Bill said he longed for a masthead, light-weather genoa to increase his sail area for light winds.

In Falmouth we met Ingrid and Khristian Lagerkrantz, a young Swedish couple who planned to sail to Yugoslavia to research Khristian's master's thesis on the anthropology of the island people. Ingrid managed to get a year off from her job as a criminologist to sail on their Swedish-built IF boat which they planned to use as both accommodation and transportation once they reached the Dalmatian coast. As Khristian said to us, "Yes, she is a small boat, but as students we could not afford to live and travel in the many islands without our little moving home." The Lagenkrantzes had sailed their Folkboat from Stockholm to Falmouth, then from Falmouth to Bayona, Spain, and from there down the coast of Portugal to Gibraltar, where we lost track of the tiny scientific sailboat. (We assume they arrived in the Dalmatian Islands although we have not heard a word since Gibraltar.)

The IF (International Folkboat) is built of fiberglass, designed by Jac Iverson, and is an attractive production yacht. It has a self-draining cockpit, a longer trunk cabin, and more living space below than the original Folkboat. No major modifications are necessary to set off cruising in an IF boat. And you can continue to enjoy it even after you return home. You can race in the IF boat fleet in your area.

In Gibraltar we met another Folkboat owned by three jolly English boys. Barry Hollis worked as a yacht rigger at Moody's Shipyard on the Hamble River, Will Keech was employed at Blake's galvanizing plant (both of these jobs showed in the fine outfitting of *Piratical Pipet*), and the third, Gordon Butler, worked as ship's accountant. All were in their early twenties and while they were in Gibraltar contracted to lay tiles in new apartments to replenish their cruising funds. The three were avid dinghy sailors who had pooled their resources to buy *Piratical Pipet* and outfit her for a total cost of twenty-nine hundred dollars (1973–74), including new spars and six new sails. Even though the little carvel-planked Folkboat was thirteen years old and they had sailed her hard down from the United Kingdom by way of northern Spain and Portugal, she looked almost like new.

The boys had changed the interior of *Piratical Pipet* completely by installing a galvanized tabernacle to replace the main bulkhead. This gave them an open, more spacious interior, allowing space for two quarter berths and a settee for the three average-sized crew. On a basically ultra-simple yacht without motor, they used oil lamps and a sculling oar with which muscular Barry could move *P.P.* at about one and a half knots. When they modified the rig from the original three-quarter sloop to masthead sloop, they "reduced the sail area for cruising." They all agreed this was their only mistake. They wished for a larger rig than the original Folkboat for the light winds they encountered. With jiffy reefing, shortening sail could have been simple. But even so, *Piratical Pipet* sailed so well in the cruiser races in Gibraltar that the boys had a few of the local IOR boats worried.

The last we heard, Gordon had acquired Barry's and Will's shares of *P.P.* and was cruising southern Spain with a girl crew. Barry was professional skipper on a sixty-one-foot American yacht and Will was last seen bound from Palma Majorca on a large charter yacht.

These three different crews on their modified Folkboats were having a great time. They were seeing and enjoying the same sights, the same beautiful harbors, the same interesting people as the crews on the large yachts anchored next to them.

Piratical Pipit's chart table is folded down by Gordon Butler, one of *P.P.*'s three owners. The pipe tabernacle near the mast is in place of a bulkhead.

Piratical Pipit has fairly narrow side decks and a Perspex fore hatch.

Piratical Pipit is a much-modified folkboat. The carvel planking and a large cabin are the most obvious changes from the original folkboat designs. Note the combination port and starboard oil lamp on the pulpit.

Gordon with his seven-dollar "outboard motor." *Piratical Pipit*'s windvane is of the horizontal-axis, or QME, type. The Rock of Gibraltar is to starboard.

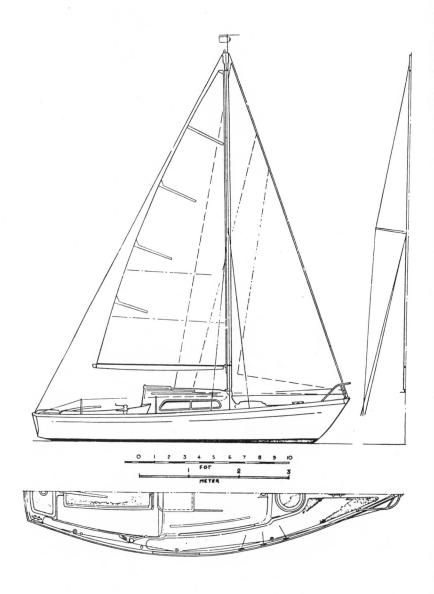

Optimist, sail plan drawing. *E. G. van de Stadt*

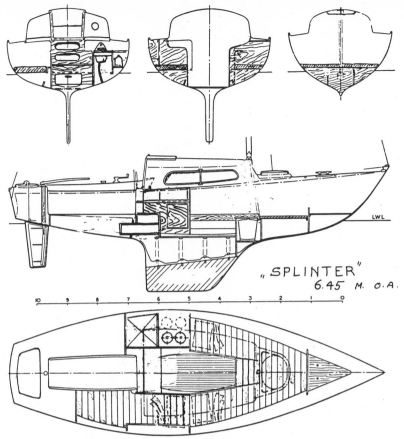

„SPLINTER"
6.45 M. O.A.

Optimist, interior views. *E. G. van de Stadt*

OPTIMIST

Owned by: Svend Kaae

Splinter class fiberglass sloop
Designer: E. G. van de Stadt
　　　　　 Scheepswerf N.V.
　　　　　 Zanndam, Holland

Built of fiberglass by G. Stead
　　　　　　　　　　　 Poole, Dorset, England

Length: 21'
Beam: 6' 3"
Draft: 3' 9"
Displacement: 1,760 lbs.
Ballast: 800 lbs.
Rig: masthead sloop
Mainsail: 90 square feet
Jib: 80 square feet

Genoa: 115 square feet
Storm jib: 45 square feet
Spars: alloy
Rudder: inboard
Self-steering: homemade, much like
　 QME
Dinghy: inflatable

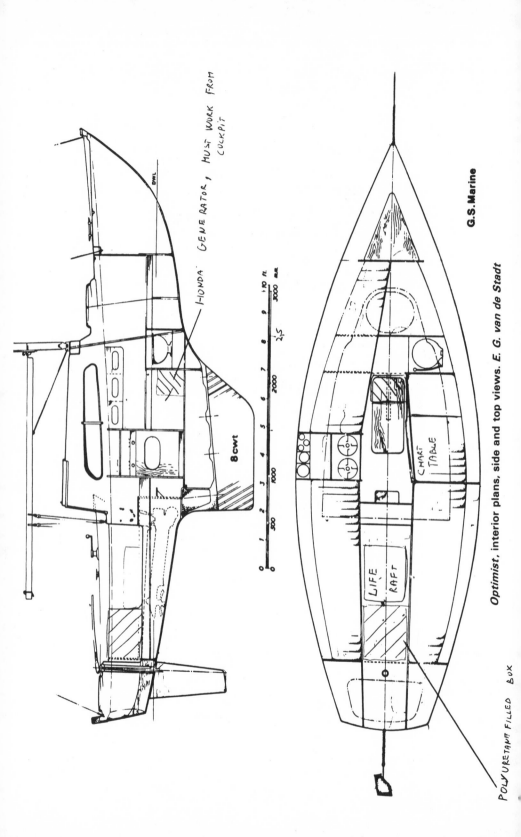

'HONDA' GENERATOR, MUST WORK FROM COCKPIT

DWL

8 cwt

| | | | | | | | | | | |
|0|1|2|3|4|5|6|7|8|9|10 ft.|

500 1000 2000 3000 mm

2,5

POLYURETHANE FILLED BOX

LIFE RAFT

CHART TABLE

G.S.Marine

Optimist, interior plans, side and top views. E. G. van de Stadt

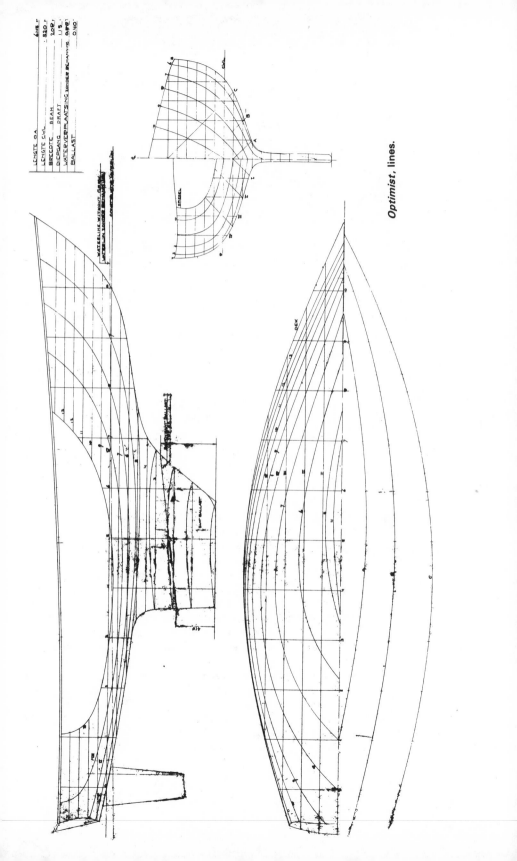

Optimist, lines.

Svend Kaae rowing his inflatible back to *Optimist*, Bayona Harbor, Spain.

Optimist is not Svend Kaae's permanent home, probably because Svend is six foot three and weighs 190 pounds and his yacht measures only twenty-one feet overall. But *Optimist*'s size has not stopped Svend from making various single-handed voyages from his home and job in Aarhus, Denmark—including a circumnavigation of Iceland and a voyage from Denmark to England, Spain, Madeira, the Canaries, the West Indies, and then a return to Denmark. In six years Svend has voyaged over twenty thousand miles on board *Optimist.*

We met Svend in Bayona, northern Spain, when he was on his way to the West Indies in 1974–75. In answer to a recent letter of ours, Svend wrote:

> I agree with you that people should stop dreaming of forty-five-foot boats and go now, provided they know the smaller boat they have. Some people I met had only sailed in sheltered waters before they started to the West Indies. Usually it went okay, but in my opinion they were too dependent on good luck in the beginning.
>
> Go simple! I prefer electric lanterns, but on *Optimist* the generator must be in the cockpit; when the battery was recharged in the middle of the Atlantic heading back from the West Indies, it got soaked and never recovered. I would have liked a Tilley storm lantern [pressure kerosene] instead of the paraffin [kerosene] anchor lantern.
>
> Overload is a problem on such a small boat. At departure from St. Thomas, U.S. Virgin Islands, with food and water for two months, the waterline was approximately ten centimeters [four inches] lower than at home. I put more weight on the starboard side because in the beginning I would sail close-hauled in the trade winds and the sailing performance was good but wet.

The return trip was full of "small" accidents. The second night (Force 5) the small genoa parted into two pieces, causing twenty hours of repairs the next four days. After three or four hundred miles in the trade winds I ran into many days with weak variable winds and Sargasso seaweed. The last was a great trouble, because a piece of it would fasten at the top front of the rudder and destroy the laminar flow, so it was impossible to sail close-hauled in Force 3 or more without running into the wind. Down with the sails, look out for sharks, swim down to the rudder (I always have a lifeline), away with the seaweed, up again, up with the sails, and the situation was okay—at least for two hours. This continued for two or three weeks. Four hundred miles east of Bermuda I read an article about thunder and lightning. Five hours later I had it (only Force 4)! I did not read the article about stormy weather.

In the middle of the Atlantic the generator got soaked and never recovered, so I used a paraffin lantern the next three weeks and battery the last five days in the Channel.

I had no wind stronger than Force 7 and a maximum headwind of Force 6, but one time (downwind) the waves were at least six meters high. I had fog southwest of the Scilly Islands, a lot of haze in the Channel, and (of course) easterly winds in the Channel. It took forty-seven days, eighteen hours, and fifty-two minutes from St. Thomas to New Haven, England.

After a month it was a little boring to sail—I had very few books —but one of the reasons for sailing directly to the Channel was to find out how I liked such a long voyage.

Single-handed sailing such as Svend does is definitely an extra risk. I personally don't recommend it, but I can appreciate a person's desire to go it completely alone. This should always remain one of man's choices, to risk his own life the way he sees fit. On the other hand, the Rules of the Road do require that a twenty-four-hour watch be kept at all times, not only to avoid collisions but to see and hear distress calls. The single-hander can't keep a twenty-four-hour watch and could possibly miss a distress flare or sail right past a dismasted yacht without seeing it. The single-hander is on his own and must be extra well prepared. Svend was, and carried

2 mainsails, 7 headsails, 2 spinnaker poles, 3 halyards for headsails. Compass in cockpit, compass on bulkhead that can be seen from bunk; Sailar receiver with D.F. and a shortwave converter from Brookes and Gatehouse. Kelvin Hughes sextant and one plastic sextant. Echo sounder, sum log and tuning fork watch. Combined

Optimist is a tiny little yacht with three reefs in the main and a large self-steering vane. *Svend Kaae*

lantern on top of mast plus lanterns in stem and stern. A 60-watt Aldis 66-amp/hour battery, Honda generator, and paraffin anchor lantern. Emergency equipment: life raft, 1-watt transmitter, (safety link) rockets, orange smoke flares, 2 fire extinguishers. Self-made windvane, 2 anchors, 50-gallon rubber water tank, 50-gallon kerosene tank, plastic containers for more water, Seagull outboard, 2 bilge pumps, radar reflector, spare rigging, and a lot of tools.

Svend also served a good apprenticeship during his sailing holidays to Aland, the Faroes, and western Norway before he set off across the Atlantic. He knew his boat's limitations, and that her gear was good. But most important, he was mentally and physically prepared for a long voyage on a small yacht.

But no matter how well prepared a single-hander is, he must be an optimist, and most of them eventually hope to find a good mate. This is when *Optimist*'s main drawback becomes obvious. She is just too small for two.

Wylo **is a masthead cutter with a large staysail. Note the battonless loose-footed main with vertical panels for less chafe on shrouds.** *Nick Skeates*

WYLO

Owned by: Nick Skeates

Designed and built by: Berthon Boat Company
Lymington, England
(1930)

Hull: wood
Length: 29'
Beam: 8'
Draft: 4' 4"
Displacement: 14,000 lbs.
Ballast: 4,000 lbs.
Rig: cutter

Mainsail: 225 square feet
Jib: 110 square feet
Staysail: 120 square feet
Spars: wood
Rudder: outboard
Self-steering: sheet-to-tiller method
Dinghy: 7' 6" sailing dinghy

Wylo's large, clean foredeck is natural pine for good footing, a safe deck for working at night. *Nick Skeates*

Nick Skeates and his boat.

Nick Skeates and *Wylo* are a classic example of a love affair between a young man and an older lady. When we cruised the south coast of England we met many love matches like theirs. While working as a government weights and measurements inspector Nick, who was in his early twenties, bought his 1930 twenty-nine-foot cutter and refitted her himself in 1972 for the very low price of twenty-four hundred dollars plus "a great deal of labor."

Since we met him in Dartmouth, England, he has sailed to New Zealand taking three years and going via the West Indies, Panama, and the Galapagos to the Marquesas, where he made a fantastic six-day run of a thousand miles (including one day of one hundred eighty miles), broad-reaching in Force 5 to 6 winds with all sails set and the boat self-steering at all times. *Wylo* does not have a windvane. Instead, Nick uses the cheaper but less convenient method of tiller-to-sheet steering (see John Letcher's book, *Self-Steering for Sailing Craft,* pp. 36–73). Nick usually has crew but did try single-handing from Tahiti to New Zealand.

He recently wrote us an interesting seaman-like summation of his yacht's performance:

You ask for comments on her good and bad points. Her comparatively shallow draft is a good point; I certainly would not want any more—it is actually about 4′ 4″. Much less than this and she'd need a centerboard to go to windward at sea. She is very full-ended and straight-sided. Thus her comparatively narrow beam extends a good proportion of her length, giving good deck space and volume below. Her full bow makes it possible to drive her hard off the wind; she never shows any signs of nose-diving. This feature also gives her a long waterline, twenty-seven feet or so, and is reflected in her good passages. A friend with a similar-size boat, but with pinched-in ends (and a similar keel profile), said his boat became "busy" at high speed and he had to reef down to self-steer properly. [We agree with Nick on this point because *Seraffyn* has fine ends and also gets busy at six knots and has to be reefed down to self-steer.]

Full ends can't be all good, otherwise all boats would have 'em. Her full bow does slow her down in a chop to windward, by comparison with a fine bow under the same conditions. This was proved by sailing in company with the boat mentioned above, but *Wylo* was faster on a reach in the same sea.

Her keel profile makes her very steady on the helm and she has never, ever refused to come about, probably due to her good cutaway forward.

Channels are handy for resting against the ways car so the whole topside can be painted in one go. The long keel makes *Wylo* easy to haul out. *Nick Skeates*

Wylo's stern view, showing her easy bilges (dead rise) and English-style boom-kin. *Nick Skeates*

Wylo's full bow. *Nick Skeates*

One bad feature is a large hole entirely through the rudder for the 17 1/2-inch propellor. This makes the rudder unnecessarily heavy to turn. It ought to be at least partly in the keel (stern post) and very possibly a quarter installation would be better; she doesn't steer going astern under power anyway.

I would like a bit more beam, giving more room inside, particularly in the main hatch area, which can become congested with a few people aboard. However, she is a surprisingly slippery boat and I fancy her narrow beam (by modern standards) may have something to do with this, also her fairly shallow draft.

Nick, like his boat, is practical. While cruising he has worked as a bus driver, yacht painter and carpenter, and writing articles for the English magazine *Yachting Monthly*.

When commenting on the cost of living and cruising on *Wylo*, Nick said, "Food can cost as little or as much as you like. Eating out is expensive, as is hauling out (use tides where possible). Engine troubles are a curse and costly, so are electrics—do without for cheapness. Labor is very expensive—do your own. Above all, keep it simple and strong. Live aboard rather than ashore when in port for economy, and sail—don't motor unnecessarily. Use what you've got, not what's in the shop."

Nick's philosophy has taken him a long way and he has had three years of fine cruising. He wrote us, "Now I have a blonde Kiwi crew who is really keen on cruising. She's done a fair bit before. I have a feeling she'll be with me for quite some time." He was right. They got married in the United Kingdom during Christmas 1977.

Nick Skeates sailing his fiberglass dinghy in Dartmouth, England, a great little tender with spars that stow in the boat.

Brian notes: "She handles very well. The fact that I can tack her up and down the [confined] Hamble River proves this. . . ." *Brian Craigie-Lucas*

Mouette at her mooring in front of the Elephant Boatyard. *Brian Craigie-Lucas*

MOUETTE

Owned by: Brian Craigie-Lucas

Designer: Peter Brett
The Pitts, Bonchurch
Ventor, Isle of Wight
England

Built of wood by Enterprise Small Rock Ferry Craft Company, 1938

Length: 32'
Beam: 8' 10"
Draft: 6' 0"
Displacement:
16,000 lbs. gross
Ballast: unknown
Rig: cutter

Spars: wood
Sails: seven in all
Rudder: inboard
Self-steering: homemade, similar to
  QME
Dinghy: hard fiberglass

Brian Craigie-Lucas is one of the old school of sailors, weaned on Stockholm tar and Italian hemp. He is a reformed single-hander, and Chris, his cute, red-headed crew who has been sailing with him for the past three years, has transformed the interior of *Mouette* from bachelor's quarters to "a tidy home for two, complete with oil paintings, comfy cushions, and a mounted whale's tooth from the Azores engraved with a full-rigged ship."

When we first met Brian in the Azores (August 1972) he was sailing alone. He wore ancient high, multipatched fisherman-style boots and rowed an old rubber dinghy with patches to match the boots. His mailing address was "Yacht *Mouette*, c/o Elephant Boatyard (find me at the Jolly Roger Pub), Old Burlesdon, Hants." Now the reformed solo sailor has a new hard fiberglass dinghy and a very respectable London bank to forward his mail.

Brian bought his lovely forty-year-old *Mouette* in very rundown condition for approximately three thousand dollars in 1968, and with the practical skill of the complete sailor, started to work on her. She had a large diesel with a broken crankshaft that stole most of what is now her galley area. Brian hoisted the motor out, sold it to a passing fisherman, and has sailed ten years to date, "doing without." Then he carefully and methodically checked the hull, especially the floors and garboards which are the most likely area to give trouble in an older outside-ballasted wooden boat. The total refit of *Mouette* cost Brian five hundred pounds, which he spent mostly on new keel bolts, new garboards, and new sails. (When we met Brian in the Azores, he showed us his battenless red mainsail. He had sailed the Atlantic twice with it and never had to repair chafe or damage caused by battens. Seeing the condition of his battenless sail convinced me. Our next sail was just like his and has worked great.) Brian used heavy, reliable galvanized fittings on *Mouette,* no stainless-steel "yacht" gear. So he ended up buying and refitting his thirty-two-foot cruising home for less than forty-eight hundred dollars.

Not all sailors have the practical knowledge needed to eye up an old boat and appreciate an originally well-built, well-designed hull under the neglect and abuse of the years. Brian did, and with thousands of hours of his own labor made *Mouette* into a reliable cruiser which has taken him to the Azores, Canary Islands, Cape Verdes, Brazil, and beyond. As of 1978 *Mouette* and Brian have crossed the Atlantic six or eight times.

Brian in
the companionway
of *Mouette. Brian Craigie-Lucas*

Mouette at rest
somewhere
in Brazil. *Brian Craigie-Lucas*

Mouette, hauled out for a
refit in 1975 at Moody's
yard on the Hamble River.
Brian Craigie-Lucas

Mouette makes "a tidy
home for two, complete
with oil paintings, comfy
cushions, and a mounted
whale's tooth from the
Azores engraved with a
full-rigged ship." *Brian
Craigie-Lucas*

A recent letter from Brian gives a glimpse of the tall, quiet, prudent English sailor with "no problems":

Well, as you will have gathered I am under way again—once more to South America. This time I have a crew, believe it or not. Takes quite a lot of readjustment after single-handing for so long. We left England last June, heading for the Azores first (of course), my fifth visit. Horta is changing a bit with over thirty yachts in port at a time and more tourists on shore. But the people are as nice as ever. . . . We spent two months in the Azores, visiting San Jorge, Terceira, and San Miguel, apart from Fayal. Then headed for Madiera and Porto Santo—the latter delightful but landing sometimes awkward. After that we spent six weeks in the Canaries before heading across the Atlantic. The crossing was slow but easy, like most of the trip so far. Mostly light winds and calms so that we took forty-nine days for about thirty-three hundred miles. No problems.

Two months were spent at and around Salvador [Brazil], a wonderful cruising area. Beautiful sheltered anchorages, completely deserted except for an occasional dugout paddling by, and this within a few miles of a large city. From there we came here direct, having a heartening welcome from friends I made at a small yacht club when I was here before. We shall stay for about another two or four weeks, then go to Ilha Grande, a day's sail south and supposed to be beautiful, a sort of Brazilian south seas archipelago. I gather we can keep the boat in Brazil for six months only, and when this is up in about three months we are going down to Uruguay and Argentina. . . . As I said, it has been an easy trip so far, with no mishaps and *Mouette* has behaved beautifully as always.

In a second letter Brian gives us some information about *Mouette:*

Load waterline [is] listed as twenty-four feet but actually about twenty-five feet now. About twenty-five years ago her keel was deepened from a draft of four feet six inches to six feet. This was very nicely done with the designer's approval. At that time she was owned by a syndicate of Harley Street doctors who were keen ocean racers and the alterations were done for improved windward performance and sail-carrying ability, and also accounts partially for the difference in her load waterline. . . . I believe her racing career was fairly satisfactory although she was never designed for it. She is now cutter-rigged with a bowsprit, although originally a sloop. Under this she handles very well. The fact that I can tack her up and down the [confined] Hamble River proves this, I think. No engine and no electrics apart from dry-cell battery-operated lights to galley and compass.

Some time ago she had a fire on board and was run ashore. I have no exact details of this, but she was a complete write-off and had to have a Lloyd's Certificate of Seaworthiness before being put back on the register. I have owned her for ten years, living and cruising on her through that time.

Brian works at anything that comes along (yacht agent, jig maker, clerk, writing) to supplement a very small pension. These endeavors and an inexpensive-to-maintain yacht are the reasons he can afford his cruising habit.

Broad-reaching off the Brazilian coast. Note the windvane, fiberglass dinghy, heavy galvanized rigging, and red mainsail. *Brian Craigie-Lucas*

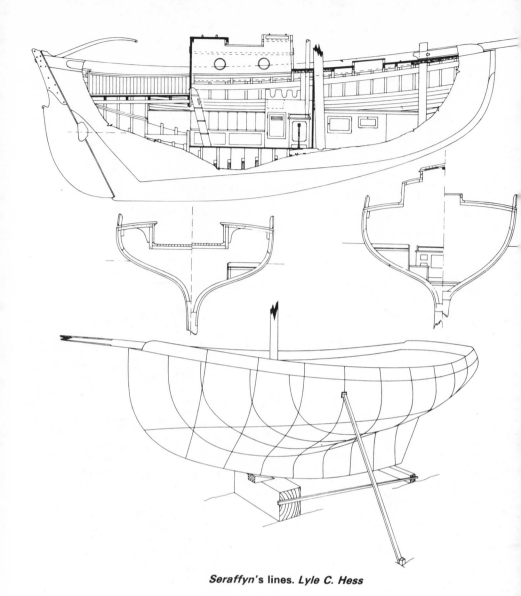

Seraffyn's lines. *Lyle C. Hess*

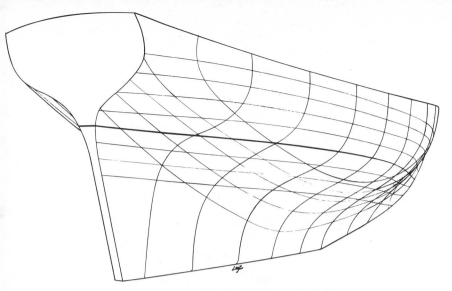

Isometric plan of our dream cutter. *Lyle C. Hess*

SERAFFYN

Owned by: Lin and Larry Pardey

Builders: Lin and Larry Pardey (launched November 1968)

Designer: Lyle C. Hess
        1907 W. Woodcrest
        Fullerton, California

Built of wood

Length: 24' 4"
Beam: 8' 11"
Draft: 4'8"
Displacement: 10,687 lbs.
Ballast: 2,700 lbs.
Rig: cutter
Sail area: 180 square feet in mainsail,
104 square feet in staysail,
265 square feet in working genoa
Spars: wood
Self-steering: trim tab on main rudder
Dinghy: fiberglass lapstrake pram with
  sail rig

OUR DREAM CUTTER

Designer: Lyle C. Hess
        1907 W. Woodcrest,
        Fullerton, California

To be built of wood by Lin and Larry Pardey

Length: 29' 9"
Beam: 10' 9"
Draft: 5' 0"
Displacement: approximately 16,000
  lbs.
Ballast: approximately 5,500 pounds
Rudder: outboard
Spars: wood
Self-steering: trim tab on main rudder
Dinghy: fiberglass lapstrake stem
  dinghy with sail rig

Preliminary sail plan of our dream cutter. *Lyle C. Hess*

When Lin and I built *Seraffyn*, we planned to cruise six months, maybe a year. If we liked cruising, we would carry on. If anyone had said nine years ago that we would have lived on her since 1969, cruised to twenty-seven countries from California to Malaysia (February 1978), I would have answered, "She's too small to live on for so long!" We never planned it this way; we just kept looking forward to the next country, the next island, or the next sailing season—and it's been fun! The little twenty-four-footer has been adequate to live on except in cold weather.

Since we never planned on using *Seraffyn* as a long-term home, we have lately been thinking about building a boat that would have all of *Seraffyn*'s great seakeeping and sailing qualities but also a more comfortable interior, especially since we would like to cruise in colder climates. We'd like to have two tables (galley and chart table) so that both Lin and I could work on our writing at the same time. We'd like an inside sit down bath and loo, and a piano for Lin, and we've found it can be done because Yamaha produces a portable tuning fork piano for traveling bands which measures about twelve inches high, eighteen inches deep, and forty-nine inches high (nonelectric). We plan to have the piano under the foldup chart table. Anyway, that is our dream.

Lyle Hess has drawn the plans for us, and for the last two years we've been savoring the delightful experience of getting our next yacht designed just the way we want it while we enjoy cruising on board *Seraffyn*.

We haven't laid the keel yet. In fact, we're still cruising enjoyably on *Seraffyn* over eight thousand miles away from the place we'd like to build our dream ship. But we have bought a Plath hand-operated anchor winch, opening ports, prismatic deadlights, and now as we cruise the Orient, we are looking for nice long-grained quarter-sawn teak to make the decks and cabin.

The greatest problem Lin and I have is deciding to part with our child substitute, *Seraffyn*. It is almost unthinkable to sell our fine little cutter which has never disappointed us or let us down. *Seraffyn* is a "right now" cruising reality, while the new boat would be at least three years of hard work away. *Seraffyn* is small enough so that we can afford to keep her indefinitely if we decide to live ashore. We could happily use her for local cruising and racing. To justify the larger boat with its extra maintenance and extra costs, we must think very carefully. Do we want to make our home permanently on a yacht? Can we part with *Seraffyn*? Do we want to give up three years of cruising time just to gain some creature comforts? This is the dilemma. If we do decide to build, then the twenty-nine-foot nine-inch Lyle Hess–designed dream cutter will become our reality cutter.

~~~~~

Some Thoughts on Heavy Weather

But in running before it your vessel may go along quite comfortably and dry for a time, and then with dreadful suddenness, a sea may come over the stern and put you and your ship out of business. . . .
—Captain Voss, *The Venturesome Voyages of Captain Voss*

A few years ago *Tzu Hang* was running from Reykhavik to the northwest point of Iceland in a southwest gale. It was a dark night and the wind force 9 with a heavy sea on her quarter. *Tzu Hang* had only her storm headsail set and in order to prevent it jibing over and back again, with sudden strains on sheet, halyard, and stay, we were running with the wind on our quarter, which gave us a nice offing from the inhospitable shore. *Tzu Hang* was tearing along through the night in the conditions that she seems to like best, and I was happy and singing at the tiller, since we were going fast in the direction we wished to go. Suddenly I felt, rather than saw a monster wave breathing down my neck and coming at a slightly different angle. The next moment we were hit with a shock that felt as if a ten-ton lorry had run into us. *Tzu Hang* was knocked bodily sideways and the tiller was wrenched out of my hand and thumped against the leeward coaming at the limit of its travel. . . . *Tzu Hang*'s masts went down to the horizontal. . . .

[In another instance] *Tzu Hang* was running before a gale which I should estimate now to have been force ten or more. At no time was she running too fast, nor was she particularly difficult to steer. . . . When she pitchpoled a very high and exceptionally steep wave hit her, considerably higher than she was long. It must have broken as she assumed an almost vertical position on its face. The movement was extremely violent and quick. There was no sensation of being in a dangerous position with disaster threatening. Disaster was suddenly there.
—Miles Smeeton, *Because the Horn Is There*

It was becoming more and more difficult to hold *Joshua* before the seas because the trailing hawsers made her less and less maneuverable as the seas got bigger. She was yawing more even with the helm right down, and what I had vaguely feared eventually happened. But it was my fault, for my attention must have momentarily wandered after fifteen hours at the helm. Carried by a wave *Joshua* suddenly came beam on to the seas and when the breaker arrived it was too late. A rush of icy water hit me in the neck and the next moment *Joshua* was heeled rapidly over. The angle of heel increased steadily but not abruptly while noise became dim. Then the silence was suddenly broken by the unholy din of a cascade of objects flying across the cabin . . . three or four seconds . . . then *Joshua* righted herself.

[Later that night] the boat was running exactly stern on to a fast approaching wave, nicely curved but not excessively large, on the point of breaking . . . or maybe not breaking. . . . I was wide awake, I think I was even extra lucid at that moment.

The stern lifted as always and then, accelerating suddenly but without heeling the slightest, *Joshua* buried her forward part in the sea at an angle of about 30 degrees, as far as the forward edge of the coachroof. Half the boat was under water. Almost immediately she emerged again. . . . We had almost been pitchpoled by a slightly hesitant wave—I would not have believed it possible.
—Bernard Moitessier, *The First Voyage of the Joshua*

Our technique for the entire period of storms was to run with the prevailing wind and wave set on the starboard quarter, holding a fair course and surging down the faces of the rising swells. As the crests caught us, they would kick the stern over, and *Sorcery* would round up slightly till she luffed; then she would fly along the top of the wave. . . . Steering was never difficult in these gale conditions, but it did require some concentration and by the tenth day of real wind, everyone on board had put in many hours of heavy-weather helm time. . . . Then the freight train hit us. There was no time to react. As the starboard locker emptied onto me, the engine which had been battery charging, kicked off. I pile-drived into the amazingly white surface of the overhead, right where the cabin sole used to be: then the port lockers emptied out. Sometime in between it seemed that a wave had washed through into the forepeak, but I barely noticed it. . . . the first definite sounds that penetrated the chaos were the piercing screams from one deck, then a shout of "Man overboard! Man overboard!"
—Aulan Fitzpatrick, "360 Degree Roll Sweeps Sorcery Clean," *Sail*,
August 1976.

All Monday it was staysail only. To hold the course without flogging its 300 square feet in accidental gybes required constant attention at the helm... [The wind was an estimated] Force 9, over 46 knots...And so dawned the fateful morning...the wind had veered. We'd come over to the port gybe... We remarked the abating seas; at the same time our pace diminished to eight knots. "Were we racing," I said, "we'd be upping the main." We agreed in the interest of rest and comfort to postpone this until I came on watch again at 1300...

Bill had impressed me as an alert helmsman more than once the past ten days. I could see him through the companionway checking the tillermaster [electric autopilot]...I read the first sentence of the first six volumes of Anthony Trollope. Then Bill shouted, "Look out..."

A second to rise up, another to swing my legs off the bunk. Four seconds. Bill's next agonized cry coincided with the creaking slapping sound of a flat surface slamming water with maximum impact...Even as the mast must have struck the water and *Streamer* lay like a wing-crippled swan on her side I still felt confident...A second shattering smack. Then gently as the mast subsided below the surface the bunk revolved around my head. I stood calf deep in water on the cabin ceiling.

[Later Bill told me] "I'd been looking ahead. I turned around. This wall. Forty feet high. It had two crests just off the stern. I kicked tilly clear. Grabbed the wheel and pulled her off with all my weight. Three spokes. I thought she'd come back until I saw the mast hit the water. Then the second crest hit us."

—Philip S. Weld, "Five Nights Upside Down—Then Rescue for *Gulf Streamer*," SAIL, August 1976.

Seraffyn's broach as described in Chapter 16 was a classic case of running too long under bare poles.

Seven different instances, five very different types of boats. *Seraffyn* is twenty-four feet long with short overhangs and heavy displacement. *Gulf Streamer* is a sixty-foot-long lightweight trimaran. *Sorcery* is a sixty-one-foot-long light-displacement IOR racing boat. *Joshua* is a forty-foot double-ended heavy steel ketch. *Tzu Hang* is a forty-six-foot-long wooden canoe-stern ketch. Each encountered waves that could have been disastrous, yet only two of these instances happened near Cape Horn. Smeeton's first account was near Iceland. *Sorcery* got into trouble in the North Pacific, *Gulf Streamer* in the North Atlantic, and *Seraffyn* in the Baltic. All of us got into trouble while running with no warning and with dreadful suddenness.

Why do yachtsmen continue to run in heavy weather? It's because they are not aware of any danger. The yacht feels like it is completely under control. In some instances it is even being steered by vane or autopilot. The motion is relatively comfortable. The wind speed seems lower because you are running away from it. To round up and heave to means a definite decision, backed by action and hard work. It means setting some sort of riding sail, sea anchor, or drough. Rounding up to heave to can be frightening, especially if you have left it too long. And that's what happens. You hang on longer than is prudent, hoping the wind and sea will lay down. That's usually when disaster strikes.

Heaving to requires gear preparation before leaving port. It requires experimentation to learn the adjustment and trimming of sails and or droughs necessary to get your particular boat into the proper hove-to position. Every boat heaves to differently and the only way to learn which way works best for yours is to practice at sea in winds of gale force. Few of us choose to go out in heavy winds just to practice. It is easier to accept a pat solution like running under bare poles, with or without warps or droughs. We have been lulled into a false sense of security by other yachtsmen who have fortunately survived to write about "running with it."

In the author's notes in his book *The First Voyage of the Joshua*, Bernard Moitessier says, "The following lines are only a very incomplete testimony, and perhaps quite mistaken. Just because we have once got away without suffering damage I cannot pretend to talk like an authority on the handling of a yacht in the high latitudes of the South Pacific."

Miles Smeeton makes a similar statement in *Because the Horn Is There:* "I write of the management of a ship in heavy weather with hesitation, because my experience, although gained in many seas, is confined to one ship."

These men don't profess to be authorities on heavy weather. But their opinions, along with those of other famous yachtsmen, have been influencing us to run in heavy weather using various methods—with warps, with bare poles, with storm sails.

In Allen Villers's book *The War with Cape Horn,* he tells of sailing the grain ship *Parma* from Australia west to east around the Horn. In the roaring forties they were running with little sail set and were suddenly swept by a large wave, suffering extensive damage. The captain was the famous Ruben de Clouix. He hove the ship to and *Parma* suffered no more.

Captain Voss, another master sailor, has recommended heaving to when heavy weather is encountered, and gives details on how this can be done in vessels of all types and sizes in the appendix of his book *The Venturesome Voyages of Captain Voss*. This appendix is worth careful study and, in my opinion, should be carried on board every seagoing yacht for reference.

Miles Smeeton notes in his section on heavy weather in his book *Because the Horn Is There*, "I have been unable to find in Adlard Cole's books [*Heavy Weather Sailing*] any record of a yacht incurring damage while hove to." We have hove-to on *Seraffyn*. I have lain hove-to in various boats while I was delivering them. Never once while lying hove-to have we suffered any damage.

I think we should reconsider the question of storm tactics and follow the example and advice of the master sailors instead of yachtsmen. We should listen to the men who spent up to nine months of every year working at sea, who often made thirty or forty trips around the Horn during their lifetimes, men who had experience on various types of sailing ships in all kinds of weather, men like Ruben de Clouix and Captain Voss.

To finish the quote that started this appendix, Voss says, "So once more I repeat my advice: be most careful in running and heave to rather a little earlier than deemed necessary by others."

*Read *Storm Tactics Handbook*, also by Lin and Larry Pardey, for more on heaving-to.

Afterword to the Third Edition

The tide rushes past *Taleisin*'s hull as I listen to the shipping forecast on the BBC. "Dover, Wight, Plymouth: southeasterly force 5, increasing 6. Showers, visibility poor."

"Lousy wind for us to go down channel," Larry says. I agree wholeheartedly, feeling pleased we've no pressing schedule. I am quite content when he suggests we stay where we are and spend the day reading through this book. It seems right somehow, to be reading about our cruising through European waters on *Seraffyn* as we wait for fair winds in the same waters 23 years later. We are anchored on the Blackwater, one of the rivers of the Thames estuary, only 30 miles as the crow flies from London, yet centuries away in mood and appearance from the hustle and bustle of that capital city. The low rolling hills of England's eastern shore, dotted with small villages and solid-granite church spires, shelter us from the cold winds of autumn. The dream cutter Lyle Hess was designing back in 1977 has been a reality for 14 years now. We've visited over 20 countries on her and have just sailed south from a summer in Scotland and Norway, two of the European countries we missed during our time on *Seraffyn*. As we both read through these earlier adventures it is fun to reflect on the changes that have occurred during the past two decades.

One of the delights of our voyage on *Taleisin* has been revisiting a few of the places we sailed to on *Seraffyn*. There are only a few so far, as after launching *Taleisin* our route led us first into the familiar waters of Baja California, but when we left there we headed west instead of east and south as we had on *Seraffyn*. This route led us across the equator and into the southern hemisphere, an area where, despite completing a 47,000-mile eastabout circumnavigation, *Seraffyn* never once put her bowsprit. So from the time we left Cabo San Lucas on Baja California's southern tip, *Taleisin*'s path did not cross that of *Seraffyn*'s for over 10 years and 40,000 miles of voyaging. Not until we stopped in the Azores, bound for Ireland, did we see any familiar landfalls. So it was with a bit of trepidation and a lot of anticipation that we finally sailed between the welcoming forts of St. Mawes and Pendennis Point, the entrance to

Falmouth Harbor.

The vistas that greeted us had changed little. There were more yachts on moorings inside the bay, fewer big ships at the shipyard. The customs boat was alongside just as quickly, but clearance consisted of "Hello, where you in from, what's your boat name?" instead of a pile of paperwork, since England is now part of the EU and clearance in the Azores serves as final clearance for most of Europe. The Falmouth working boats are still the glamour girls of the harbor, and we were delighted to see that the old boats we once sailed have become collectors items, used hard and restored often. But now there is a fleet of fiberglass replicas swelling the ranks of working boats on race days. The increased competition has led to ever-bigger rigs, so on light-wind days it is not uncommon to see 28-foot working boats spreading 2,000 square feet of canvas for a reach down Carrick Roads. Oyster dredging is still done under sail, though catches were down for several years after a fungal disease decimated the oyster beds. Fortunately stocks are slowly regaining their health, and it is like stepping back 100 years when you stand on the shores of Mylor Creek on a cold wintry day and watch as these old gaffers dredge under sail, their scandalized mains holding them beam-on to the tide, their crew shouting across the water to each other, the lively race that often ensues as the dredging day ends and *Magdelena* or *Winnie* or one of the other boats we watched at work 23 years ago short-tack back to their moorings.

With the passing of so many years we were not surprised to hear that some of our old friends had gone on their last sail. On the other hand, every week we've spent in the south of England has been spiced up by at least one person rushing over to say, "Hey, glad to see you back, where have you been?" Arfie Trenier married his lovely lady, Sue, and still races and fishes on *Magdelena*, though now he has a motorized fishing boat he uses for offshore fisheries during the summer. His 15-year-old daughter works as his crew. Frank Jarrett, now in his late 70s, is still an eager participant in Royal Cornwall Yacht Club regattas. Paul Lees and Vicki are now married with two romping young sons and have worked together to expand Crusader Sails into a very successful business. They were part of a warm welcome we received at the Parkstone Yacht Club in Poole. Now, instead of mooring almost a mile offshore in that tide-racked, open harbor, we tied up in the club's new marina that is protected by the westerly breakwater and could easily walk right up to the clubhouse to join many of our old friends for dinner.

We tried to find one of our favorite British characters—Henry North and his wife, Josephine—when we were in Dartmouth. But though well remembered by local folks, no one knew of their whereabouts. Trevor Vincent and his wife, Eva, who owned *Mary and Elizabeth*, the boat pictured on page 201, generously showed us how little has changed along the river Dart where we once again sheltered from the first winter gales on board *Taleisin*. The anchorage still becomes a bit uncomfortable when wind blows against tide, just as it did so many years before when we sheltered here on *Seraffyn*, but the local sailors still welcome overseas visitors to their club, and the tidal grid still costs only £5.00 per night to use.

The cruising grounds along England's south coast have become much more crowded with boats and ships of all sorts. With the crowds have come dozens of new marinas and higher harbor fees. We found it better in 1997 to visit this area outside the normal cruising season, which runs from the first of June to the middle of September. But when we sailed 100 miles away from the south coast, be it farther south to Britanny, north and east to the Thames Estuary, or north and west to Ireland, Scotland, Norway, and Sweden, the crowds thinned, free anchorages abounded, and local people seemed to spoil anyone flying a foreign flag.

Yachting facilities have increased throughout Europe, in some cases opening completely new areas to cruising. The French government has built dozens of small marinas and created excellent charts and leading marks along the rock-strewn coast of Britanny all the way to the Seine. Now adventuresome cruisers can explore an area once limited strictly to those with local knowledge.

Back in 1972 to 1974, we found the cost of living and cruising in British waters to be slightly higher than those for cruising along the east coast of the United States; in Spain they were lower; in Scandinavia two to three times higher. If you use the same inflation figures as you would for the U.S. dollar over a similar period (in other words, multiply any figure in this book by five), you'll get a pretty accurate picture of today's prices. Although many marine items are double the price of those in the United States, a cost-conscious person can cruise here for a little more than he/she could in the U.S. Caribbean. Ireland and Scotland could be more costly except for local hospitality and the free or low-cost seafood. But be prepared for a shock if you visit any mainland northern European country or Scandinavia. A glass of wine in a café in Norway costs $7, an ice cream cone $5. On the other hand, by stocking up in England or France before sailing north, you can have a wonderful Scandinavian summer at low cost, as there is now little need to pay a harbor fee and fresh local produce is relatively affordable. Better yet, the people of Scandinavia are still delighted to see overseas-flagged yachts.

Looking at the small boats shown in the appendix of this book brings to mind the question we still hear from most of the people who come to cruising seminars we give during our occasional visits to the United States: What size boat do I really need? We still feel 25 to 30 feet is enough. Nick Skeates unfortunately lost *Wylo* on a reef near Fiji five years after our time together in England. By that time he had married his blonde crew, Dorothy. Together they built and outfitted a 30-foot steel-hulled, wooden-decked boat that Nick designed. It took them only two years to get afloat again, and together they completed a leisurely circumnavigation onboard *Wylo II*. Although they then went their separate ways, Nick is still voyaging on *Wylo II* and echoes our feelings when he said, "Any bigger and it would have taken another year or two to get going. We'd have had to work a lot more every year to pay for cruising and to keep the boat ready to go to sea at any time."

Although some of the boats you see in the appendix look a bit old-fashioned, remember—they were old-fashioned when we wrote this book. Yet boats like this are still out cruising, some of them offered as newly built "classic cruisers." Tania Aebi made her famous voyage in a folkboat exactly like the one used by the Swedish couple, the Lagerkrantz, and similar to P. Pippet. Inflation and changing times have meant that many Americans are wealthy enough to buy boats 40 or even 50 feet long to go off cruising for a few years. But we still see people of all ages out in small affordable boats like the Orion 27, Triton 28, Norsea 27, Bristol Channel Cutter (28 feet), Cape George Cutter (30 feet), Twister (28 feet), just to name a few. Even boats normally not pinpointed as perfect voyagers have been used successfully. We saw two beefed up Catalina 30s in the South Pacific with families on board. A young couple completed a circumnavigation (and had two children along the way) on board a well-fitted-out Cal 25. Small boats are not only affordable and seaworthy but can provide more sheer sailing pleasure than their bigger sisters, as Mike Whipp, a fortunate sailor from the Isle of Man, made clear. Mike and his wife, Tricia, built a 28-foot Twister (a classic cruiser designed by Holman and Pye) from a bare hull and set off cruising until their first child came along two years later. They returned from the Caribbean to take over the family farm. With a growing family and growing financial reserves, they were able to buy a 45-foot steel boat to use for exploring high latitudes all the way from Iceland and the Faroes to the Arctic coast of Norway. But they also kept their 28-foot Twister, which they use for cruising along the shores of Scotland and Ireland. Why do they keep two boats? Both Mike and Tricia agree, "We simply have more fun, do more sailing and less powering, meet more people and feel less hassled on the Twister than we do on the bigger boat."

Few of us can afford the luxury of one boat for high latitudes and another for middle latitudes. But the boat that was only a dream when we first wrote *Seraffyn*'s European Adventure is a fine compromise. The 29-foot, 6-inch cutter that Lyle designed started to become a reality in 1979 when we sailed back to California at the completion of an eastabout circumnavigation. Larry worked full-time building (teak planking, walnut-trimmed interior), part-time earning our construction funds. I worked full-time earning, part-time building. The reward for three-and-a-half years of 50- to 60-hour work weeks was *Taleisin*, a boat that has now carried us over 47,000 miles. She has been a worthy successor to mighty little *Seraffyn*. But there are times when we miss the ease with which either of us could sail *Seraffyn* on our own and the simplicity of haulout time, with far less surface area to scrub and paint. On the other hand, voyaging to less-temperate climates is more comfortable on her bigger sister. We now have a safe, vented heating stove to warm the cabin, a simple-to-use shower/sitz tub arrangement with pressurized and metered water so we are independent of shoreside showers and can keep warm and clean even as we cross oceans. Larry has dedicated a work bench and a tool-stowage area plus room for two folding bikes on board. But no, we did not incorporate a piano into our reality ship. In the Orient, a guitar found its way on board *Seraffyn*. Its portability and the fun sing-alongs it promoted soon made it the more logical instrument choice for a sailing life.

As we reread this book, it causes us not only to reflect back but also to look forward. As younger, less-memory-filled voyager/adventurers, our goals were chosen almost at whim—influenced only by the direction of the wind, the need to earn cruising funds, the desire to see a new place, any new place. Now it is in some ways more complicated. It is tempting to retrace *Seraffyn*'s steps and visit places firmly etched in our memories. But will they be anti-climatic? Should we instead try to visit only places that are completely new to us? There are many destinations to choose from. The shorelines of the Bay of Biscay, the fjords of western Norway, the Shetland Islands, or the far side of the Atlantic with the completely new-to-us coast of New England and Maine. Or maybe we should go back and explore some of the Swedish coast we missed last time, revisit Danish friends, and savor the Rias of northern Spain. But that is the magic of our life, the life our two small cutters have opened to us. Whichever direction we turn when we sail out past Pendennis Castle, hopefully more opportunities, more new friends, and more heartwarming adventures lie ahead.

On board *Taleisin*,
England 1998

The authors

About the authors

Larry, a Canadian born in Victoria, British Columbia, dreamed of going exploring under sail from the time he was a young boy. He learned his skills racing, skippering charter boats, and doing boat repairs in Vancouver and later in Newport Beach, California. There, in 1965, he met Lin, an American (from the San Fernando Valley of California). Together they built *Seraffyn*, the boat used for the adventures written about in this book. During their 11-year circumnavigation, they began writing articles, which appeared in magazines around the world, including *Cruising World, SAIL, Cruising Helmsman, Australia, South African Yachting, Practical Boatowner, UK, Yachting Monthly UK, Die Yacht, Germany*, and others. Nine books have developed from their sailing, some of which have been translated into German and Japanese.

For the past 14 years their home has been 29-foot, 6-inch *Taleisin*, the boat they built for themselves in the mountains of Southern California. She, like *Seraffyn*, uses only renewable energy—the wind. During the course of their cruise on her, they found a home base in northern New Zealand and spent two-and-a-half years fixing it up, but the urge to move on saw them off on more voyages around the south of Australia and onward to Africa, Brazil, and Europe. As they did on *Seraffyn*, they still earn their cruising funds by writing articles and doing boat repairs, wooden-boat restoration, and the occasional yacht delivery.

Lin and Larry Pardey also return to the United States every few years to give seminars on storm tactics and cost-conscious cruising.